Brimming with creative inspiration, how-to projects, and useful information to enrich your everyday life, Quarto Knows is a favourite destination for those pursuing their interests and passions. Visit our site and dig deeper with our books into your area of interest: Quarto Creates, Quarto Cooks, Quarto Homes, Quarto Lives, Quarto Drives, Quarto Explores, Quarto Gifts, or Quarto Kids.

First published in 2017 by Motorbooks, an imprint of The Quarto Group, 401 Second Avenue North, Suite 310, Minneapolis, MN 55401 USA.
Telephone: (612) 344-8100 Fax: (612) 344-8692

QuartoKnows.com

Motorbooks titles are also available at discount for retail, wholesale, promotional, and bulk purchase. For details, contact the Special Sales Manager by email at specialsales@quarto.com or by mail at The Quarto Group, Attn: Special Sales Manager, 401 Second Avenue North, Suite 310, Minneapolis, MN 55401 USA.

10 9 8 7 6 5 4 3 2 1

ISBN: 978-0-7603-5236-6

Library of Congress Cataloging-in-Publication Data

Names: Schorr, Martyn L., author.
Title: Day one : an automotive journalist's muscle-car memories / by Martyn L. Schorr.
Description: Minneapolis, Minnesota : Motorbooks, 2017.
Identifiers: LCCN 2017009915 | ISBN 9780760352366 (hardback)
Subjects: LCSH: Muscle cars--United States--History--20th century. | Schorr, Martyn L.--Anecdotes. | BISAC: TRANSPORTATION / Automotive / History. | TRANSPORTATION / Automotive / Pictorial. | TRANSPORTATION / Automotive / Antique & Classic.
Classification: LCC TL15 .S35 2017 | DDC 629.2220973--dc23
LC record available at https://lccn.loc.gov/2017009915

Acquiring Editor: Darwin Holmstrom
Project Manager: Jordan Wiklund
Art Director: James Kegley
Layout: Ashley Prine, Tandem Books

On the front cover: Laying down some serious tracks in a preproduction SS454 LS5 Chevelle in June 1971 at the GM Proving Ground. With automatic and 3.31 Posi gears, the Chevelle was not ideally suited for the quarter-mile. Our loaded production test car with the same powertrain ran 93 miles per hour in 15.10 seconds (see page 191 for more).

On the frontis: Because of its "vintage" 401 Nailhead engine, the Skylark GS was not a serious GTO competitor. It did, however, offer a great combination of luxury, ride and handling, and performance. We had Pacers Auto's George Snizek tune our GS before testing in New York.

On the endpapers: Ace Wilson's Royal Pontiac and Yenko Chevrolet. *Don Snyder*

On the back cover: It took me a while to get used to the giant wing that followed me everywhere I drove. Driving an M-plated preproduction Daytona on the street was a major thrill and I never crossed paths with another one (see page 152 for more).

All photographs are from the author's archives unless noted otherwise.

Printed in China

FSC
MIX
Paper from responsible sources
FSC® C008047
www.fsc.org

DEDICATION

For Sharon, my editor, wife, and best friend.

ACKNOWLEDGMENTS

To write a book (or build a car) is seldom accomplished alone. I would like to acknowledge the following people and organizations that gave me help and support: Automotive History Preservation Society (AHPS), Dick Brannan, John Craft, Joe Curley, Scott Davies, Charlie Gray Jr., Randy Hernandez (Fran Hernandez Collection), Gary Jean, Ken Kayser, Don Keefe (Poncho Perfection), Peter Klutt (Legendary Motorcar Collection), Dennis Kolodziej, Rick Kopec (SAAC), Charley Lillard, Fred Mackerodt, Denny Manners, Mike Matune, Bob McClurg, Bill McGuire, Jon Mello, Jeff Murphy, Joe Oldham, Steven Perry, RK Motors (Charlotte, North Carolina), Diego Rosenberg, Rocky Rotella, Bill Schultz, Nick Smith (Factory Lightweight Collection), George Snizek, Scott Snizek, Kevin Suydam, Adam Tuckman, Rick Voegelin, and Jim Wangers.

Special thanks go to:

- Ray Day, VP Communications, Ford Motor Company; Sara Tatchio and Dean Weber, Ford Archives.

- Terry Rhadigan, General Motors Communications; Larry Kinsell, GM Media Archives; and Christo Datini, GM Heritage Center.

- Brandt Rosenbusch, FCA (Chrysler) Archives.

- Darwin Holmstrom and the Motorbooks team, who kept me on point through tens of thousands of words and hundreds of photos.

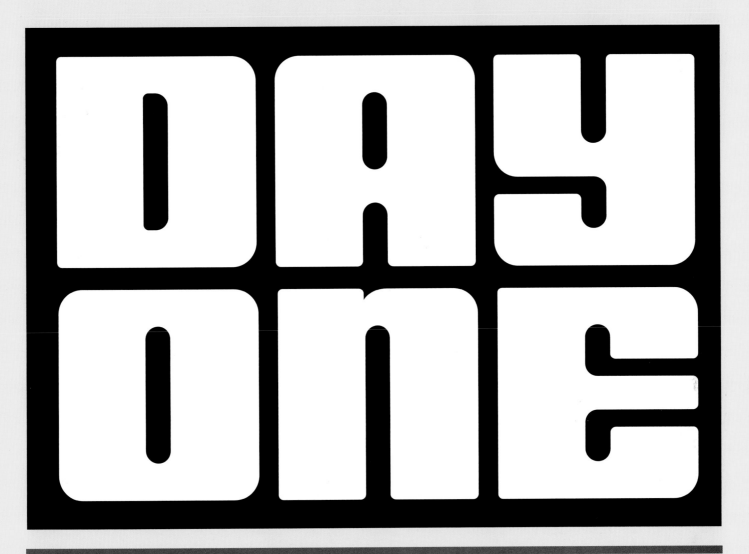

DAY ONE

AN AUTOMOTIVE JOURNALIST'S MUSCLE-CAR MEMOIR

MARTYN L. SCHORR

motorbooks

CONTENTS

DEDICATION AND ACKNOWLEDGMENTS 2

FOREWORD 6

INTRODUCTION 8
   THE WAY IT WAS

CHAPTER 1 13
   AMERICA'S LOVE AFFAIR WITH SPEED & POWER

CHAPTER 2 23
   PERFORMANCE IN PRINT

CHAPTER 3 27
   DAY TWO ON DAY ONE

CHAPTER 4 33
   1962: GO BIG OR GO HOME
      CHEVY 409: FIRST OF CHEVY'S BIG-BLOCK LEGENDS
      TEMPEST FOR TWO

CHAPTER 5 47
   1963: TOTAL PERFORMANCE, TOTALLY
      RPO Z11: CHEVY 427 LIGHT HEAVYWEIGHT
      MARK II: CHEVY'S MYSTERIOUS 427
      SWISS CHEESE SD-421: THE LIGHT FANTASTIC
      FINE WHINE: CHRYSLER'S TURBINE BIRD

CHAPTER 6 65
   1964: THE YEAR OF THE SUPERCAR
      MUSTANG SETS THE PACE
      CHRYSLER'S 800-POUND ELEPHANT
      427 INCHES OF ROLLING THUNDER

CHAPTER 7 79
   1965: THE MORE THE MERRIER
      THE GOLDFISH THAT ATE MUSTANGS
      DODGE'S HYBRID "STREET" HEMIS

CHAPTER 8 91
   1966: POWER TO THE PEOPLE
      DAY 1.5: FROM SALT TO SUBURBIA
      THERE'S NO SUBSTITUTE FOR CUBIC INCHES
      427 SOHC: AN ENGINE IN SEARCH OF A CAR

CHAPTER 9 . . . . **107**

1967: SUPERCARS, PONY CARS,
& MAJOR MUSCLE

427 CAMARO: THE THOMAS NICKEY AFFAIR

ROYAL PONTIAC GTO: BEWARE THE BOBCAT

OPTION Z28: CHEVY BUILDS A BOY RACER

CHAPTER 10 . . . .**121**

1968: SOMETHING FOR EVERYONE!

455 HURST-OLDS: LANSING'S EXECUTIVE EXPRESS

A-BODY HEMIS: THE KILLER BEES

428 COBRA JET: KING OF THE ROAD

CARS PROJECT: 390 SUPER JAVELIN

1968–1969 Z/28 CAMARO: THE BEAT GOES ON

CHAPTER 11 . . . .**141**

1969: WILD IN THE STREETS

ZL1: ZORA'S LIGHT ONE

CHARGER DAYTONA: IT'S ALL ABOUT THE AERO

RAM AIR V GTO: THE MYTH & THE MAGIC

454 CAMARO: RAREST OF THE RARE

OLDSMOBILE ROCKET SCIENCE

STING LIKE A (SUPER) BEE

CHAPTER 12 . . . . **163**

1970: MAGNUM FORCE FROM MOTOWN

BUICK GS: SPEAK SOFTLY & CARRY A BIG STICK

STAGE II GSX: BUICK'S PHANTOM SUPERCAR

CHALLENGER T/A & AAR 'CUDA: SIX-PACK TO GO

CHAPTER 13 . . . . **185**

1971: THE TURNING POINT

CHAPTER 14 . . . .**191**

1972: LAST OF THE GREAT ONES

PONTIAC 455 VENTURA II: ONE OF NONE

CHAPTER 15 . . . . **199**

1973–1974: SAVED BY THE SUPER-DUTY

INDEX **206**

FOREWORD

It was one of those life-defining moments. I had flown to Los Angeles to cover a press event, and had asked Pontiac PR to loan me a car for three days. No Avis *rent-a-blob* for me. I was thrilled when they rolled out a red GTO convertible.

"Here you go, buddy. Have a nice day." Yes, indeed.

As the engine throbbed through the Goat's dual exhaust, I put the top down and headed north. It was a glorious day—clear, warm, sunny. I rolled onto the Pacific Coast Highway, California Route 1, the blue Pacific Ocean to my left and the sheer cliffs of Malibu on my right. Then suddenly, it dawned on me.

Hey, I'm getting paid to do this. This is my job.

From 1965 to 1976, I worked as a writer for Magnum-Royal Publications in New York City, publishers of *Hi-Performance CARS*, *Speed and Supercar*, and *Supercars Annual*. As such, I lived through the golden age of muscle cars as an insider. With just a phone call, I had access to almost every muscle car from every manufacturer. I drove them, I photographed them, I street raced them, and I lived with them. And got paid to do it. If you were a car guy, as I was from the time I was a little kid, it was a dream job.

How did a dumb kid from Brooklyn wind up with such a cool gig?

For one thing, I had the guts to simply walk into the Magnum-Royal offices one day and ask for it. That day I was lucky enough to meet Editorial Director Martyn L. Schorr, the author of this book, and his managing editor, Fred Mackerodt. They saw a kid with a degree in journalism from New York University in one hand, writing samples in the other, and a background that included street racing a tri-power Pontiac.

They decided to give me a shot. To this day, I am forever grateful to them. Marty and Fred remain two of my dearest friends.

My writing had a definite New York edge to it, an attitude. Marty encouraged and fostered a tough-but-fair, tell-it-like-it-is attitude, and my writing fit right in. It's what set us apart from competitors, mainly the West Coast–based *Hot Rod*, *Car Craft*, and *Motor Trend*.

The other thing that set us apart from them was car company advertising—or lack of it. Those magazines had loads of it, and that made for a politically correct, tread lightly editorial direction. Their editors were like the Will Rogers of car magazines—they never met a car they didn't like. They didn't *personally* like us very much either. They were the establishment and we were kind of like the wiseass outlaws from New York.

Joe Oldham with his legendary Baldwin-Motion SS-427 Camaro, outside Motion Performance, after having it dyno-tuned in late 1968. It was his daily driver until it was stolen and never recovered in 1969.

But Magnum editors had no such obligation to make nice to car manufacturers. They didn't advertise much with us anyway so we had nothing to lose. Our first obligation was to the readers who plunked down their money every month and bought our publications off newsstands. They supported us and we supported them. I can remember times going to Marty and telling him that a car I had just tested was "a piece of crap."

"I have to blast it, Marty," I'd say. And he would say:

"Tell it like it is. But make sure you have your facts straight and tell the truth."

When car companies loaned us cars to test, they knew they were going to get a tough, but fair, shake. We reported exactly how the car actually performed, good or bad. They didn't always like what we wrote. But that was on them. Hey, make better-performing cars!

A classic example occurred in 1972 after we tested a 401 Javelin AMX that literally fell apart around us, culminating in the right rear axle actually snapping off on the street. We took a photo of the crippled car, and printed our truthful report.

Several days later, I got a call from Gerald C. Meyers, executive vice president at American Motors. Gerald C. Meyers calling me? Yes, and he's pissed. I picked up the phone and he berated me for the next ten minutes, accusing me of abusing his car and deliberately damaging the vehicle. He also banned me personally, and everyone else at *Hi-Performance CARS*, from ever attending AMC press events. As it turned out, the ban actually lasted only a couple of years, as AMC soon after went out of business.

While many automotive journalists were slobbering all over the 426 Street Hemi engine, telling readers how fantastic it was, we were telling readers the truth. It really didn't run very well off the showroom floor. It was a high-rpm racing engine with huge ports and valves and breathing through a restrictive exhaust system. It developed minimal low-end torque. Yet, you'd never know it reading most of the other car magazines. But our readers knew because we told them. On the street, the 440 Six-Pack could give the much more expensive Street Hemi a run for its money. Sure, with professional tuning and headers, the 426 would run rings around just about anything. But that's not how they ran off the showroom floor.

For our troubles, we got hate mail and death threats. But we prided ourselves on telling the truth. Serve the reader. That's what Marty said.

Which is why I wrote the first article ever, in any magazine, that addressed the issue of street racing in a truthful and realistic way. Yes, it was politically incorrect and we were berated by the likes of mayors, police officials, even the NHRA. But we didn't give a rat's ass. It existed and we told the truth.

Smokey burnouts were also politically incorrect and you rarely saw them in the high-circulation West Coast magazines. But you saw tons of them in our publications. Our readers liked them, and frankly, we enjoyed doing them. But sometimes, even burnouts got us in trouble.

One day while photographing new cars at Black Lake at GM's Milford Proving Ground, we started doing burnouts. A vast blacktop surface literally acres in size, it's officially the Vehicle Dynamics Test Area. It's used by engineers for testing suspension setups and is so big you could spin out in any direction and not hit anything for miles.

Off in the distance a Chevy pickup was approaching at high speed. It screeched to a stop, all four wheels locked up, right in front of the car we were photographing. Out jumped Doc Whitworth, the guy in charge of safety at the Proving Ground.

"That's it!" he screamed at me. "You guys are shut down! What the hell do you think you're doing?" he yelled, waving his arms like a madman.

"Err, uh, burnout photography?" I answered.

"Burnout photography my ass!" he screamed. "You're making holes in *my* blacktop! You guys are out of here! Leave the premises immediately!"

And with that, we were kicked out of the GM Proving Ground. In trouble again, just for trying to please the reader. At least it wasn't a lifetime ban.

This book continues Marty's philosophy of pleasing the reader. I think you'll find some of the best stories about some of the most fascinating muscle cars Marty encountered in his years as an editor. And all with a New York attitude.

—*Joe Oldham*

DAY ONE
THE WAY IT WAS

It was the golden age of muscle, when American carmakers stuffed their biggest, most powerful engines into midsize supercars and long-hood, short-deck pony cars. Automobile manufacturers supported racing—and discovered that *winning on Sunday* actually did *sell cars on Monday*. DAY ONE is about muscle cars from 1962 to 1974, presented *the way they were*.

Enthusiasts rarely leave things the way they are. So it wasn't unusual that new 1960s and 1970s high-performance cars, even while still under warranty, were tweaked to extract more power, and often cosmetically enhanced as well. Speed shops selling "horsepower" flourished from coast to coast. If you wanted to buy an already modified new car, specialty dealers were ready to take your order.

During this time, I was not only an enthusiast, but also an automotive photojournalist, magazine editor, and publisher. I also partnered with Joel Rosen in

Author Marty Schorr, circa 1959, with his potent Ford Flathead V-8 60-powered MG TC. Dubbed the "Jag-Porsche Hunter," it displayed membership in the Draggin' Wheels hot rod club and Foreign Car Club of America, covering all bases.

While editing car magazines, my "office" moved each summer to carmakers' proving grounds for test driving next year's cars. I'd try to spend as much time as possible at straightaways used as drag strips. I'm running a pre-production unmarked '67 Dodge Coronet 426 Street Hemi against a Hemi-Charger at Chelsea, Michigan, in June 1966.

1967 and created Baldwin-Motion supercar catalogs and advertising and co-founded the Motion Supercar Club. It was a glorious time to be a car guy.

During my early years, my fantasy was to be a magazine staff writer-photographer. In the early 1960s, I freelanced articles and photography to enthusiast magazines. While delivering a story to Larry T. Shaw—who was editor of *Custom Rodder*; *Car, Speed and Style*; and *CARS* at Magnum-Royal Publications' Manhattan offices—my life changed. I discovered that Larry was going to be devoting all his time to *CARS* and the publisher would need an editor for the other two magazines. A few minutes later, Magnum's publisher, Irwin Stein, came into Larry's office and he offered me the job of editor for *Custom Rodder* and *Car, Speed and Style*. Not the job I always fantasized having, but one giving me *total* responsibility for producing *two magazines*. Too numb to answer, I simply nodded until I could get the words out. I thought my head was going to explode that day.

Except for a surprise "sabbatical" between October 1961 and August 1962 courtesy of Uncle Sam, I remained with the company for approximately thirteen years. On August 12, 1961, Russians started building the Berlin Wall, isolating East Berlin from the West. On August 30, 1961, President John F. Kennedy activated the National Guard and Army Reserve. With me being a reservist, at the end of September my wife and I packed a trailer, hitched it to our new tri-power '61 Bonneville, and headed south. On October 2, I reported for duty at Fort Eustis in Virginia. We lived off-post, sharing a house with friend and fellow reservist Joel Wasserman and his wife. After more than fifty-five years, we are still friends, but unfortunately my wonderful 389/348 Bonneville is long gone.

DAY ONE is my ticket to ride down memory lane, flashing back to coming of age as a hot rodder in New York City. I joined the Draggin' Wheels Hot Rod Club in Yonkers, New York, in 1955 and proudly displayed our club plaque on my rare '40 Mercury convertible sedan. Mildly customized and powered with a Flathead V-8 with twin Strombergs and dual exhausts, the car had bark that was much worse than its bite. However, back then it was the only one I had ever seen.

I've been able to relive hanging out with club members and rivals from the Highwaymen club at the Raceway Inn on

ABOVE: The author's first new performance car, a '61 Bonneville tri-power hardtop, in Virginia, June 1962. This photo is while he was on active duty at Fort Eustis. The spider wheel treatment was later replaced with Cragar S/S mags. Interior had a Sun tach and extra gauges. The engine had already been modified and fitted with hot ignition, '62 Pontiac alternator, and engine dress-up goodies.

LEFT: Dilbert Farb was in charge of our magazine display at the 1967 New York City Hot Rod & Custom Show and treated showgoers to Josel, the exotic snake dancer. It was one of the most successful attractions of the show, but people hardly noticed my hot rod.

the east end of Gun Hill Road in the Bronx. The "menu" was always the same: burgers, fries, cokes, trash talking, and street racing. Late at night, we would often head to the Cross Bronx Expressway, still under construction at the time. There you could see everything from fuel bikes to supercharged Caddys and Chrysler Hemi-powered Fords running for bragging rights. It was an incredible adrenalin rush for a nineteen-year-old newbie hot rodder!

Back in the day, our club raced a '32 Ford three-window coupe and rear-engined dragster, both powered by fuel-burning supercharged Caddy engines. We also produced a hot rod and custom car show at the Westchester County Center. Serving as the club's publicity director put me in touch with magazine editors, thus igniting my passion for writing about cars.

On weekends I would drive my hopped-up Merc to tracks in the tri-state area to photograph cars with my $6 Kodak Brownie Flash Six-20. One of those photos, a Cadillac-Allard shot in 1956 in Allentown, Pennsylvania, was published in 2011 in Nicholas Pettitt's *British Drag Racing: The Early Years*.

In 1957 I purchased a unique, cycle-fendered '49 MG TC that had been converted to left-hand drive and repowered with a pro-built Ford V-8-60 Flathead. The engine had a hot cam, headers, duals, and Edelbrock aluminum heads and manifold with dual Strombergs. It was my scaled-down '32 Ford roadster. My quirky MG, with louvered hood and spindly 19-inch wire wheels, always had a fresh coat of gray primer and was never painted. On weekend nights, I would troll areas around Bruckner Boulevard and on the Post

Author Marty Schorr with one of his heroes from the 1960s, Roy Lunn, godfather of the 1966–1969 Le Mans–winning Ford GT40s. Photo taken in 2016 with Schorr's Tungsten Grey '06 Ford GT and photographer Gary Jean's Mark IV Red GT. We took Roy out for lunch to celebrate his induction into the Automotive Hall of Fame. *Gary Jean*

Road in the Bronx looking for unsuspecting Jag and Porsche drivers. They were easy prey for my "hot rod" MG—as long as the road was straight.

I left Magnum-Royal in 1973 and started Performance Media Public Relations (PMPR, Inc.). I also produced magazines such as *Chevy Action* and *Vette* for other publishers. In the late 1970s, my wife, Sharon, and I started publishing *Thunder Am* magazine and Marque Series Books under the Quicksilver imprint.

My media experience and car guy cred figured heavily in Buick choosing us to handle its East Coast PR and media relations in 1982. Buick was a client for almost eighteen years. We also did work for Aero-Tec Labs, Nicola Bulgari and the BVLGARI-Cadillac relationship, Mercedes-Benz, Panoz, Piero Rivolta (Iso and Zagato), and Volvo.

Since 1960, when I started editing automotive magazines, my avocation has been my vocation. *DAY ONE* is my latest contribution to the hobby.

Ab Jenkins's iconic *Mormon Meteor* was a custom-bodied '35 Duesenberg SJ fitted with a J-557 supercharged 400-horsepower engine with dual carbs. Jenkins set a number of records, including averaging 145 miles per hour for 10 miles, over 152 miles per hour for one hour, and clocked as high as 160 miles per hour.

CHAPTER ONE

America's Love Affair With Speed & Power

We've been obsessed with more horsepower and faster cars for more than a century—and it's not fading anytime soon.

The horsepower and speed race have been going on since the second car was built. If you were a carmaker craving attention at the turn of the twentieth century, building fast cars and winning races was the surefire route to take. Nobody proved that more definitively than Henry Ford.

At a 2001 celebration of the Ford Motor Company's motorsports centennial, Henry Ford's great-grandson, Edsel Ford II, said: "Not only is our racing tradition older than our company, but there might not

even have been a Ford Motor Company without racing. My grandfather needed to get the world's attention—and he knew how. Henry Ford built a race car."

On October 10, 1901, Henry Ford raced his home-built *Sweepstakes*, powered by a 26-horsepower, horizontally opposed two-cylinder engine, in a ten-lap, 10-mile race in Grosse Pointe, Michigan. The odds-on favorite was Alexander Winton, a successful racer and car builder best known for luxurious, powerful, and technologically advanced vehicles. His Winton *Bullet* sported a 70-horsepower engine and he had little trouble leading the field. On the eighth lap, Ford caught up and passed Winton to win. Winning that seminal race set off a chain of events that led to the formation of the Ford Motor Company in 1903. One hundred and fourteen years later, Ford Motor Company is still involved in building high-performance cars and racing.

As early as 1904, racing was used to showcase brands and influence car buyers. Buick was then heavily involved in a variety of racing activities. Buicks had excelled in competitive events, and in 1905, a Buick won the Two-Cylinder Class at the 1,000-Mile Glidden Tour and Mount Washington Hillclimb. In 1910, one year before the first Indy 500 race, Buick took its massive Bug race cars to the Brickyard for testing. Driving a raucous, red Bug powered by a massive 622-cubic-inch, 57.6-horsepower four, Bob Burman clocked 105.87 miles per hour and set a national record.

Decades before Cadillac and Oldsmobile introduced powerful, game-changing overhead-valve V-8 engines in 1949 and Pontiac unveiled the GTO in 1964, carmakers

ABOVE: Louis Chevrolet (Yes, *that* Chevrolet!) and Bob Burman successfully campaigned Buick Bugs, powered by 622-inch Fours, during the first decade of the twentieth century. In 1910, Burman ran almost 106 miles per hour at Indy to set a national record. *General Motors*

BELOW: Ford's Flathead V-8, introduced in 1932, was the engine of choice for hot rods and race cars until the first Cadillac and Olds OHV V-8s appeared in 1949. This beautifully detailed Flathead boasts a positive-displacement supercharger.

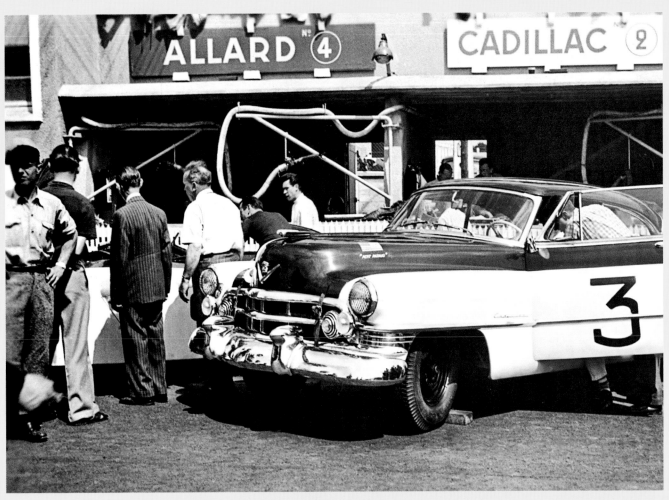

ABOVE: In 1950, Briggs Cunningham took two Cadillacs to Le Mans to contest the premier international endurance-racing event. After twenty-four hours, the relatively stock-bodied hardtop, driven by Sam and Miles Collier, finished 10th. The streamlined race car version, *Le Monstre*, driven by Cunningham and Phil Walters, finished 11th. *General Motors.*

RIGHT: During the early 1950s, Flathead Six Hudsons dominated stock car racing thanks to Marshall Teague and Smokey Yunick. Starting in 1952, Hudson offered dual-carb Twin H- power engines as optional in passenger cars. This slightly modified Twin H engine is in the *Satan of Morimar*, an original road racing and hillclimb Hornet.

Chevrolet introduced the 265-inch small-block, a new design, lightweight V-8, in 1955. Its power pack options and displacement increased to 283, 327, and 350 cubic inches and revolutionized road and track performance. Its descendants can still be found in the latest Camaros and Corvettes.

had been keenly aware of the public's passion for power. And they responded accordingly. Pontiac started the supercar revolution by stuffing a 389-cubic-inch engine into a midsize Tempest and branding it a GTO. Low-volume, high-performance cars first surfaced in the early 1900s, when most cars were little more than motorized buggies. During this time, Mercer and Stutz were feared on racetracks and ruled the roads.

Even though the automotive industry was still in its infancy, Mercer and Stutz built limited numbers of pricey, stripped-down, high-performance roadsters. The 1911 Mercer Raceabout and 1914 Stutz Bearcat were designed and engineered specifically to appeal to wealthy enthusiasts who craved bragging rights and on-road fun.

At the time, Mercer's Raceabout came with an inconceivable performance promise: "Guaranteed to Cover the Flying Mile in 51 Seconds at 70 MPH." Powered by a 300-cubic-inch, 60-horsepower T-head four, America's first highly tuned sports car was scary fast.

In 1914, the Stutz Bearcat delivered more power and was faster than just about any production car on the road. Its 361-cubic-inch, 80-horsepower T-head four was considered state of the art. Race-prepped Stutz roadsters were stock car champs—and a 92-horsepower Stutz placed second at Le Mans in 1926.

Duesenberg, one of the most prestigious American marques of the 1920s and 1930s, earned its reputation for power and engineering years before its nameplate graced a grille shell. Between 1912 and 1916, Duesenberg Engine Manufacturing Company produced walking beam two-plugs-per-cylinder fours, displacing 298 to 361 cubic inches for automotive and aircraft use. The company's advertising slogan was "Power of the Hour." Eddie Rickenbacker, with his Duesenberg Speedway engine–powered car, won at Ascot in 1916.

Henry Ford actually made going fast affordable at the turn of the century and into the 1920s. Between 1908 and 1927, Ford built more than 15 million Model Ts with prices starting at $260. Enthusiasts wanting to go very fast for very little money flocked to Henry's cars. Speed and performance garages that specialized in coaxing more power from 20-horsepower Model T flathead fours proliferated from coast to coast during almost two decades of production.

Ford dealers got into the action as well, converting mostly used Model Ts into hot rods and race cars using Mercury and Langdon Speedster bodies, Ruckstell two-speed rear ends, Franklin steering, Buffalo 20-inch wire wheels, and modified engines. This was some forty years before dealer-built Chevy muscle cars from Baldwin-Motion, Nickey, and Yenko first appeared.

Enthusiasts could choose from OHV, SOHC, or DOHC conversion heads made by Clemons, Cragar, Frontenac, Gemsa, Hal, Hunt, Rajo, Roof, Winfield, and others. The Frontenac or "Fronty" DOHC sixteen-valve conversion, manufactured by Arthur and Louis Chevrolet, was extremely popular with racers and hot rodders searching for maximum performance.

In California in the 1920s, the Model T Ford is credited with giving birth to the hot rod movement. When Ford introduced its new and improved 40-horsepower Model A in 1928, it took over where the T left off. When the 65-horsepower flathead V-8 Ford debuted in 1932, it assured Ford's domination of the hot rod field until the advent of OHV V-8s.

By the late 1920s and early 1930s, the formerly elusive 100-mile-per-hour mark was old news. Magnificent, short-wheelbase '32 Duesenburg SJ Speedsters with supercharged 320-horsepower DOHC engines could top 120 miles per hour. Factory racer Ab Jenkins set a number of records at the Bonneville Salt Flats, averaging over 150 miles per hour in a streamlined and supercharged Model J Dusey. In 1935

Jenkins returned to the salt and averaged 135.58 miles per hour for twenty-four hours, setting a record that stood for many years. Jenkins's custom-bodied Bonneville record-setter was modified after the record runs and became the legendary *Mormon Meteor*.

Buick actively campaigned race cars through the 1920s and 1930s, and in 1941 introduced compound carburetion, a high-performance dual-carb option for its popular OHV Fireball Eight Century. Fitted with dual two-barrel carburetors and rated at 165 horsepower, Buick's Century was the highest-power standard production vehicle built in America in 1941.

During the early post–World War II years and into the 1950s, automakers actively participated in stock car racing. In 1952 Twin-H (dual carb) 308-inch flathead six Hudson

Hornets won twenty-seven of thirty-four NASCAR Grand Nationals. The Hornet proved tough to beat, even when the competition went to OHV V-8s. Marshall Teague, with help from Smokey Yunick, put Hudson on the map with his NASCAR racers powered by special 200-plus-horsepower 7X flatheads with aluminum high-compression heads, multi carbs, and racing cams. Hudson offered Twin-H power as a regular production option on Hornets starting in 1952.

The flathead's domination was seriously challenged in 1949 when Oldsmobile introduced an all-new, 303-cubic-inch OHV Rocket V-8. At approximately $2,000, a showroom-stock 135-horsepower Olds 88 had a top speed of 100 miles per hour. In 1949, an Olds 88 coupe won six of nine NASCAR Grand Nationals and in 1950 an Olds won the first Mexican Road Race.

From 1955 through 1958, Chrysler letter series cars (C-300 to 300D) were available with potent Hemi engines, displacing 331 to 392 cubic inches. This is a 354-inch Hemi in Ralph Gorenstein's ultra-rare, one-of-twenty-built, three-speed-stick Chrysler 300B.

Rochester mechanical fuel injection was available in 1957 and 1958 Pontiac Bonnevilles. The 347-inch fuel-injected engine here is vintage 1957 and rated at 300 horsepower. In 1958, engine displacement jumped to 370 cubic inches and the fuel-injected engine was 310 horsepower. Production was limited.

The mid-1950s proved to be pivotal years for Detroit and high-performance vehicle production. Gasoline was cheap, the economy was strong, and performance was very easy to sell. That's when we started to see carmakers use provocative engine branding as sales tools: Power Pack, Ramjet FI, and Super Turbo Thrust (Chevrolet); Interceptor (Ford); J-2 Rocket (Oldsmobile); Fury and Golden Commando (Plymouth); and Tri-Power (Pontiac) (among others). Even Cadillac offered dual-quad and tri-power Eldorado engine options.

In 1955, Chevrolet introduced its all-new, lightweight 265-cubic-inch small-block V-8, available with optional Power Pack four-barrel and dual exhausts. Two years later, displacement jumped to 283 cubic inches and Chevys could be fitted with four-speed and fuel injection. Chrysler also jumped on the bandwagon in 1955 with its 300-horsepower C-300.

Chrysler's letter series entry in the horsepower wars, weighing in at more than 4,500 pounds, could accelerate to 60 miles per hour in the nines and top out at 130 miles per hour. In NASCAR competition, Kiekhaefer's legendary Chrysler C-300s were *the* cars to beat. Chrysler's Hemi, one of the most successful engines in American racing history, was unstoppable on super speedways and drag strips in the 1960s and 1970s.

While Chrysler's letter series 300s were heavy luxury cars, they offered true muscle car performance. A 331-cubic-inch Hemi with two four-barrel carburetors, solid lifter camshaft and valvetrain, beefed suspension, and dual low-restriction exhaust system powered the '55 C-300. A stock C-300 could go to 60 miles per hour from a standing start in ten seconds flat and cover the quarter-mile in the mid-seventeens at over 80 miles per hour. A prepared C-300 clocked almost 128 miles per hour in Flying Mile competition in 1955.

In 1956, Chrysler upped its game and the 300B was available with 340- or 355-horsepower, 354-cubic-inch Hemis. Fitted with the optional 355-horsepower engine, a 300B ran almost 140 miles per hour in the Flying Mile. It was the first American car to deliver 1 horsepower per cubic inch, a year before Chevrolet's fuel-injected 283-cubic-inch, 283-horsepower engine.

Chrysler continued its lead position in the performance car marketplace in 1957 with the restyled 300C, powered by a stock 375-horsepower, 392-cubic-inch Hemi or optional 390-horsepower version. Performance was blistering for the time, with magazines reporting 0- to 60-mile-per-hour times in the high eights and quarter-mile times of low seventeens at over 90 miles per hour. Running on the old Daytona Beach sand course, a Chrysler 300C won its class with an impressive 138.9-mile-per-hour pass.

In 1958, the 300D received the last version of the dual-quad 392-inch Hemi, rated at 380 horsepower. A small number of fuel-injected 390-horsepower, 392-inch Hemi 300Ds were built, but the system proved to be unreliable and was quickly discontinued. A 300D, piloted by Norm Thatcher, ran over 156 miles per hour at Bonneville to set the Class E record.

Starting in 1959, Chrysler 300 letter series cars received new 413-cubic-inch Wedge engines, first with inline dual quads and later with long (30-inch) and short (15-inch) cross-ram dual-quad induction systems. In 1960, the 300F came with a stock 375-horsepower engine; approximately fifteen 400-horsepower models with 15-inch short ram manifolds were produced. The short ram cars were fitted with exotic Pont-à-Mousson four-speeds built in France for Chrysler-powered Facel Vegas.

By 1961 most American carmakers were involved in building performance cars and racing. The Chrysler 300G was once again restyled and was still available with long and short ram 413-cubic-inch Wedge engines rated at 375 and 400 horsepower, respectively. While the four-speed was no longer available, you could order a three-speed manual racing transmission—if you were well connected. Only a few of these Option Code 381, three-speed 300Gs were built for competition and first surfaced at the 1961 Daytona Flying Mile Trials. In articles and advertising, letter series Chryslers were often referred to as "banker's hot rod" and "gentleman's express."

Another luxury brand, Buick, was also ahead of the curve when it came to high-performance, big-engined production cars that were also successfully raced. By simply fitting a dressed-up 1955 Century body on a shorter wheelbase Special chassis and then coupling it with the highest horsepower Roadmaster engine, Buick created one of Detroit's first muscle cars.

In 1955 and 1956, Buick Centurys competed favorably with smaller, lighter hot Fords and Chevys. They came with 322-cubic-inch Nailhead V-8 engines rated at 236 and 255 horsepower, respectively, which were good for mid-nine-second 0- to 60-mile-per-hour sprints and consistently clocked low-seventeen-second quarter-mile times. While this may not sound impressive when discussing muscle cars, the Century was a heavy, full-size car.

On a roll with the Century, Buick upped the ante in 1957 with a 364-cubic-inch, 300-horsepower engine, creating a big car that could accelerate to 60 miles per hour in nine seconds flat—or less. Buick's 364-inch V-8 had big-port heads, big valves, 10:1 pistons, high-lift camshaft, Carter AFB four-barrel, and header-like exhaust manifolds. The '57 Buick Century was right on the money and hard to beat at a time when Detroit was in the middle of a horsepower race.

During the late 1950s, Buick had a special program for marketing heavy-duty components—thinly disguised

Ford rated its optional supercharged '57 F-Code 312-inch engine at 300 horsepower, but that was very conservative. It was available in all body styles and sedans racked up an impressive number of NASCAR Grand National and USAC wins. On the street, supercharged Fords held their own against fuel-injected '57 Chevys. *Gary Jean*

speed equipment—through dealership parts departments. Listed as Export Kits, the heavy-duty parts were for cars being shipped out of the country where driving styles and conditions called for additional engine output. Included in these kits were high-lift, long-duration camshafts and solid lifter valvetrains, high-compression 11:1 forged aluminum pistons, adjustable rocker arms, and assorted hardware. When installed on a stock 300-horsepower '57 Century engine, horsepower increased by a solid 10 percent. There's little doubt that a greater percentage of Export Kits were sold to domestic hot rodders and racers than put on cars being exported, though.

Just about all carmakers in the 1950s offered high-performance options and models, setting the stage for the 1960s and early 1970s—the golden era of performance cars. Starting in 1956, Pontiac marketed dual quad, tri-power, and even fuel-injected engine options. In 1957 Oldsmobile offered a 300-horsepower Tri-Power J-2 Rocket engine option. Following Chrysler 300's lead, Plymouth and Dodge offered lower-priced specialty models powered by Wedge and Hemi engines.

The same was true of Chevrolet, with its fuel-injected and multi-carbed 283/327 small-blocks and pre-396/427 big-block 348/409 Super Sports. Ford had skin in the game prior to its 1963 Total Performance marketing blitz. Think multi-carbed and supercharged Fords, starting in 1957.

In 1957, the Automobile Manufacturers Association (AMA) responded to Detroit's rampant promotion of high-performance and racing by announcing its infamous anti-racing edict. The AMA "encouraged" carmakers to play down performance and horsepower and play up safety in advertising and marketing, and it banned direct factory participation in racing. Initially Detroit caved, but it was a very short-lived victory for the AMA as carmakers continued to "unofficially" supply racers with cars and parts.

Henry Ford was fed up with the ineffective AMA racing ban and had no qualms letting the public know about it: "The AMA ban on auto racing is null and void within Ford Motor

One of Detroit's sexiest and most powerful engines, the 375-horsepower long-ram, dual quad 413-inch Wedge with 30-inch tuned runners, appeared first in the '59 Chrysler 300F. Versions with long and short (30-inch) ram-induction would later appear on 413- and 426-inch Mopars, including the legendary Max Wedge & Ramcharger–equipped Dodges and Plymouths.

In the mid-1950s, carmakers often used the Daytona Beach International Safety and Performance Trials, Pure Oil events, on the old Daytona Beach sand course to set flying and standing mile records. The '57 Chevys with dual four-barrel and fuel-injected 283 engines were quite successful. *General Motors*

Company in 1962." On June 11, 1962, Ford's board chairman who, ironically, was president of the AMA, sent a letter to the trade association stating, "The [racing ban] resolution adopted in the past by the AMA no longer has either purpose or effect. Accordingly, we are withdrawing from it."

Detroit's competitive spirit during the mid- to late 1950s set the stage for some of the most exciting years in performance automotive history. The 1960s was a time when Detroit's landscape was overflowing with high-performance cars and powerful engines. Chrysler and Ford openly participated in racing and vigorously promoted their involvement. GM participated via a backdoor approach, keeping its promotional efforts minimal in accordance with corporate policy. The end game was to satisfy the public's need for speed and sell more cars. It worked.

Credited with creating the supercar (a midsize car with a big-car engine) market segment in 1964, Pontiac's GTO was a dressed-to-thrill Tempest with 389-inch V-8 power rated 325 (four-barrel) or 348 (tri-power) horsepower. A GTO could be ordered with three- or four-speed stick, automatic, and a host of comfort, convenience, and performance options. It wasn't the quickest or fastest, but it offered the absolute best possible combination of power, ride, and handling and head-turning appeal. The industry's most creative, in-your-face advertising and marketing promotions supported it. The GTO became a legend in its own time. And it still is.

Long before carmakers started using focus groups to test new ideas and develop sales and marketing strategies, savvy marketers were already aware of how speed, power, and winning races positively affected potential buyers. With the advent of the phenomenon known as the youth market in the early to mid-1960s, it was hard to find a brand that didn't include a high-performance model in its latest offering. The same is true today.

Bill Mitchell put our magazine-sponsored Baldwin-Motion 427 Camaro into the NHRA record books quite often in 1968 and 1969. He continued his record-breaking performances from 1972 to 1974, driving *CARS*-sponsored Motion Minicar H/Gas VW and Porsche.

performance in print

Hi-Performance CARS was a David battling Goliaths such as *Hot Rod*, *Car Craft*, and *Popular Hot Rodding* for newsstand display space, advertising revenue, and the hearts of enthusiasts. *CARS* didn't do that well competing for prime newsstand display and advertising dollars, but we did succeed in winning the loyalty of enthusiasts who appreciated a magazine with a New York City attitude. A magazine that told it like it was—advertisers be damned!

Launched as *CARS Hot Rods – Super Stocks – Customs*, the first issue, December 1959, was published by Royal Publications and edited by Larry T. Shaw. I was listed as a photographer. Shortly thereafter, Royal became Magnum-Royal Publications and its portfolio included bi-monthly, digest-size *Custom Rodder* and *CAR, Speed and Style* (changed in 1961 to *SPEED and CUSTOM*), previously published by Magnum.

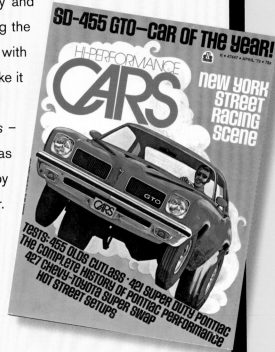

Typically, our Top Performance Car of the Year issue is one of the year's best selling. When we honored the Super-Duty 455 GTO in 1973, it was *the* best selling issue. The only problem was that Pontiac decided not to build any, including the one I personally ordered. Whoops.

It all started when I began freelancing for these digest-size hot rod and custom car magazines while I still had a "day job" in the mid-1950s. I became editor of them in 1960.

In 1960, I was named editor of the bi-monthlies. I became editorial director and editor of *CARS* in 1965 and changed the title to *Hi-Performance CARS*. In 1970 there was a public offering and our name changed to Magnum Communications Corporation and my new title was vice president, editorial.

Even though our secondary magazines such as *Rodder & Super/Stock*, *SPEED and SUPERCAR*, and *SUPER/STOCK & FX* had grown in number and size and acquired new titles, *Hi-Performance CARS* was our flagship publication. It was editorially aligned with the top magazines on the West Coast that had large staffs and budgets and monopolized newsstand display space. They also boasted substantial advertising revenue that supported sizable editorial staffing. We had neither!

What we did have was an abundance of New York attitude—and our readers loved it. Our circulation grew accordingly. Joe Oldham, a Brooklyn street racer who viewed every traffic light as a Christmas tree, got his start at *Hi-Performance CARS*. He turned burnouts into an art form, and was a valued columnist and contributor of road tests and muscle car features.

In April 1965, I hired Fred Mackerodt. When I brought Fred onboard as managing editor, I knew about his experience at Cowles Magazines and writing for *Nugget* and *Penthouse*. And I knew that he earned his motorhead cred starting and running Automotive Obsolete, selling vintage NOS parts. What I didn't know, however, was that he came with an alter ego whose name was Dilbert Horatio Farb. According to his business card, he was the "Exalted President and Honorable Leader of the Pitkin Avenue Street Racing & Choral Society." Fred was "Straight Outta Brooklyn" and *Hi-Performance CARS* became the only automotive magazine to have full-time humor editor, Dilbert H. Farb, on its masthead.

Dilbert also penned a Q&A column, "You're Asking, I'm Telling!" that generated most of our reader mail. His irreverent, tongue-in-cheek oddball road tests, including those of a scale model Can-Am McLaren bed and a Maine lobster boat, are legendary.

The Dilbert Farb road test that garnered the most reader responses appeared in the July 1970 issue: "Dilbert Horatio Farb delves into pollution control and wrings out a '67 White refuse vehicle in a fantastic TRASH BASH." He tested a 30,500-pound garbage truck powered by a 220-horsepower, 743-inch Cummins NH220 diesel, borrowed from Coney Island Carting.

"When Carroll Shelby heard we were track-testing a garbage truck named *Vinnie*, he supplied 32 cans of his Pit Stop deodorant so that we wouldn't be penalized during tech inspection," the magazine noted. Impeccably attired in his trademark bespoke driver's suit, he actually collected garbage with truck owner Joe Morea before heading to the track.

"When the flag dropped, I went flying down the track, deftly double-clutching and shifting the 16-speed transmission approximately every 43 feet. The 4.88 Posi gears were perfect. At the precise moment I slammed the shift lever into 16th gear, the truck rocketed through the traps. My best time was 61.1 mph in 43.88 seconds, a new class record for Formula Garbage/CR-AP!" wrote Dilbert.

To enhance our relationship with racing enthusiasts, we sponsored race cars that collected an enviable number of NHRA national records between 1964 and 1974. The fuel-burning, blown Hemi AA/A *Tasmanian Devil*, which also ran in CC/FD, was campaigned by Pacers Automotive. Motion Performance fielded A/MP and B/MP Camaros, while Motion Minicar competed with "slammed" H/Gas VWs and a Porsche 911. Some were displayed with magazine project cars as centerpieces of our auto show exhibits.

Pacers' George Snizek drove *Taz* to a class win and record at the 1964 NHRA Indy Nationals. He locked in the AA/A record at 161.87 miles per hour in 9.56 seconds, which stood for a number of years. In May 1966 at the NHRA record run at Island Dragway, in Great Meadows, New Jersey, George nailed the CC/Fuel Dragster record at 165.13 miles per hour in 9.34 seconds.

With the growing interest in pony cars, we expanded sponsorship to Camaro. driven in 1967 by Joel Rosen, in 1968 and 1969 by Bill Mitchell, and in 1970 to 1974 by Dennis Ferrara. Rosen set two AHRA world records, B/MP F-2 and B/HR F-2. His best time was 122.95 in 11.33 seconds. In 1968, Mitchell was the first to put an A/MP Camaro into the tens and in a two-year period filled a wall with NHRA records. Ferrara competed in A and B/MP with the Gen II Camaro, setting records each year, and in 1974 he set both ends of the NHRA A & B/MP records, 145.16 miles per hour in 9.54 seconds and 140.84 in 9.84 seconds, respectively.

In 1972 and 1973 Mitchell ran consistent 11.0s in the chopped Motion Minicar/*CARS Thunderbug* VW and literally *owned* the H/Gas record. His radical H/Gas Porsche 911 ran consistent 10.20s in 1973 and 1974.

ABOVE: Our *CARS*-sponsored Gen II Baldwin-Motion Camaro driven by Dennis Ferrara set NHRA A & B/MP National Records and, in 1974, set both ends of both records. It was one of the winningest Camaros in the country.

TOP: The July 1972 issue carried Dilbert Farb's off-the-wall road test of my son Stuart's McLaren Can-Am bed, built by dune-buggy pioneer Bruce Meyers: "Dilbert wrings out a real sleeper in this fantastic test of an all-out DREAM MACHINE." Here he gets a wake-up call from Stu and his sister, Collier.

We also sponsored a decade of Super/Stock and Funny Car Championship races at Cecil County and Atco Dragway, which kept us in touch with top racers across the country.

After I left Magnum in mid-1973, all efforts were put into *Hi-Performance CARS*. It survived into the early-1980s under the direction of a number of editors. Those truly were the *great* old days.

Joe Oldham's triple-black '69 SS427 Camaro was featured in "WANTED" and "the moment of truth" national advertising, and this photo was on the 1969 Baldwin-Motion catalog cover.

CHAPTER THREE

Day Two
on
Day One

In the 1960s and 1970s, unique dealerships made it possible for an enthusiast to order a new car built to "Day Two" specs. Some were hot-rodded with headers and intake and ignition upgrades. Others were low-volume serial production cars with larger, more powerful engines than normally available. A few were warrantied and most could be financed through carmakers' credit companies. Those dealers were dream merchants.

The highest profile dealer-built specialty cars were 427 Camaros marketed by Baldwin-Motion, Nickey Chicago, and Yenko Sportscars. Baldwin-Motion offered the widest range of options in both domestic and export models. Yenko was the highest volume producer. Nickey was the largest Chevrolet dealer marketing specialty cars. Its involvement in high-performance dated back to the mid- to late 1950s.

Holiday Greetings FROM OUR HOUSE TO YOUR HOUSE

CARS MAGAZINE

Joel Rosen and I founded Baldwin-Motion, a partnership between Baldwin Chevrolet and Motion Performance. In the 1960s, Ed Simonin owned Baldwin Chevrolet, which was started by his father, August Simonin, in the 1920s. Motion Performance, a speed shop owned by Joel Rosen, was known for dyno tuning and building and racing fast Chevys. They were located three-quarters of a mile from each other in Baldwin, a New York City suburb on Long Island.

Between 1967 and 1974, Baldwin-Motion marketed 425–450 horsepower SS and 500-plus-horsepower Phase III 427 and 454 Camaros, Chevy II/Novas, Chevelles, Corvettes, and entry-level $2,998 Biscayne Street Racer Specials. Its halo car was the stunningly bold, limited-production 1969–1971 Phase III GT Corvette. All cars were built-to-order at Motion Performance. Orders were processed and GMAC financing made available by Baldwin Chevrolet.

Mike Mueller wrote in *Motor City Muscle* (published by Motorbooks International in 1997): "Easily the most radical of the super Chevrolets built by superdealers were the Baldwin-Motion Phase III cars, most common of which were the Camaros. Setting records in a Baldwin-Motion Chevrolet was simply a matter of how much you were willing to spend."

Baldwin-Motion 1964–1967 A & B/Modified Production Camaros sponsored by *Hi-Performance CARS* were consistent national record holders.

ABOVE: The first Baldwin-Motion 427 Camaro was the *Hi-Performance CARS*–sponsored race car powered by an almost-stock L88 engine. Joel Rosen drove it to two AHRA world records and it was the subject of the magazine's 1967 Christmas card.

LEFT: Stunning examples of Yenko/SC '69 Camaro and Chevelle, built on 427 COPO models, and the '70 Nova 350/360 COPO *Deuce*, marketed exclusively by Yenko. *Mark Hassett/Bob McClurg*

For a short period of time in 1968, Motion partnered with Mack Markowitz Oldsmobile to market MACH 1 vehicles. Just a few were built before the partnership ended. In late 1973, Baldwin Chevrolet became Williams Chevrolet. Then, in August 1976, it became Lion Chevrolet, which shut down a dozen or so years later.

The Justice Department, on behalf of the EPA and DOT, crashed Baldwin-Motion's party in 1974 and served Joel Rosen with a cease-and-desist summons. It was Motion's 454 Vega that brought Washington's wrath down on the Baldwin-based supercar builder. Rosen paid a $500 fine and agreed that Motion-modified new vehicles could be sold "For Export Only" or in the United States with a disclaimer: "This vehicle does not comply with DOT and EPA regulations and is For Off Road Use Only."

Nickey Chevrolet opened its doors in Chicago, Illinois, in 1925. Approximately thirty years later, Edward and Jack Stephani purchased it and laid the groundwork for high-performance activities. Prior to opening its High-Performance

Center, managed by Dick Harrell in 1965, Nickey had built and road-raced the legendary *Purple People Eater* Corvettes. Driven by Jim Jeffords and wrenched by Ronnie Kaplan, they won SCCA B/Production titles in 1958 and 1959. In the mid-1960s, the Nickey logo appeared on USRRC and Can-Am cars.

Working with Dick Harrell and Bill Thomas, Nickey became one of the Big Three 427 Camaro producers. With an in-house speed shop, they also built 427 Novas and Chevelles. They closed their doors in 1977.

Yenko Chevrolet, founded by Frank Yenko in 1933 in Bentleyville, Pennsylvania, opened an additional store in Cannonsburg, Pennsylvania, in 1949. Between 1967 and 1969, the Cannonsburg-based Yenko Sportscars, run by Don Yenko, sold the most 427 Camaros. Other niche-market models included the 350/360 LT1 Yenko Deuce and 427 Novas and Chevelles. Yenko Chevrolet also produced SCCA D/Production 1966 through 1969 Stinger Corvairs, and in 1971 and 1972 Turbo-Stinger Vegas.

With assistance from Dick Harrell, Yenko built 427 Camaros and Novas in 1967 and 1968. Starting in 1969, Yenko retrimmed and rebadged factory 427 COPO (central office production order) models.

Don Yenko raced Corvair Stingers and Gulf Oil– and Sunray DX–sponsored Corvettes and Camaros in NASCAR Grand American and SCCA A/Sedan and Trans-Am Series. In 1969, it was his special relationship with Vince Piggins, Chevrolet's director of product promotions, that led to the creation of 427 COPO 9561 Camaros and COPO 9562 Chevelles. For 1970, Chevrolet built COPO 9210/9737 Novas, marketed as Yenko Deuces. Yenko Sportscars could be ordered at more than seventeen Chevrolet dealers. The last specialty car built before shutting down in 1982 was the Turbo Z/28 Camaro.

Pontiac enthusiasts were well served by Knaffel Pontiac, Myrtle Motors, and Royal Pontiac. With a direct connection to Pontiac and master-marketer Jim Wangers, Ace Wilson's Royal Pontiac, in Royal Oak, Michigan, was a primary source for modified Pontiacs. Its signature product was the super-tuned Bobcat GTO. In 1968 Royal built a few 428-engined GTOs.

In 1960, Jim Wangers drove Royal's SD-389 Catalina to a Top Stock Eliminator win at the NHRA Nationals. Wangers became the guiding force behind Royal preparing factory Pontiacs for magazines. In 1969, Ace Wilson sold the Royal Pontiac Racing Team and in around 1970 sold the dealership.

Knafel Pontiac, of Akron, Ohio, built and campaigned championship GTOs driven by "Doc" Dixon and Arlen Vanke. In 1970 Knafel built fifty Magnum 400 Tempests with 400/350 GTO engines and Judge side stripes. At $3,200, it was affordable and insurable.

Myrtle Motors, a New York City Pontiac dealership owned by three generations of the Bloom family, built new Gen I Firebirds with 428 engines. It closed down in 1992.

Berger Chevrolet, Dana Chevrolet, Fred Gibb Chevrolet, Dick Harrell's Performance Center, Scuncio Chevrolet, and Bill Thomas Race Cars also built and/or distributed ultra-high-performance Chevrolets. The big name in high-performance Fords was Tasca Ford, still going strong in Cranston, Rhode Island.

Norman "Mr. Norm" Krause's Grand Spaulding Dodge opened its doors in Chicago, Illinois, in 1962. It specialized in dyno-tuned high-performance cars and produced GSS 383 Darts and supercharged GSS 340 Demons. "Mr. Norm" left in 1977 and Grand Spaulding closed its doors in the early 1980s.

The "dream merchants" brought one-stop shopping to the enthusiast community. Their serial-production supercars ruled the streets and today are revered as symbols of the golden age of muscle.

1962

If you really wanted to make a statement in 1962, few cars were cooler (and hotter) than a '62 Impala Super Sport droptop powered by one of two potent 409 engines: a single quad 380 horsepower or dual quad 409 horsepower. *General Motors*

CHAPTER FOUR

GO BiG
or
GO HOME

Ford withdraws from the AMA auto-racing ban; Motown's Big Three increase engine displacement and force-feed the horsepower wars.

In 1957 the Automobile Manufacturers Association's ban on member auto racing participation and promotion was about as effective as the United Nations. Chrysler, Ford, and General Motors signed on, but never actually stopped developing and producing high-performance engines and "supporting" racers. Many of the high-performance brake, chassis, and suspension packages were initially hidden in police and taxi and export vehicle order books.

It was business as usual in Motown until June 11, 1962, when Ford's board chairman, Henry Ford II, let the trade association know that Ford was no longer honoring its ineffective ban. Initially, Chrysler and General Motors remained committed to the agreement, yet continued participation in the horsepower wars with impressive 409 Chevys,

421 Pontiacs, and 413-inch Max Wedge Dodges and Plymouths to combat Ford's 406 Galaxie. Racing budgets were often disguised to avoid corporate detection and, unlike Ford, racing activities were transacted through convoluted "backdoor" relationships.

Chevrolet celebrated its fiftieth anniversary in 1962, and full-size models showcased all new sheet metal and availability of two optional 409 engines. As far as hardcore enthusiasts were concerned, Chevy's focus was on Bel Air and Biscayne models with 409 engines and Impala hardtops with SS (Super Sport) trim and either 327/300 or 409 engines. It was Chevy's first year for bucket seats, available only with the RPO-240 SS package on Impala coupes and convertibles. Adding just $156.05, the package included bucket seats, shift console, passenger assist bar, special wheel covers, SS emblems, and unique console décor. For just $48.45, you could opt for RPO-331, a *state-of-the-cool* column-mounted Sun tach!

Available only with manual transmission, 409 engines were rated at 380 horsepower and 420 lb-ft of torque with a single four-barrel and 409 horsepower and 420 lb-ft of torque

with dual four-barrel carburetion. While the 409 engines delivered the most power, the new 300-horsepower Turbo Fire 327 (RPO-397) variant of the prior year's 283 was the most popular choice.

The four-barrel, dual-exhaust 327 small-block delivered 360 lb-ft of torque and, with a smooth-shifting four-speed and decent Posi gears, could propel a 119-inch-wheelbase Impala SS to sub-eight-second 0-to-60-mile-per-hour sprints. Quarter-mile performance was also impressive at high-80-mile-per-hour trap speeds in the mid-sixteens. Late in the 1962 model year, Chevrolet released aluminum front end components, first to key drag racers and later added the goodies to service parts listings. Approximately twenty aluminum front ends were produced.

Drag-prepped 409/409 Chevys with four-speed, 4.11 Posi gears and sticky tires could sprint to 60 miles per hour in the mid-sixes and cover the quarter-mile at trap speeds of just a tick under 100 miles per hour in 14.9 to 15.2 seconds. Even though 409 Chevys were victorious at major NHRA events in 1962 such as the Winternationals and Nationals, the

Before Dick Brannan was hired by Ford to work on maximum-performance, limited-build lightweight race car projects, he was a successful drag racer and salesman at Romy-Hammes. In 1962, he ran this 406/405 Ford. *Dick Brannan*

Chevy top dog, the Turbo-Fire 409, came with dual quads and solid cam, and it pumped out 409 horsepower and 420 lb-ft of torque. Later model 409s came with chrome valve covers and air cleaners. *Jeff Murphy*

380- and 409-horsepower 409's real success was on the street. That's where the much-improved 348-W passenger car and truck engine shined and earned its cred.

It did not distinguish itself in stock car racing, winning just one race on NASCAR's 1962 calendar. Rex White edged out favorite Joe Weatherly in his 421 Pontiac to win the last race of the season in Atlanta. But Chevrolet did have plans to come back to NASCAR in 1963 with a new engine, displacing 427 cubic inches and unlike any other in its lineup. The "one-year wonder" became known as the 427 Mystery Motor.

In 1963, with the AMA racing ban forgotten, Ford started on a road that would lead to its commitment to Total Performance. Prior to December 15, 1961, the hottest engine available in a '62 Galaxie was the carryover 390-cubic-inch big-block with tri-power rated at 401 horsepower. After December 15, you could opt for a new 406 rated at 385 horsepower with a single four-barrel and 405 horsepower with tri-power. One classic '62 Galaxie advertisement focused on the new 406 engine with 385 or 405 horsepower. Headlined *How Sudden Do You Want Your Car To Be? Galaxie Has The Quick Answer!*, it was a new day at Ford.

With 11.4:1 compression, these engines generated tree-stump-pulling torque—444 lb-ft at 3,400 rpm with single-carb and 448 lb-ft at 3,500 rpm with tri-power. Ford expected 406s to be raced; all were produced with special heavy-duty blocks, .500-inch-lift camshafts, 1.76 ratio rocker arms, and dual-point ignition. And, of course, dual exhausts. Its option cost was $379.70.

Ford left nothing to chance when it came to packaging 406 Galaxies, regardless of trim levels: base two- or four-door sedans or 500XL coupes and convertibles. Everything was geared to the buyer actually utilizing the 406's full potential.

Standard equipment included B-W four-speed, four-pinion differential with final drive ratios to 4.11, heavy-duty rear axles, oversize fuel lines, 15-inch wheels, police brakes, and heavy-duty radiator and special springs and shocks. Tuned cast-iron headers with low-restriction duals, such as the ones fitted on 352 Specials in 1960 and 390s in 1961, proved to be super efficient for the street.

Each 406-engined Ford came with its own status symbols. These were three Thunderbird crossed checked flag motif emblems—one on the lower right corner of the trunk lid

TOP LEFT: Carmakers often packaged high-performance models with the hottest chassis options, which also could be found under listings for Police & Taxi or Export models. I shot this photo of '62 Chevy and Plymouth Indiana State Police two-door pursuit cruisers, with the hottest engines available, from the timing tower at the 1963 NHRA Indy Nationals.

TOP RIGHT: A rare photo of a '62 Dodge Dart with 413-inch dual quad short Ram induction engine rated at 420 horsepower, at 1963 NHRA Nationals. The driver is top East Coast racer Bud Faubel, whose future Dodge race cars carried *Honker* livery.

BOTTOM: The hottest Mopar engine in 1962 was 413-inch Wedge, branded Super Stock in Plymouths and Ramcharger in Dodges. These were serious race motors, but many 11:1 engines rated at 410 horsepower ended up on the street. Tuned upswept exhaust manifolds were stock. *Factory Lightweight Collection*

and one on each front fender. Street racers often substituted emblems from smaller-engined Fords, surprising competitors at stoplight drags!

The 406 Galaxie had incredible potential as both a street and strip machine. However, its bulk, weighing in at over 4,000 pounds, was hard to overcome. While its top end with standard street gearing was a solid 125 miles per hour, sprinting to 60 miles per hour averaged 7.5 seconds and quarter-mile times were around 90 miles per hour in the low- to mid-fifteens.

In 1962, factory participation in Super/Stock and Factory Experimental drag racing took center stage at NHRA events. Even those brands still locked into the AMA racing ban worked with in-house and outside drag racers and high-profile shops to insure that enthusiasts were aware of their vehicles' performance potential. Ford hired Dick Brannan, an engineer and salesman at Romy Hammes Ford and a successful Ford drag racer. His first project at Ford's Experimental Vehicles Garage (X-Garage) was prototyping a lightweight 406 Galaxie and working with Dearborn Steel Tubing to produce approximately a dozen.

Vehicles tagged for Lightweight conversions were ordered as six-cylinder models without radio, heater, clock, or carpeting. Proprietary parts included fiberglass front fenders, hood, deck lid, doors, aluminum bumpers and inner fender panels, Lincoln aluminum brake drums, and "thin" side glass. Not all the Lightweights received all the lightweight parts. Some cars were built expressly for A/FX competition with 406 engines fitted with dual Holley quads instead of tri-power.

Brannan's team built approximately a dozen "$1.00" cars for factory-supported dealers and racers: Jerry Alderman Ford, Ed Martin Ford, Tasca Ford's Bill Lawton, Ford test driver Len Richter, Dick Brannan, Phil "Daddy Warbucks" Bonner, Les Ritchey, Gas Ronda, Mickey Thompson, and others. Six of those Lightweights, including those raced by Dick Brannan, Gas Ronda, and Les Ritchey, were re-bodied as 1963½ 427 Sport Roof Galaxies in December 1962.

Not long after Ford pulled out of the 1957 AMA agreement, Chrysler followed suit. But Chrysler did not have Chevrolet and Ford's racing heritage, nor its budgets and "supported" brand-name racers. Chrysler also didn't have the right *image* cars to compete with GM and Ford styling. Chrysler slightly downsized and restyled its 1962 Plymouth and Dodge B-body

Dodge did very little to hide its racing participation. This is NHRA founder Wally Parks with a '62 Dodge sedan and racer at a Dodge-sponsored pre-race program at the NHRA Winternationals. Dodge had a fleet of models with high-performance engines for the press to race.

car lines (Dart, Savoy, etc.), resulting in cars that looked like they'd been hit by an ugly stick. Fortunately, whatever they lacked in style, they more than made up for in performance. Much of the racing technology of the time was developed by a group of young Chrysler engineers who had formed the Ramchargers Racing Club. Tom Hoover was Chrysler's racing engines project coordinator, Dick Maxwell directed racing programs and was club president, and Jim Thornton distinguished himself as a class-winning and record-setting driver. They raced Dodges while another in-house club, the Golden Commandos, concentrated on the Plymouth brand.

As soon as Briggs Cunningham, who brought Cadillacs and Corvettes to Le Mans and built Cunningham cars, took delivery of his brand new '62 Pontiac Grand Prix, he had it modified. This photo was taken at Latham Manufacturing after the engine was boosted with a new Axial-Flow supercharger with side-draft carbs.

The Ramchargers had the higher profile and, during the mid-1960s and into the 1970s, fielded some of the most feared Dodges in drag-racing history.

Displacing 413 cubic inches and fitted with short tuned-ram intake manifolds with dual four-barrels and tuned upswept cast-iron exhaust manifolds, the Max Wedge engines were not available at new model introduction time. They appeared in the spring of 1962 and there has always been some confusion over horsepower ratings. The 413-inch Wedge engine was available in the Chrysler 300-H and rated at 380 and 405 horsepower. When the 413 was made available in Dodge and Plymouth models, other than station wagons, it was more highly tuned with 15-inch short ram intake manifold, new heads with large 2.08-inch intake valves, and upswept, tuned cast-iron exhaust manifolds. The compression ratio was 11:1 and it was rated at 410 horsepower. A second 413 engine, with 13.5:1 compression and rated at 420 horsepower, found its way into some cars.

Available with B-W T-85 three-speed manual transmission and the superb A-727 three-speed TorqueFlite automatic, 413-inch Super/Stock Mopars could run in the mid-twelves. In 1962, they recorded four class wins at major NHRA events. At the NHRA Nationals, *Hot Rod*'s Ray Brock and Leroi "Tex" Smith campaigned a 413-inch Plymouth and set the low ET record at 12.37 seconds. In the final round

for Stock Eliminator, Jim Thornton, in the Ramchargers' Dodge, fell prey to Hayden Proffitt driving his 409 Chevy. He later switched to a Super/Stock '62 Dodge. When installed in Plymouths, 413 engines were branded Super Stock; Dodges carried Ramcharger logos.

Even with impressive horsepower/torque engines and record-setting drag strip performance, the public rejected Dodge and Plymouth styling, and 1962 model sales suffered dramatically.

In 1957, Semon "Bunkie" Knudsen, son of former GM President William Knudsen, laid the groundwork that changed Pontiac's stodgy image and brought exciting, image-centric, high-performance cars to market. He loved racing and hanging out with Mickey Thompson and NASCAR greats Ray Nichels and Smokey Yunick. The GM vice president and Pontiac general manager had two favorite sayings: "Build what we race and race what we build" and "You can't sell an old man's car to a young man, but you can sell a young man's car to an old man."

Even though GM, theoretically, was still abiding by the AMA anti-racing ban, Knudsen, during his 1957 to 1961 tenure, was responsible for some of the industry's hottest and most desirable street performance cars. He actively supported the creation of Pontiac's Super Duty Engine Group and NASCAR and drag racing. By the time he left Pontiac in 1961, plans for the 1962–1963 Super-Duty 421 engine and racing programs were locked in. Pete Estes, also a strong believer in performance and racing, replaced him.

The first engine dubbed Super-Duty was the SD-389, a single four-barrel engine rated at 385 horsepower at 5,200 rpm with 10.75:1 pistons. To legally qualify for NASCAR competition, the SD-389 was listed as a passenger car option, but few if any ever left the factory. In 1961, SD-389-powered Pontiacs won almost half of NASCAR's fifty-two events.

Since the Super-Duty engines were developed primarily for racing, Pontiac also offered a huge list of optional engine parts, aluminum front ends, aluminum exhaust manifolds, and a variety of McKellar solid lifter cams and valvetrains. In 1962 Pontiac produced 177 Super-Duty cars, but it is not clear how many of them had aluminum front ends or SD-389 engines. They built just fifteen SD-389 and 225 SD-421 engines for both new car assembly and service and aftermarket sales.

You could order a SD-421 Catalina with a factory-installed aluminum front end, but it made little sense to order

ABOVE: Pontiac was right on the money in 1962, making new dual quad 421-inch Super-Duty engines available to racers. A tamer single four-barrel version was optional throughout the line. Bill Abraham and Arlen Vanke campaigned this A/Stock Catalina nationally. They later built their competition cred at Knafel Pontiac, running GTOs.

BELOW: Grumpy Jenkins tuned and prepped this Northwind 409 Bel Air running in A/Stock and driven by its owner, Joe "Tex" Gardner. Running 409/409 power and 4.56 gears, it ran consistent 12.20s at around 116 miles per hour—a top contender in NHRA Division 1.

a Lightweight for street use. With an aluminum front end, little dings would quickly turn into expensive repairs. The optional SD-421 engine was factory rated at 405 horsepower at 5,600 rpm with McKellar No. 10 long-duration cam and mechanical valvetrain, forged 11:1 pistons, and dual 500-cfm Carter four-barrels on an aluminum manifold. Actual horsepower was in the area of 450. A smooth-shifting B-W T-10 four-speed was available along with a laundry list of limited-slip rears.

A typical drag-prepped SD-421 Catalina with four-speed, quarter-mile gearing and appropriate tires would run in the mid-twelves at over 110 miles per hour. In 1962 Pontiac had the styling, a new high-profile Grand Prix, and everything you needed to go fast—on the road or track. Fireball Roberts won the Daytona 500 in a Smokey Yunick–prepped SD-421 Catalina and Joe Weatherly won the NASCAR Championship in a Ray Nichels Catalina. While GM's board supported the AMA ban, it appeared as though it forgot to tell Pontiac!

ABOVE: Ford built approximately a dozen lightweight '62 Galaxies with dual quad 406 engines to run in NHRA A/FX at the Indy Nationals. The majority of these cars were refitted with lightweight '63½ fastback Galaxie bodies and new 427 engines. The first rebodied '62 FX Galaxie was Dick Brannan's car. *Factory Lightweight Collection*

RIGHT TOP: Lightweight A/FX Galaxies with fiberglass body panels were factory equipped with unique high-compression, dual quad 406 engines fitted with tuned cast-iron header-style exhaust manifolds. *Factory Lightweight Collection*

RIGHT BOTTOM: Chevrolet and Pontiac offered the best interior packages for 1962. This is the Super Sport Chevy Impala interior with first-year bucket seats, console, grab bar, and RPO-331 steering-column-mounted Sun tach. It was a regular production option available with all engines. *General Motors*

CHEVY 409: FIRST OF CHEVY'S BIG-BLOCK LEGENDS

It may have started out as an updated truck engine, but it proved to be a force to be reckoned with. It paved the way for some of the most potent large displacement engines ever to come out of Motown.

Two years before the supercar hype and big-engined midsize cars, full-size '62 Chevys, powered by 409-inch versions of the 348 W-Series passenger car and truck engine, carried the muscle car banner for Chevrolet. While the engine first surfaced in the 1961 model year, it was a late arrival. Just 142 Chevys with RPO-580 360-horsepower, single-four-barrel (Carter AFB), and solid-lifter-cammed 409 engines were produced. With 409 lb-ft of torque coming in at 3,600 rpm, performance was outstanding.

One of the first 409s built, a Bel Air model, went to "Dyno Don" Nicholson. He waded through an incredibly tough field at the 1961 NHRA Winternationals in Pomona, California, to win Stock Eliminator in his brand new car. He was later disqualified because his engine had the latest GM valve springs and a carburetor that had not yet been approved by NHRA. To help create a performance image quickly for its new powerplant, Chevrolet supplied the 409 engines to racers, so there were a lot of them out there.

In road racing competition in the United States and the United Kingdom, Dan Gurney campaigned a '61 Impala powered by the 409/360 engine. It was fitted with factory police and taxi suspension, quick steering, metallic brakes, and Goodyear road-race tires mounted on wide NASCAR steel wheels. Bill Thomas blueprinted the engine and set up the chassis. Gurney broke the lap record at Riverside Raceway, set by Dave McDonald in a fuel-injected Corvette, and had a field day in Sedan racing in the United Kingdom.

Not to be confused with Dave Stickler's *Old Reliable* Chevys, this is a B/Stock 409 '62 Impala. The *Old Reliable* was campaigned successfully throughout the Midwest by Ralph Fisher for Crivelli Chevrolet.

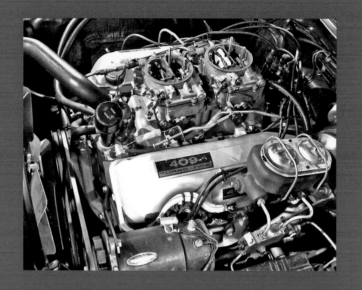

The 409 came into its own in 1962. Chevy's new big-block offered horsepower ratings of 380 at 5,800 rpm and 420 lb-ft of torque at 3,200 rpm with a single four-barrel carburetor. Also available was a 409/409 with 409 horsepower at 6,500 rpm and 420 lb-ft of torque at 4,000 rpm with dual four-barrel induction. Its success on drag strips and the street—and the June 1962 release of the Beach Boys' first car song "409"—bolstered the 409's appeal.

On the flip side of *Surfin' Safari* (Capital Records), "409" got an incredible amount of airplay and probably influenced more than a fair share of sales of '62 Chevy 409s. Almost nine thousand of them were sold in 1962, and I think you would have been hard-pressed to find purchasers who were *not* familiar with Brian Wilson and Gary Usher's lyrics, *"She's real fine my 409,"* and did not save their pennies and dimes to buy a brand new 409. Wilson recorded the intro exhaust sounds while Usher revved up the engine in his '62 409 Impala.

The key players at Chevrolet responsible for the 409, and the 427 iteration (Z11) in 1963, were project chief John T. Rausch and key assistants Howard H. Kehrl and Don McPherson. They were three of General Motor's top engine engineers who went on to work on some of GM's most iconic performance engines.

Essentially a bored and stroked ($4^{5}/_{16}$ x $3^{1}/_{2}$ inches) 348-W engine used in passenger cars and trucks, the first 409 was a strong street motor that was long on low-end and short on top-end torque. Standard equipment included a forged steel crank and .440/.440-inch lift camshaft. Weighing in at approximately 665

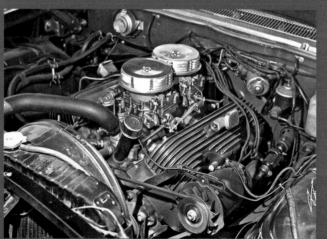

TOP: The top 409, with dual quads and 409 horsepower, proved to be very successful at major NHRA events during 1962. Chevrolet had a handful of high-profile racers at the receiving end of the latest engine upgrades, including rare aluminum front ends. Approximately twenty sets of lightweight body panels were produced for A/FX competition.

CENTER: A picture-perfect Day Two '62 Impala Super Sport, customized when brand new by Herb Gary, of Gary's Auto Body, in Seal Cliff, New York. Gary took some trim off the body, hand-formed a custom grille, added chrome-reverse wheels, and Candy Apple Red lacquer. It was street-driven.

BOTTOM: The Day Two Impala 409/409 engine was also customized with Pontiac Super-Duty air cleaners, finned alloy valve covers with breathers, and period pin striping on the inner fender panels. The engine treatment is typical of the period.

pounds, a 409 big-block was just 35 pounds heavier than the base six. It's potential as a race engine was enhanced when Chevrolet came out with a service package upgrade in mid-1962. Many of the parts in the package had earlier been sent to factory-supported drag and NASCAR racers.

Chevy's top performance 409 for 1962 boasted dual four-barrel Carters with progressive linkage on an aluminum manifold, 11.0:1 pistons, improved heads with 2.20-inch intake valves and larger ports, high-lift camshaft with solid lifters, stiffer valve springs, and a 75-psi oil pump. The actual compression ratio of the 409/409 was 11.04:1 with 83 to 85cc combustion chambers. With two factory-installed head gaskets on each engine bank, chamber capacity would reach 91ccs and the compression ratio would drop to 10.20:1 for more manageable street driving.

Some of the components of the 1962½ 409 Engine Service Package No. 3822953 included a new dual-point distributor, .480-inch lift camshaft, improved single four-barrel aluminum manifold, and Carter No. 3345-S carburetor. It was primarily geared to upgrade the 380-horsepower engine.

Considering the engine was only available in full-size models, including convertibles with or without RPO-240 SS trim, real world street performance was impressive. I recall going to Westhampton Raceway on Long Island to do some stories and check out some new 409 Impalas. We were able to get a couple of owners to allow us to clock some 0-to-60-mile-per-hour times using a stopwatch. A 380-horsepower 409 Super Sport Impala with close-ratio four-speed and 3.70 Posi gears could sprint to 60 miles per hour in the low to mid-sevens. Quarter-mile times ranged from 92 to 95 miles per hour in 15.0 to 15.5 seconds. A hotter 409/409 Bel Air with 4.11s and four-speed ran high-fourteens to low-fifteens at 96 to 99 miles per hour. Sprinting to 60 miles per hour from a dead stop took just 6.3 to 6.6 seconds. It should be noted that these cars' engines had headers and were shod with the ultimate traction tire of the day—Atlas Bucrons.

TOP: If you were serious about maximum performance, a 409/409 Bel Air was the way to go. It was lighter and cheaper than an Impala. Note period sticky blackwall tires on painted rims with dog dish hubcaps. *General Motors*

BOTTOM: I shot this 409/409-powered B/gas '59 El Camino in June 1962 at ⅕-mile Freedom 7 drag strip, an old converted military landing field (Creeds Field) in Virginia Beach, Virginia. Chevy built more than 15,000 409 engines in the 1962 model year and this guy wasted no time getting one and setting it up for serious competition.

Drag racers and Chevrolet had a good year in 1962. "Dyno Don" Nicholson won Street Eliminator at the NHRA Winternationals, Hayden Proffitt won Stock Eliminator at the NHRA Indy Nationals, and Dave Strickler beat Hayden Proffitt to win Super/Stock. Other popular drag racers such as Butch Leal, Hubie Platt, and Dick Harrell successfully campaigned 409s in 1962. Most of the A-list racers had direct support from Chevrolet. Records at GM's Tonawanda, New York, engine plant show that it produced 15,019 409 engines; 8,909 went to new car assembly and the balance of 6,110 for warranty service and aftermarket sales.

ABOVE, BOTH: From this angle, it's not really apparent that 15 inches (between its doors and rear wheels) have been taken out of the Monte Carlo's overall length. Custom egg-crate grilles are painted black. *General Motors*

BELOW: A custom marine-style flame-arrestor air cleaner tops off the Carter AFB four-barrel. A Mickey Thompson supercharging system makes use of a much-modified GMC 3-71 blower to force feed the 195-inch four. *General Motors*

Strickler's *Old Reliable* '62 Chevy was tuned by Bill "Grumpy" Jenkins and owned by sponsor Ammon Smith Chevrolet in York, Pennslyvania. When fitted with an aluminum front end, *Old Reliable* competed in NHRA's A/FX class. Chevrolet supplied approximately twenty sets of aluminum front ends in 1962 to key racers.

It was a landmark year for the 409 and Chevrolet. The 409/409 with dual quads was the car to beat in 1962, on the street and on the track. For 1963, the top-rated dual-quad 409/409 received a performance bump to 425 horsepower along with chromed valve covers and air cleaner. Chromed engine accessories continued for 1964 and 1965 model years.

When fitted with single Carter four-barrel carburetion, the carryover 409/380 engine was rated at 400 horsepower. Multiple carburetion was discontinued after the 1964 model year. For 1965, 409s were rated at 340 and 400 horsepower before being phased out for the incoming, much-improved Mark IV big-blocks, displacing 396 cubic inches.

The 409 had its day in the sun and Brian Wilson and Gary Usher absolutely got it right: "Nothing can catch her— nothing can touch my 409, 409!"

TEMPEST FOR TWO

Built on a shortened prototype '62 Pontiac Tempest convertible, the Monte Carlo was a hit at auto shows and major road racing events. It shared the spotlight with GM Design Chief William Mitchell's Corvair Sebring Spyder.

One thing was a given at GM in the 1960s: Chevy's Corvette was a sacred cow and no other division could bring a two-seat sports car to market. The only way Buick, Pontiac, Oldsmobile, or Cadillac could reveal branded two-seat, high-performance sporty vehicles was to have Mitchell's GM Design create concepts that became part of GM's traveling auto show displays. The Tempest Monte Carlo, powered by a supercharged 195-cubic-inch four rated at 250 to 300 horsepower, featured 15-inch shortened unibody architecture with four-wheel independent suspension. With a wheelbase of 97 inches and overall length of 175 inches, it had a 5-inch shorter wheelbase and was 2 inches shorter overall than a '62 Corvette.

Pontiac already had a relationship with Mickey Thompson, having supplied him with four- and eight-cylinder engines for some of his high-profile, multiple-engine Bonneville and drag racing cars. Thompson came up with a supercharger package for the Tempest Four, incorporating a modified GMC 3-71 Roots-type blower driven by a 2-inch-wide ribbed Gilmer belt and a manifold with a huge built-in pop-off valve. An offset adapter allowed for installing a Carter four-barrel. As with most GM showcars, the Monte Carlo's engine received abundant chrome and polished aluminum accessories.

A 15-inch section was removed from the four-passenger Tempest, converting it into a sporty two-seater. The Tempest's four-wheel-independent suspension was retained, though the controversial flexy shaft between the engine and the rear-mounted, Corvair-based four-speed was shortened considerably, making the drivetrain more efficient.

Since Pontiac's plan included showing the Monte Carlo at major sports car races, it was treated to a full complement of gauges, racing mirrors, dual thin blue racing stripes, tri-spoke steering wheel, hood louvers, and Firestone Super Sport tires mounted on polished Halibrand knockoffs.

Wholly impractical but responsible for drawing a crowd wherever the Monte Carlo was displayed, the severely chopped wraparound plexiglass windscreen looked as though it had come off a full-tilt race car. It offered absolutely no protection, but tied in nicely with the slick fiberglass tonneau cover with headrest fairings.

Finished in White Pearl, the Monte Carlo was also shown in 1962. The only change was knockoff wire wheels with Goodyear Blue Streak tires in place of the Halibrand-Firestone combo. Unlike most concept/show cars, the Monte Carlo was not crushed after it was retired. It was gifted to Ed Cole, vice president and head of GM's Car and Truck Group. Before taking delivery, he had the Monte Carlo re-powered with a stock 215-inch aluminum V-8. The windscreen was replaced with a production Tempest windshield, and they also added a small convertible top.

The net result was a somewhat awkward-looking, short-wheelbase Tempest with an oversize top. The Tempest survived and is currently in a private collection. But Mitchell's original Monte Carlo styling did not.

1963

The Pontiac Grand Prix was all new for 1963, but the carmaker didn't build a convertible you could buy. This is the XP-400 concept, the centerpiece of Pontiac's display at the 1963 New York Auto Show.

CHAPTER FIVE

TOTAL PERFORMANCE, TOTALLY

The displacement race peaked in 1963. Chevrolet and Ford led the charge with 427-cubic-inch big-blocks, followed by Dodge and Plymouth with 426 and Pontiac with 421 cubic inches.

It was a glorious time for performance enthusiasts. Chrysler, Ford, and General Motors were offering large-displacement engines that could be ordered as traditional power options from *any* new car dealer. Special versions were available for drag racing and for use on NASCAR and USAC high-speed tracks. To keep the displacement race from getting out of hand, two major sanctioning bodies, NHRA and NASCAR, imposed displacement limitations of 7.0 liters or 427.5 cubic inches on passenger car engines that could quality for competition. Detroit could now concentrate on further development of its existing big-blocks instead of tooling up for new mega-displacement engines to stay in the game.

LEFT: The hottest production Chevy you could buy in 1963 was 409/425 powered. This two-door Biscayne post sedan was the hot setup. *Joe Oldham*

RIGHT: The new 426 Dodge Ramcharger and Plymouth Super Stock engines broke cover in time to make our November 1962 issue.

In 1963 Frederick Donner was chairman and CEO of General Motors, the biggest of Detroit's Big Three. GM was experiencing approximately 55 percent market share, with Chevrolet accounting for an astounding 25 percent of that share. While GM shareholders were enjoying the rewards, Donner was under attack in Washington. In 1962 and 1963 congressional hearings were pounding away at Donner and GM for investing too much money and resources in racing and performance programs and not enough in safety. Not that many years later, Henry Ford II would find himself in the exact same position and throttle back Ford's racing efforts.

The trust-busting folks over at the Department of Justice had another agenda. They started attacking GM at the same time the congressional hearings were being held for being too big and monopolizing the marketplace. Frederic Donner was the recipient of Washington's multipronged attacks.

Donner was a brilliant bean counter and steered GM to record sales and profits. He didn't much care about performance cars or racing. At the end of 1962, Donner issued an internal memo to Jack Gordon, president and COO, ordering GM divisions to discontinue all involvement in competitive events. Word spread down the chain of command to Chevrolet, Pontiac (the major players), and Oldsmobile general managers.

While clandestine backdoor participation continued on a very limited and quiet basis, Pontiac's Super-Duty 421 engine and lightweight body component programs and Chevrolet's RPO Z11 lightweight 427 drag car and 427 Mark II NASCAR Mystery Motor were dead in the water. A Pontiac memo dated January 24, 1963 advised dealers not to accept any orders for SD-421 models. By the time the ban actually took place, Chevrolet had built fifty-seven Z11s.

While Chevrolet's RPO Z11 option was strictly for drag racing, bow-tie enthusiasts could choose from three optional and streetable high-performance 409 engines, with horsepower ratings of 340 to 425. On the RPO Z11, you received aluminum body panels and a stroked 409 W-series engine with new heads, intake, and 13.5:1 compression pistons. Factory rated at 430 horsepower at 6,300 rpm, Z11 engines pumped out in excess of 475 horsepower. They were purpose-built race cars.

The single four-barrel, 10:1 compression 409 produced 340 horsepower and the single and dual four-barrel engines

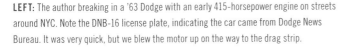

LEFT: The author breaking in a '63 Dodge with an early 415-horsepower engine on streets around NYC. Note the DNB-16 license plate, indicating the car came from Dodge News Bureau. It was very quick, but we blew the motor up on the way to the drag strip.

RIGHT: A Dodge two-door post sedan mixed in with other new production cars is actually a factory-built drag racer, complete with Ramcharger 426 Max Wedge engine and aluminum front end. *FCA Archives*

with 11:1 compression generated 400 and 425 horsepower, respectively. Changes made to 409 engines in mid-1962, such as cam, carburetion, and intake manifold upgrades, were carried over for 1963.

Ford kicked off 1963 with a Galaxie available with a 406-cubic-inch big-block rated at either 385 horsepower with a single four-barrel carburetor or 405 horsepower with three Holley two-barrels. Both engines had 11.4:1 pistons and solid lifter valvetrains, good for 5,800-rpm redlines. Six months after new model introductions, Dearborn launched the industry's first mid-model-year barrage of new engines and models specifically geared toward enthusiasts and racing. With GM pulling back, Ford's timing couldn't have been better.

The singular, most important weapon in Ford's 1963½ arsenal was the fastback Galaxie Sports (and Mercury Marauder) hardtop powered by a new 427-cubic-inch Wedge engine, which replaced the 406. Essentially a bored-out 406, the 427 came stock with cross-bolted mains, forged steel rods, 11.5:1 pistons, solid-lifter valvetrain, and choice of single or dual

Holley quad intake. Like previous Ford big-block performance engines, tuned header-type exhaust manifolds were utilized with full, low backpressure duals. Two power levels were available: Q-Code 410 horsepower at 5,600 rpm with a single Holley 780-cfm four-barrel and R-Code 425 horsepower at 6,000 rpm with dual Holley 650-cfm four-barrels.

As delivered, with skinny tires and stock tuning, an R-Code Galaxie could go from 0 to 60 miles per hour in 7.5 seconds and run through the quarter-mile at 95 to 96 miles per hour in the low-fifteens. With typical Day Two tuning, headers, and open exhausts and "cheater" slicks, 427/425 Galaxies were capable of 105 to 108 miles per hour in the mid-twelves.

I was fortunate enough to drive a pre-production 427/425 Galaxie in early January 1963 at Ford's press introduction and International Road Rally in the Maritime Alps above Monte Carlo. We also got to drive new four-speed Falcon Sprints powered by 260-inch V-8s and to check out the Holman-Moody Monte Carlo Rally Falcons.

ABOVE: Lincoln-Mercury's racing guy Fran Hernandez (left) stands beside Bill Stroppe, who prepared new '63½ fastback 427 Marauder factory NASCAR cars. *Ford Motor Company*

BELOW: Chrysler-Plymouth dealer Norm Thatcher set numerous Bonneville and drag records in the early- to mid-1960s. This '63 Plymouth had a 513-inch blown Wedge under its hood, and ran in the high-170s in B/Supercharged Coupe class. *FCA Archives*

Nothing since has equaled the exhilaration and terror of driving a four-speed, 425-horsepower Galaxie behemoth with drum brakes on some of the world's most beautiful and dangerous roads. With a 119-inch wheelbase, the new Galaxie tipped the scales at over 3,700 pounds. The four-speed 260 V-8 Falcon Sprints proved to be best suited for the Alps' twisty roads with almost endless switchbacks and sheer, unprotected drop-offs. The 1963½ lineup also included a Fairlane optioned with the high-revving 271-horsepower 289 small-block.

Besides being more attractive than its boxtop predecessor, the new Galaxie fastback hardtop boasted an approximate 25 percent aerodynamic advantage. While this offered little advantage on the street or on drag strips, it paid off in spades on high-speed stock car racing tracks. Ford engineer Dick Brannan refitted his '62 Ford drag car lightweight chassis with a '63½ fastback body complete with fiberglass panels. At NHRA's York U.S. 30 Divisional, Brannan set the Super/Stock record at 12.42 seconds. It was the first Ford in history to set an NHRA Super/Stock record.

Fords dominated the field at the Daytona 500 on February 24, 1963. New '63½ Galaxies finished 1-2-3-4-5. Tiny Lund crossed the line first in the No. 21 Wood Brothers car, originally prepared for and qualified by Marvin Panch who was sidelined by track injuries. Fred Lorenzen, Ned Jarrett, Nelson Stacy, and Dan Gurney followed Lund. A month earlier, Gurney had won the Riverside Raceway Grand National race in a Holman-Moody Galaxie.

Dodge and Plymouth high-performance offerings in popular B-body models were limited to a lukewarm, four-barrel 383-cubic-inch version of the previous year's 361 or a scalding-hot 426 Wedge (¹⁄₁₆-inch stroked 413) rated at 415 horsepower at 5,600 rpm with a pair of quads on a short-ram aluminum intake manifold. The 383 was nice for street driving, but certainly no match for the competition. The 426 Mopars were essentially race cars that could be driven on the street. And mid year saw upgrading of the 426 to 425 horsepower, 426-II specs with 13.5:1 compression, making it even less street-friendly. On drag strips from coast to coast, the Stage II Super/Stock Plymouths and Ramcharger Dodges became *the* cars to beat.

Al Eckstrand kicked off Mopar domination on drag strips, taking Top Stock Eliminator at the 1963 NHRA Winternationals in one of the Ramcharger Club's cars. He waded through a field of the country's top fifty stockers to post the win at 115.08 miles per hour in 12.44 seconds. It

Ed Martin Ford of Indianapolis campaigned some of the hottest Ford drag cars in the Midwest. I shot this '63½ 427 fastback with steel body running in A/SA at the 1963 NHRA Nationals. Mopars usually dominated automatic classes.

was the first time an automatic transmission car had won this prestigious national event.

I borrowed a plain pipe rack '63 Dodge Polara post coupe powered by an early 415-horsepower engine from Dodge PR for a road and track test for *CARS* magazine. My plan was to street-drive it during the week, catch a few runs, and then take it to Westhampton Raceway on Sunday. One of my Army buddies, Martin Hanish, and one of his friends met me early Sunday morning with tools and spare wheels with cheater slicks and we headed out to 'Hampton. We knew it would be a long trip as the Dodge had mid-four-series rear gearing and our cruising speeds would be severely limited. We never actually made it to the track. An hour or so out on the Long Island Expressway, oil pressure (small aftermarket Stewart-Warner gauge mounted in the dash) dropped, and by the time I pulled over and turned it off, I could hear the metallic sound of death. We never made it to the track, but we did experience the violent wrath of the 426 Ramcharger engine on the street.

When the ax fell on Pontiac's hugely successful Super-Duty 421 engine and lightweight aluminum body components

Like the '62 XP-400, a supercharged engine fitted with Mickey Thompson speed equipment powered the latest iteration. The blower is a multi-V-belt-driven positive-displacement GMC 4-71. It has Corvette Six side-draft carbs fitted with marine-style flame arrestors.

programs, it affected serious racers, competing with factory and dealership support, on drag strips and NASCAR high-speed tracks. The brand's ego was unquestionably dented, but performance enthusiasts were not denied access to some of the market's best-looking and highest-performing models.

For 1963, the Grand Prix, first introduced the previous year as an uplevel Catalina hardtop, was totally restyled with smooth, trim-free body panels; an exclusive roofline; great interior; and a unique sports-luxury look and feel. Pontiac still offered high-performance 389 engines, but the potent HO (High Output) 421, available in Catalina to Bonneville, was the top choice. Essentially a detuned and streetable SD motor with four-bolt main block, forged crank, and bulletproof McKellar .414-inch lift hydraulic cam, the 10.75:1 compression 421 HO engine could be ordered with single-four-barrel at 353 horsepower or tri-power at 370 horsepower. An optional smooth shifting four-speed was the hot ticket.

In 1963, engineer and journalist Roger Huntington was our valued contact with Pontiac engineers and Royal Pontiac. He was involved in track testing a '63 Grand Prix with the 421/370 engine for a story he was writing for *CARS*. "With wide-ratio T-10 four-speed and 3.23 street gears, that 4,000-pound-plus GP could turn quarter-mile ETs in the low-15s at 92 mph without winding above 5,000 rpm. That was the easiest *belt-in-the-back* I could remember up to that time," he wrote.

It was a great time to be a car guy. Production cars were getting quicker and faster than ever before, and new car dealerships had an endless choice of high-performance models. But a pall came over the country before the year was out. On November 22, 1963, President John F. Kennedy was assassinated by Lee Harvey Oswald in Dallas, Texas. The war in Southeast Asia was heating up. The road ahead was looking like it would be a rocky one.

RPO Z11:
CHEVY 427 LIGHT HEAVYWEIGHT

By checking off RPO Z11 on a 1963 Chevrolet new car order form, you could buy a factory-built race car. Only fifty-seven people made that choice before GM pulled the plug.

The first time I saw a Z11 Chevy was not at a GM press event, drag strip, or even at a Chevrolet dealership. It was at Ford's Dearborn Proving Ground. That's right, FORD!

Some have said: "You never forget your first time." Well, I'll certainly never forget the first time I got up close and personal with a Z11 Chevy. It was in June 1963 and I was driving a 427/425 Galaxie on the test track. Frank "Zimmy" Zimmerman, a sales and marketing executive who would later become a Special Vehicles Activity manager, was riding shotgun. He was breaking one of the Proving Ground's cardinal rules not to allow an "outsider" to drive on the banked, high-speed track.

After positioning the red Galaxie in the 110- to 120-mile-per-hour groove, I spotted a black '63 Chevy coming on strong. I thought my eyes were playing tricks on me. Suddenly he dropped down a slot and the black Chevy was next to me. I figured he was looking for a run. Zimmy said: "Blow his doors off and show him what Total Performance is all about." He didn't seem concerned about the Chevy's hood and fender signs that read: ***ALUMINUM—DO NOT TOUCH***. Maybe he didn't notice. At more than 100 miles per hour, we both nailed it. Then, the Chevy's driver waved goodbye and proceeded to make my Ford look like four spark plug wires had been disconnected. It was *not* a pretty picture.

We caught up with the Z11 later in SVA's experimental garage. Ford had purchased, from a dealer, a 427-engined Chevy with aluminum front end for its Competitive Vehicle Fleet. It was the first time I had seen Chevy's new big-block based on a stroked 409 engine and fitted with cowl induction. The next time I would see Z11s was months later at the NHRA Indy Nationals—where they cleaned house.

Drag racing and pit parking confrontations took a heavy toll on lightweight body parts. Bill Clay drove this Silver Blue A/FX Z11 Impala, sponsored by Hattan Chevrolet of Wichita, Kansas. I took this shot during FX eliminations at the 1963 NHRA Indy Nationals.

TOP: For $1,240, you could opt for RPO Z11 and end up with a lightweight '63 Impala powered by a stroked 409 displacing 427 cubic inches. Campaigned by Frank Sanders, this is the only Z11 painted Azure Aqua. *Factory Lightweight Collection*

BOTTOM: The unique big-block Z11 was produced only in 1963 and just fifty-seven cars were built before the GM racing ban killed off the program. Rated at 430 horsepower, the engine, in drag racing setup, produced 500. It was Chevy's first use of cold air ram induction, similar to NASCAR cars. *Factory Lightweight Collection*

The Z11 was a Regular Production Option 427 that added $1,240 to the MSRP of an Impala. A Z11 Impala Sport Coupe cost approximately $4,000. Rated at 430 horsepower at 6,000 rpm, actual output, when prepped for the track, was a solid 500. That translated to quarter-mile speeds in the 115- to 122-mile-per-hour range with elapsed times in the twelves. By the end of the season, I remember Z11s running in the elevens.

The Z11 engine was essentially a stroked 409 with Code QM 4.31-inch bore block, 3.65-inch stroke crank, heads with large oval intake ports and 2.19-inch intake and 1.72-inch exhaust valves, and a unique two-piece intake manifold with a pair of Carter AFBs. Other proprietary components included a .556-inch-lift, 325-degree-duration solid-lifter cam, 13.5:1 pistons, and deep-sump oil pan. It was Chevrolet's first production engine to utilize NASCAR-style cowl induction. Cool, fresh air was inducted at the high-pressure area at the base of the windshield and ducted to the carburetors.

All Z11 Chevys were factory-fitted with twenty-six-gauge aluminum body parts, including hood, front fenders, front and rear bumpers, assorted brackets and hardware, front splash pan, grille filler panel and brackets, and fan shroud. It was never clear just how many of the fifty-seven cars came through without insulation, sound-deadening materials, and heater. Talking with Z11 racers back in the day, I always received conflicting weight-saving estimates, ranging from a minimum of 112 to maximum of 233 pounds, compared with a 409 Impala. Typical curb weight was 3,405 pounds. When Z11s started turning up on the match-racing circuit, they had shed at least 300 pounds.

Chevrolet's short-lived Z11 was more than just a 427-cubic-inch engine. An Impala sequenced for RPO Z11 production received a beefed Posi rear with 4.11 gears, close-ratio Borg-Warner T-10 four-speed, electronic 6,200-rpm-redline tach, sintered metallic brakes with rear screens and air cooling scoops, heavy-duty suspension with special coil springs, and larger wheels. The front anti-sway bar was automatically removed on Z11 cars. It was a complete race car—not a dual purpose high-performance street car.

In 1963, the Z11 Impala became a legend in its own time, thanks to outstanding regional and national wins by Malcolm Durham, Dick Harrell, Butch Leal, "Dyno Don" Nicholson, Hubie Platt, Hayden Proffitt, Frank Sanders, Ronnie Sox, and Dave Strickler. In addition to Southern-style match

One of the winningest Z11 Impalas during 1963, Frank Sander's original car with original 427 engine has survived. *Factory Lightweight Collection*

racing, Z11 Chevys ran in a variety of classes, depending on time frame and sanctioning body.

They competed in FX, S/S, and LP classes at AHRA, NHRA, and NASCAR events. Dick Harrell won Super/Stock at the AHRA Winternationals and Frank Sanders took the Limited Production win at the NHRA Winternationals. Dave Strickler won the NHRA Summernationals in the Jenkins-tuned *Old Reliable IV*. At the 1963 NHRA Indy Nationals, Strickler beat Nicholson for Factory Experimental honors. Nicholson had received the first Z11, which was built in December 1962. Don Kimball drove a Z11 to the Eliminator win at Indy, beating Bill Lawton in the one-off Tasca A/FX 427 Fairlane.

It's safe to say that Z11s were the fastest production cars in 1963. A Z11 Impala was the first production stock car to exceed 120 miles per hour in the quarter-mile. On the *Drag News* match-racing circuit, the three top cars were Z11 Chevys. Frank Sanders's Z11 Impala was on the *Drag News* Top Stock Eliminator chart for the entire year and an overall national points champion. It was the only Z11 painted Azure Aqua and it has survived with its original 427 engine, transmission, and interior.

MARK II:
CHEVY'S MYSTERIOUS 427

The real 427 Mystery Motor, unlike the Z11, was not available in a car or to the public. You had to have serious NASCAR cred to get one of the twenty built.

In the 1960s, Semon "Bunkie" Knudsen always seemed to be one step ahead of GM Chairman Fred Donner's missives disallowing factory involvement in racing. While running Pontiac, Knudsen had supported the Super-Duty Group that, after he left, managed to get 421 Catalina Lightweights to drag racers before the ax fell. In 1961, he moved on to Chevrolet, and supported the RPO Z11 drag racing and clandestine NASCAR 427 Mystery Motor projects. Both pure racing programs survived, even though GM was officially out of racing. In the case of the Mystery Motor, *everything* was conducted through Chevrolet's backdoor.

Except for cooperating with Ray Brock for a story in the May 1963 issue of *Hot Rod*, Chevrolet PR did not distribute any photos or information or discuss the Mark II 427 with media.

As far as Chevrolet was concerned, the engine did not exist. The Mystery Motor rattled the troops at Daytona, generated reams of misinformation, and became a cult engine.

The 427 Mystery Motor makes use of the same bore/stroke block—4.31-inch bore and 3.65-inch stroke—as the Z11. But that's where the similarity ends. Unlike W-Series engines with combustion chambers in the cylinders, the Mark II utilized canted and staggered-valve (porcupine) heads with conventional chambers. This style head debuted in production 396/427 Mark IV big-block engines, affectionately dubbed "Rat Motors" by enthusiasts.

Although developed primarily as a NASCAR engine, Chevrolet did produce a singular variant for street applications. Most likely the Mark II in street trim, displayed for many years at GM's Tonawanda, New York, engine plant, was built to justify the expenses of building a racing-only engine. It is possible that at some point the project was referenced internally as RPO Z33. That would have been done only to disguise the 427 as an optional production engine so as not to attract unwanted attention. Interestingly, the Mark II engine was not produced at Tonawanda, the facility best known for Mark IV 396, 427, and 454 engines.

Junior Johnson's legendary '63 Impala, powered by the Mark II 427 Mystery Motor, was parked after the 1963 season and Goodyear tire testing. *RK Motors*

LEFT: Ken Kayser, business case manager for Mark IV engines at the Tonawanda, New York, engine plant, poses with the lone surviving Mystery Motor in 1991. It had been on display at the engine plant for years and was now back in Detroit. *Ken Kayser*

RIGHT: Junior Johnson, in the Mystery Motor Impala, was in good company in this shot from the 1963 Firecracker 400 at Daytona on July 4, 1963. That's race winner Fireball Roberts in the No. 22 Ford, trailed by Tiny Lund in the No. 10 Ford. Both are Holman-Moody Galaxies.

One of the industry's top engineers, Richard "Dick" Keinath, had the lead in designing and developing the Mark II engine. The program started in 1960, before Bunkie Knudsen arrived and wrapped up in November 1962. To keep it off the radar, development of the Mark II and its testing by pro drivers in NASCAR race cars was conducted at GM's Winter Proving Ground in Mesa, Arizona, rather than in Milford, Michigan.

Part of the mystery surrounding the Mark II engine can be attributed to its planned public debut on February 24, 1963, at the Daytona 500. The first couple of engines were shipped to Smokey Yunick for use in Chevys being prepared for the 500. Junior Johnson and Johnny Rutherford were two high-profile racers originally slated to run this engine.

However, Mark II 427s were in two Z06 Corvettes competing in the 250-mile American Challenge Cup at Daytona on February 16. This was a race for sports cars and one-offs, not NASCAR stockers. Few people at the time realized that two of the split-window Sting Rays in the Challenge Cup had Mark IIs under their hoods. They were actually the *first* big-block Corvettes.

To better understand how this happened, you only have to look at some of the major players involved in Chevrolet and Corvette racing: Zora Arkus-Duntov, Vince Piggins, Mickey Thompson, Smokey Yunick, and, of course, Chevrolet boss Bunkie Knudsen. Bunkie was extremely close with Thompson since his days at Pontiac, and he helped Mickey set up Thompson Enterprises to front for Chevy racing activities. He also had a long-standing relationship with Smokey and his Best Damn Garage in Florida.

Smokey prepared two Corvettes like NASCAR Grand National stockers and installed Mark II engines with heavy-duty three-speed transmissions. Small, unobtrusive Mickey Thompson hood scoops were installed in the center of

The race-only Mark II 427 had the same bore-stroke as the Z11 big-block, but the head design was all new, with staggered valves and new combustion chambers. Like the Z11, it had a cowl-induction air cleaner. It was the forerunner of the Mark IV 396-454 engine. *RK Motors*

the Sting Rays' hoods for intake and magneto clearance. Scheduled drivers were Junior Johnson and Rex White. During practice, Junior was not comfortable with how his Corvette was handling at 160 miles per hour and decided not to drive. Bill Krause replaced him and went on to finish third. He beat other Corvettes, Ferrari GTOs, and Porsche Carrera Abarth GTLs. Driving a Pontiac Super-Duty 421 Tempest, Paul Goldsmith won the three-hour race, followed by A. J. Foyt driving a Nickey Corvette. Bunkie was thrilled!

Unfortunately, Chevrolet was more of a disrupter than a winner at the Daytona 500. The Mark II 427 was less-than-legal for NASCAR since it was not a true production engine. Chevrolet had a huge fan base—and Bill France simply looked the other way.

Johnny Rutherford drove Smokey's No. 13 car and finished ninth, the best finish for a Mystery-motored Chevy. Rutherford lapped the track at 165.14 miles per hour, setting a closed course record. A broken distributor in the No. 3 Ray Fox/Holly Farms Impala sidelined Junior. He did win seven

of the fifty-five Grand National races in 1963, including the Charlotte 400. With no factory support for the engine, the car was parked. It ran its last "race" on the 5-mile Goodyear Tire test track in Texas. Goodyear used it for baseline testing when finalizing tire development for the 1964 Mopar NASCAR Hemi stockers.

While no longer a mystery, there remain a variety of opinions as to the quantity built and power output of the Mark II 427. According to a 1963 internal Chevrolet memo from Vince Piggins, twenty Mark II 427s were built. It's doubtful that all were complete and running. Smokey never returned one to GM for disposal. After his 1986 shop auction, the Mark II 427 went into collector-racer Tom McIntyre's Silver Blue lightweight Z06. It's the very same car that finished third at the 1963 Grand American Cup.

Power output of the Mark II 427 varies from 500 to 600-plus horsepower. Regardless of actual output, it is a living legend from the golden era of performance when GM *wasn't* racing.

SWISS CHEESE SD-421:
THE LIGHT FANTASTIC

You had to be on a very short list to receive a lightweight '63 Super-Duty Pontiac. Mickey Thompson got the first two.

One of the first people to use the words "Swiss cheese" to describe Pontiac's lightened Super-Duty chassis was Roger Huntington, a regular contributor to *Hi-Performance CARS* and other magazines I edited. It came to him after he counted 120 holes drilled in the perimeter frame of Royal Pontiac's Catalina.

A total of eighteen aluminum body parts were used to reduce the weight of a Super-Duty 421 Pontiac. The result was the Lightweight Catalina, weighing in at approximately 3,300 pounds. Plexiglas side windows and aluminum deck lids helped lighten it further. Some of the early cars ran with stock aluminum hoods that later were ventilated for use with scoops from Ford Super-Duty trucks.

For 1963, the SD-421 drag racing engine was improved considerably. Head castings were modified with taller intake ports and oval-shaped exhaust ports, and it was fitted with larger 2.02-inch intake and 1.76-inch exhaust valves. New forged aluminum pistons raised the compression ratio from 11:1 to 12.5:1. Factory listing for the Group 35 Super-Duty 421 cars shows the B-W T-85 three-speed as standard and B-W T-10 four-speed optional.

Jim Wangers (left) and Frank Rediker, with the SD-421 Lightweight that won B/FX at the 1963 NHRA Indy Nationals. This shot was taken before the aluminum hood was cut and the hood scoop from a Ford pickup was installed.

Pontiac's Malcolm "Mac" McKellar came up with a new cam and dual valve springs that allowed shift points as high as 6,400 rpm. The tuned aluminum exhaust headers, just 27 pounds per set, were mated to a weight-saving single muffler system. While Pontiac upped the 421's horsepower from 405 to 410, the new heads, camshaft, valvetrain, and compression increase translated into a solid 40 to 50 horsepower bump. Racers experimented with a variety of cams, including Number 10 and 12 McKellar grinds.

Early in 1963, Royal Pontiac's B/FX Lightweight tuned by Frank Rediker and driven by Jim Wangers, posted times in the low-twelves at 117 to 119 miles per hour. Wangers went on to a class win at the NHRA Indy Nationals. Howard Maselles later drove the Packer Pontiac lightweight into the NHRA record books, setting the C/Stock record at 114.64 miles per hour in 12.27 seconds.

Total production of 1963 SD-421 Pontiacs is pegged at eighty-eight. This includes fourteen lightweight full-size models and twelve Tempest compacts, plus steel-body cars and development vehicles.

While it is hard to deny the performance of lightweight Pontiacs or the romance attached to factory lightweight cars, the decision to drill out the chassis was questionable. Lightening the chassis resulted in a lack of structural integrity that affected safe, reliable performance. They had to be braced and, in many cases, replaced. In retrospect, it was not a smart decision.

Pontiac's Super-Duty racing programs were officially discontinued on January 24, 1963, a victim of GM's racing ban. It was the end of the road for the Bunkie Knudsen programs that had successfully reversed Pontiac's early 1950s stodgy image. But all was not lost. Less than one year later, Pontiac would jump-start the supercar revolution with a car called the GTO.

OPPOSITE: The SD-421 engine with aluminum exhaust manifolds on the dyno at Pontiac Engineering on December 21, 1962. Early advertised horsepower was 410; actual output was 450 to 460. Some racers got close to 500.

BELOW: A drilled-out chassis presented structural integrity problems, causing racers to add bracing and often replacing the frames. Note the single exhaust system.

Cruising in the white prototype turbine car at Roosevelt Raceway during the New York Press Preview on May 14, 1963. It could have been the white turbine with blue racing stripes that was in the 1964 movie, *The Lively Set*.

FINE WHINE:
CHRYSLER'S TURBINE-BIRD

I didn't make any friends at the turbine car press preview after asking a Chrysler engineer, "Is there room under the hood for a 413-inch Wedge?"

On May 14, 1963, I slipped behind the wheel of the white prototype at the New York City Press Preview at Roosevelt Raceway and I was confused. It wasn't the well-organized dash and luxurious appointments that baffled me. Nor was it the engine's whine, rightfully sounding like an airplane engine exhaling through a car's exhaust system. It was the tach, redlined at 60,000 rpm—not 6,000. And the engine temperature gauge showed hot at 2,000 degrees—not 200.

I really didn't feel less confused when an engineer said, "The redline was closer to 44,500 rpm. And, normal engine operating temperature is just a little less than 1,000 degrees and it idled at 22,000 rpm." I felt as though I had just entered *The Twilight Zone*.

The first thing you notice when driving a turbine is a total lack of engine and powertrain vibration, incredibly smooth acceleration, and tremendous low-end torque. It felt like a luxurious GT. We ran stopwatch 0- to 60-mile-per-hour sprints, with most runs in the low elevens. It actually felt quicker since the air-cooled 140-horsepower CR2A gas

turbine delivered 425 lb-ft of torque at idle. Acceleration was equal to that of a then-average 200-horsepower midsize car. The turbine has few moving parts and half the weight of an average V-8 and could be nourished on just about any liquid, from perfume to booze. Smelly Diesel #2 and kerosene were the preferred fuels. Leaded gas could not be used because of potential corrosion issues.

Two ex-Ford designers at Chrysler—Chief Stylist Elwood Engle and Stylist Charles Mashigan—were responsible for the turbine car. That may explain its similarity to the '61 Thunderbird. It also features styling cues from the easily forgettable '58 Ford La Galaxie and Mashigan's '63 Chrysler Typhoon concept cars.

The turbine's luxury appointments, fit, finish, and overall quality were superior to that of any car built by any US carmaker in 1963. Ghia, in Turin, Italy, handcrafted bodies for final assembly in Detroit. Chrysler and Ghia were early adopters of using aluminum body panels (hood and trunk lid) to reduce weight and structural adhesives for bonding inner and outer sections together.

Chrysler built fifty-five turbine cars in 1963 and 1964, keeping five prototypes and distributing fifty for consumer road tests. A total of 203 people were loaned cars for three-month evaluations. All program cars were painted Turbine Bronze. Eventually forty-six cars were crushed, owing to tax and liability issues; Chrysler retained two and sold two to private individuals. One of these was consummate car guy, Jay Leno. It remains one of Leno's favorite cars.

TOP LEFT: While trying to find the turbine car engine's carburetor, I learned that it had just one spark plug, no pistons or cylinders, no carburetor, and it would run on a variety of fuels, other than the leaded gas available everywhere.

TOP RIGHT: Chrysler's Italian stylists drove home the turbine theme when designing the rear end of the car.

BOTTOM: I found the turbine car's ride and handling to be more like that of a European luxury GT than a typical Chrysler product. At the time, we were not aware that all the production cars would be painted bronze.

1964

Plymouth and Dodge featured models with 426 Street Wedge engines with more horsepower and torque than the competition offered. This is a four-speed 426 Sport Fury ragtop that I drove around San Francisco in 1964. With stock tires, a four-speed with Hurst linkage, and 3.23 Sure-Grip rear, it hit 0 to 60 times in the mid-low sevens. Note the M plates.

CHAPTER SIX

THE YEAR OF THE SUPERCAR

The year 1964 was all about the birth of the supercar, Hemis, and factory-built race cars. Ford added a Mustang to the mix midyear. It was pure, unbridled sensory overload.

Pontiac called it "a device for shrinking time and distance." Magazine editors called it a supercar. And, from coast to coast, enthusiasts flocked to Pontiac dealers see the new GTO, an option that breathed life into a Tempest. Pontiac—not Ford, Chevy, or Plymouth—essentially created the option that ignited the supercar revolution and an almost cult-like movement. The GTO's extensive performance, comfort, and convenience menu was the envy of the industry. It was the supercar for all seasons—and reasons.

Because the GTO became an overnight sensation, fiction often gets in the way of reality when discussing responsibility for its concept and creation. Pontiac's primary players were Pete Estes, general manager,

To further stimulate sales, GM Design created a slick Day Two GTO—*Flamme*—with trendy chrome-reverse wheels, custom rocker trim, rectangular Cibie headlamps, and exhaust cutouts under the front fenders.

and John DeLorean, chief engineer. DeLorean's staff included a number of racing enthusiasts. The concept of putting a 389-inch engine from a full-size Pontiac into a Tempest evolved from meetings DeLorean had with two performance-savvy guys—Bill Collins and Russ Gee, who headed up the Experimental Engineering Department. One of the key meetings was not, however, about creating a high-performance street car. It dealt with building a slightly longer wheelbase Tempest to replace the NASCAR Super-Duty 421 stockers that had become history.

Gee revealed that since 326 and 389 engines shared the same motor mounts, a 389 could be shoehorned into a Tempest in about a half-hour. With NASCAR in mind, Russ Gee's team built a '63 Tempest 389 prototype with a 3-inch longer wheelbase: 115 versus 112 inches. It worked and it was fast. But DeLorean couldn't find any support for stock car racing at Pontiac. All efforts shifted to creating a product that would appeal to performance enthusiasts, preferably young ones. That proved to be a far better route.

During the discussion of a unique 389-engined Tempest, Jim Wangers—who was a successful Pontiac drag racer and account executive at Pontiac's advertising agency, McManus,

John & Adams—got involved. He also had a relationship with Ace Wilson, owner of Royal Pontiac. Wangers presented youth-market-targeted GTO concepts to Pete Estes. Estes passed them along to DeLorean, and the 389 Tempest GTO program was greenlighted. Ferrari originally used the model designation GTO—Gran Turismo Omologato—for its 250 GTO. It means that the vehicle meets the standard specifications for racing in the Grand Touring category.

Prior to the GTO option, the most powerful engine you could get in a Tempest was a 326-inch V-8 rated at 280 horsepower. A GTO-optioned Tempest could be equipped with a standard four-barrel 389 rated at 325 horsepower at 4,800 rpm or the optional tri-power 389 rated at 348 horsepower at 4,900 rpm. Both engines generated 428 lb-ft of torque. Buyers could choose from three- or four-speed manuals with Hurst shifters or a two-speed automatic and limited-slip rears with 3.08 to 3.90 gearing.

Since no GM division had done this before, Pete Estes was apprehensive about how the marketplace would receive the new car. While he did sign off on producing five thousand units, Estes voiced concern: "If Pontiac doesn't meet its GTO sales target, it will not be around in 1965."

Jim Wangers did not share Este's concerns. McManus, John, and Adams came up with advertising for the GTO's launch. It was the first of many years of GTO campaigns that set the standard for high-performance car advertising. The ads spoke to young enthusiasts—and they responded. By January 1964, dealers had already taken orders for more than ten thousand GTOs, securing the model's future. Waiting lists were growing longer each day. The GTO emerged as a huge success, with total 1964 GTO production of 25,806 hardtops and 6,644 convertibles.

GM Design created a dynamite follow-up for the 1964 auto show circuit—the tri-power GTO *Flamme*. Fitted with Cibie rectangular headlamps and under-fender exhaust cutouts and, of course, painted Flame Red, it debuted at the 1964 Chicago Auto Show. It was first shown with a white interior and wire wheel hubcaps. By the time I saw it at the New York show, its interior was also red and trendy chrome-reverse wheels had been installed.

Oldsmobile's response to the GTO was a midyear 4-4-2 that excelled in ride and handling. An offshoot of its successful police-option F85, the 4-4-2 came stock with a 310-horsepower dual-exhaust, four-barrel 330-inch V-8 with four-speed. Even though the 4-4-2 showcased a Police Pursuit chassis with heavy-duty springs and front and rear sway bars, the 4-4-2 lacked the GTO's power and youth market appeal. Oldsmobile sold only 2,999.

I can remember feeling like the proverbial kid in a candy store in 1964. I was editor of *Custom Rodder* and *Speed & Custom* (formerly *Car, Speed and Style*) magazines and managing editor of *CARS*. Not only was I making a living doing what I loved, but I was able to borrow the latest and greatest performance cars. It was like Fantasy Camp for car guys!

Of all the cars I borrowed that year, one stands out for delivering the ultimate pulse-quickening experience. Nothing else even came close and the encounter has been indelibly recorded on my internal hard drive.

It was early in the week of April 13, after the close of the 1964 New York International Auto Show, when I received a call from Dodge News Bureau's Bernard Francis "Moon" Mullins. One of the best, most creative PR operatives in the industry,

TOP: Oldsmobile's 4-4-2 paled by comparison to the GTO, but its one-off GM design concept gave the GTO *Flamme* a run for its money on the auto show circuit. *General Motors*

BOTTOM: Jim Wangers was a guiding force in the GTO's growth and influence in the youth market and the creation of the supercar category. A successful drag racer and key player in the creation of the Royal Pontiac Bobcats, he was an executive at Pontiac's advertising agency. *Jim Wangers Collection*

he wanted to know if I'd like to borrow the Ramchargers' S/SA *Candymatic* Dodge for a week or so. Somehow during all my stuttering and stammering, I managed to get a *YES* out. "Just go over to the Chrysler West Side Service Center and pick it up. Tell them I sent you!" he replied.

The Ramchargers' *Candymatic* I drove was not *the Candymatic*, Jim Thornton's Candy Apple Red and White Dodge that had won S/SA at the NHRA Winternationals. That car was a lighter two-door sedan and "my" *Candymatic* was a hardtop. Blueprinted and race-ready Stage III 426 Max Wedges powered both. However, unlike Thornton's, the one I played "hero driver" in had never turned a wheel in anger on the quarter-mile. It was a backup race car that served primarily as a show car and had been displayed at the New York show. Loading the car in and out of shows, teamsters racked up most of its miles.

One might expect that a lightened race car powered by a 12.5:1 Max Wedge backed up with a bang-shift Torqueflite and 4.56 Sure-Grip rear gears was less than ideal for driving around New York City. It also had jacked torsion bars and cheater slicks, and was built without insulation or sound deadeners. Being a young car guy editing enthusiast magazines, I thought it was a dream come true.

Originally factory-built as a steel race car, it was retrofitted with aluminum body panels. Dodge's in-house drag-racing engineers put it on a diet, reducing weight by approximately 150 pounds.

During my first drive, nine miles from Chrysler's Manhattan West Side Service Center to my apartment in Forest Hills, Queens, I was

TOP: Lincoln-Mercury contracted with Logghe and DST to build 427 High-Riser Comets to run in A/FX. Bill Schrewsberry won A/FX in Jack Chrisman's Comet and Ronnie Sox won Stock Eliminator at 1964 NHRA Winternationals. *Fran Hernandez Collection*

MIDDLE: The small-block Chevelle was no match for the GTO or 426 Street Wedge Mopars, but this Chevelle kept Chevrolet in the spotlight during 1964. Washington D.C.–based Malcolm Durham put his '63 Impala Z11 engine into the *Strip Blazer* Chevelle and raised havoc in modified classes and on the match race circuit.

BOTTOM: Chrysler and Ford built the two hottest factory race cars in 1964: The 426 Hemi Dodges and Plymouths and the 427 Ford Thunderbolt. Jim Thornton stages his *Candymatic* Dodge and Butch Leal his Thunderbolt at 1964 NHRA Nationals. Thornton won S/SA and Leal copped S/S in Mickey Thompson's T-Bolt.

overwhelmed by endless detonation, multiple carburetor flameouts, and stalling. And I sweated profusely because heat was coming through the noninsulated firewall. The solid-lifter 426 liked to idle between 1,500 and 2,000 rpm and low-end performance left a lot to be desired. Once I got it over 3,500 rpm, the tach hit around 6,500 rpm in what felt like nanoseconds.

Its engine didn't feel right. After blowing up a Dodge Ramcharger on the way to the track in 1963, I knew that I needed help. I also went through a half-tank of gas that I later discovered was probably *no-octane* regular. Maybe I should have taken the booklet and warning card in the glove box seriously:

> The 1964 Ramcharger 426 engine is designed for use in supervised acceleration trials. It is not recommended for general everyday driving because of the compromise of all-around characteristics which must be made for this type of vehicle.
>
> To protect the working parts of the Ramcharger 426, it should not be run over 6,500 rpm. Wide open throttle bursts should be limited to 15 seconds duration.

After losing valuable driving time foolishly thinking that a Chrysler service center could make it right under warranty, I visited a local speed shop and had a friend, Bill Howell, take it for a spin. Dealer techs had done some work on it and billed Dodge News Bureau $42 for labor. We discovered that valves were set too tight, timing was way off, and the spark plugs were two ranges short of a spark. The tank was drained and refilled with 104-octane Sunoco 260.

We got the idle down to around 1,250, flameouts were history, and throttle response was what you would expect from a 426 engine built by the

Ramchargers. Getting it to hook up on New York's mean streets was problematic. The *Candymatic* was fitted with cheater slicks that were designed for traction on a smooth, clean road surface. That ruled out New York City streets. And, unfortunately we ran out of time before we could take it to Westhampton. Because of the car's stance, appearance, and sinister exhaust note, it was not easy finding runs. It was way too intimating. It did, however, attract a lot of interest from New York City's Finest. I was pulled over more than half a dozen times, mostly to check what was under the hood. Even though the Dodge didn't have a trace of yellow paint, a number of pedestrians hailed me, thinking it was a taxi!

Before having to return our *candy-striper*, I managed to spend one Saturday running on Woodhaven/Cross Bay Boulevard in Queens. I dusted off a few 409 Chevys, 421 Pontiacs, and even a fuel-injected Sting Ray. On the Cross Bay extension heading out to the Bow Wow and Pizza City street racer hangouts in Howard Beach, I met my match. An Olds-powered '40 Willys coupe with an exposed GMC blower made quick work of me.

What made it all worthwhile that day was beating a modified Day Two 409 Impala ragtop, three for three. After

For one week in 1964, author Marty Schorr played the great imposter. He street-raced the Ramchargers' 426 Max Wedge *Candymatic* backup race car in New York: "I stopped off at Pizza City on Cross Bay Boulevard to see if I catch a run . . . and grab a slice for lunch."

the third run, I pulled over to the side to let the engine cool and the Chevy pulled up next to me. "Are you Jim Thornton and is this the real *Candymatic*?" the Chevy driver asked. Since Thornton and I had a lot in common—we're both tall and he and the Ramchargers really did build the car I was driving—I answered in the affirmative. At that point the guy's girlfriend handed him a copy of *Hot Rod* and opened to a full-page Dodge *Candymatic* ad, which he handed to me. "Do you think you can autograph it?" "No problem."

After scrawling a barely legible *Jim Thornton*, I felt as though we really did have something in common. The *real* Jim Thornton continued his winning ways and I returned to reality . . . driving a Royal manual typewriter.

Pontiac owned the supercar niche market, even though other carmakers were building performance cars. Chevrolet continued with 340-, 400-, and 425- horsepower 409 Impalas and Biscaynes, but the midsize 327/300 Chevelle couldn't cut it. Dearborn's 289/271 Comet and Fairlane had neither the power nor the image to compete with the GTO. Mopars had more powerful engines, but lacked the image.

Ford *skunked* the competition with its new Mustang, available with 289/271 power. It launched a new generation of pony cars. In the first four months, Ford sold in excess of one hundred thousand Mustangs. Galaxies and Marauders could be optioned with R-Code 427s, but they were full-size cars. For NHRA Stock to Super/Stock and FX competition, Ford and Mercury offered enthusiasts a veritable menu of

TOP: To keep the 409 Impala fresh, GM Design created this Day Two convertible with Cibie headlamps, custom hood, fender-mount exhaust tips, one-off wheels, and a chopped windshield. *General Motors*

BOTTOM: This is *the* first 426 Hemi Dodge Lightweight racecar to be built at the Chrysler Hamtramck, Michigan, assembly plant. The front end is aluminum. The dual four-barrel Hemi engine has 12.5:1 compression and 425 horsepower. Note the front mags.

steel and lightweight 427 Galaxies and one of the hottest factory-built Super/Stocks—the 427 Thunderbolt.

By mid-2004, and after driving pre-production 2005 models at carmakers' proving grounds, I knew the best was yet to come. What I didn't know was that I would become editor of *CARS* and editorial director of the Magum-Royal Automotive Group.

MUSTANG SETS THE PACE

If NASCAR had a class for compact convertibles in 1964, all the Holman-Moody-built Indy 500 Pace Car would have needed was a roll cage, fuel cell, and race tires.

Three of the first new Mustangs built in 1964 never made it to Ford dealerships, press introductions, or even to members of the Ford family. They were shipped from Dearborn, Michigan, to Holman-Moody in Charlotte, North Carolina. H-M was Ford's NASCAR, USAC, and FIA race car builder of choice and charged with converting stock Mustang convertibles into Indy 500 Pace Cars capable of getting out of the way of race cars at speeds up to 140 miles per hour.

Lee Iacocca wanted to showcase the all-new Mustang at the 500-mile classic, but it was obvious that a stock, early-build Mustang would not be up to the job. His only option was to have three of the first convertibles built professionally race-prepped. Holman-Moody was chosen based on its experience building class-winning 1963–1964 Monte Carlo Rally Falcons with powerful 260/289 engines and developing 289s for Ford's GT road racing program. A blueprinted and balanced 289 engine, based on the optional Mustang 289/271 small-block, was chosen to replace the Mustang's stock 260. Only one of the three Wimbledon White convertibles actually served pace car duties.

The race-prepped 289 with deep oil sump, forged crank and rods, ported and polished heads, and 10.5:1 pistons utilized a solid-lifter valvetrain and stock Autolite-Ford four-barrel induction. A Galaxie radiator was installed to aid

Henry Ford II's younger brother Benson drove the highly modified Mustang to pace the Indy 500. It was capable of speeds up to 140 miles per hour. *Ford Motor Company*

ABOVE: This H&M 289 engine still retains its original valve covers with Ford Engine & Foundry "Experimental" stickers. Externally, it looks pretty stock, but the block and heads received extensive machine work and forged crank, rods, and pistons were installed. *RK Motors*

LEFT: One of the three Holman-Moody Mustangs paces the 1964 Indy 500. The actual pace car has survived and has been restored. The other two were never used during the race. *Ford Motor Company*

engine cooling under stop and start and high-speed track conditions. The Mustang's stock drivetrain was replaced with a Ford Toploader four-speed and narrowed Galaxie limited-slip rear like those used on factory drag cars.

One of the major concerns of running a powerful, compact convertible under Indy "pacing" conditions was structural integrity. This is where Holman-Moody's experience building NASCAR stockers and pro rally cars came in handy. The Mustang's engine compartment had tri-point bracing between the fenders and cowl. The brakes were beefed and a larger sway bar installed along with chopped coils and de-arched leaf springs. Koni shocks were used front and rear with left and right side units valved (80/20 left and 50/50 right) to accommodate banked track conditions. The Mustang's platform was also beefed to compensate for its powerful engine and high-speed capability.

The actual Indy Pace Car was driven by Benson Ford at Indy and, after the race, was shipped back to Dearborn. After a freshening at Holman-Moody, it was shipped to Sebring where it was used for a decade for parades, loans to race car drivers, and pacing races. After years of storage, it was sold in the 1990s. The new owner had it professionally restored to exactly how it was seen by millions at the track and on TV, pacing the 1964 Indy 500. It survives today, complete with dual stanchion-mount checkered flags, two-way radio, and other pace-car-only accessories. It stands ready to pace again.

CHRYSLER'S 800-POUND ELEPHANT

The 426 Hemi was the first new Hemi engine since Chrysler's original 1951 to 1958 FirePower V-8 dominated motorsports and sent competitors back to their drawing boards.

Four years after the last 392-cubic-inch Hemi was installed in a '58 Chrysler 300D, work started on the next generation Hemi. In December 1962, Chrysler Engineering received an internal memo from senior management requesting development of a new race engine. They were to come up with an engine and vehicle combination capable of winning NASCAR-USAC stock car races.

Engineering considered a variety of engine configurations, quickly narrowing it down to one that would displace 426 cubic inches and feature cylinder heads with ultra-efficient hemispherical-shaped combustion chambers. That program was expanded so that the same engine could be easily adapted for drag racing. Since Chrysler had reams of test and development data on Hemi engines used in a variety of

vehicles for nine model years, the choice to develop a new Hemi was obvious.

Chrysler targeted the 1964 Daytona 500 for public debut of the new engine. On December 6, 1963, the first 426 Hemi, a single-four-barrel NASCAR motor, ran on a dynamometer. Instead of having to tool up for a new block, Chrysler was able to use its 426 Wedge block, reducing development time considerably.

For development as a Hemi, they beefed the carryover 4.25-inch bore/3.75-inch stroke block with cross-bolted mains and forged steel crank and rods. The 12.5:1, 852-pound Hemi received cast-iron heads with 2.15-inch intake and 1.94-inch exhaust valves. A single Holley four-barrel was slated for circuit racing, while dual four-barrels on an aluminum short ram manifold was for drag racing. Because of its bulk, it was dubbed *Elephant*.

The 426 Hemi burst on the circuit-racing scene at the Daytona 500. The rest is history. On February 23, Hemi-powered Plymouths and Dodges dominated NASCAR's premier 500-mile race. It was at the very same race, only one year later, that Ford had swept with its 427 Galaxies.

Led by Richard Petty in his legendary No. 43 Plymouth, '64 Plymouths driven by Jimmy Pardue and Paul Goldsmith completed the Hemi's 1-2-3 win. Jim Paschal filled in the

ABOVE: Highly underrated at 425 horsepower, the new 426 Hemi could be ordered in a factory-built Lightweight Plymouth or Dodge. Automatic transmission models owned S/SA. *Factory Lightweight Collection*

LEFT: Jim Thornton, president of the Ramchargers Club (left), after winning S/SA at the 1964 NHRA Nationals. He was also runner-up for Top Stock Eliminator to Roger Lindamood's *Color Me Gone* Dodge. Thornton won class in the Hemi *Candymatic* with a 128.20 mile-per-hour run in 11.37 seconds.

fourth spot in Cotton Owens's Dodge. With eight wins and thirty-seven top-five finishes, Petty nailed his first NASCAR Championship. Hemi-powered Mopars won twenty-six of sixty-two Grand National races. NASCAR Hemi engines were pulling 550-plus horsepower and could run at 6,500 to 6,800 rpm all day. The Hemi cars ran so fast and so reliably that NASCAR's Bill France, prodded by Ford, banned the engine for the 1965 season for not being production-legal.

While Hemi cars were dominating NASCAR superspeedways, Code A864 Plymouths and Dodges claimed ownership of NHRA Super/Stock classes. In September 1964, I spent five days in Indianapolis at the NHRA Nationals and my coverage appeared in the December issue of *CARS*. In most of the high-profile categories—Top Fuel Eliminator, Top Stock Eliminator, AA/Fuel Dragster, Super/Stock Automatic, and Factory Experimental—426 Hemi cars ruled.

After posting the first official 200-plus-mile-per-hour (201.34 miles per hour) run in his 426 Dodge *Wynn's Jammer* dragster on August 2 at Island Dragway in New Jersey, Don "Big Daddy" Garlits continued his winning ways at the NHRA Nationals. He took AA/FD class and Top Fuel Eliminator (7.67/198.22 miles per hour) gold.

Ramchargers' President Jim Thornton ran 11.37/128.20 miles per hour in the *Candymatic* Dodge to win S/SA, and was runner-up to Roger Lindamood for Top Stock Eliminator. Lindamood ran 11.31/127.84 miles per hour in his *Color*

TOP: Dodge's man on the West Coast, Dick Landy blasts off the line in his S/SA Hemi. Landy switched later to four-speed cars and raced Dodges well into the Pro Stock 1970s. He was a feared competitor.

BOTTOM: Single four-barrel stock car racing 426 Hemi–powered Plymouths secured 1-2-3 wins at the 1964 NASCAR Daytona 500. Unlike drag racing engines factory equipped with dual AFBs, the circuit-racing Hemi came with a single 850-cfm Holley with sealed cowl induction to pick up high-pressure airflow at the base of the windshield. *FCA Archives*

Me Gone Dodge. Former Chevrolet superstar Dave Strickler switched to Dodge in 1964 and won A/FX with an 11.04 run. Fred Cutler, in the only Hemi Dodge station wagon, ran 11.81/120.48 miles per hour and won B/FX.

In my *CARS* story, I wrote: "Just as Chrysler-powered products reigned supreme in Top Gas and Fuel competition, they also ruled top stock classes. In fact, you would swear that the staging area during eliminations was part of a Mopar assembly plant!"

427 INCHES OF ROLLING THUNDER

Named after the legendary World War II P-47 Thunderbolt fighter plane, Ford's Thunderbolt honors its namesake.

To remain competitive in Super/Stock racing in 1964, Ford needed a smaller, lighter car than the previous year's 427 Galaxie. The '63 Fairlane was powered by a 406-inch big-block and equipped with fiberglass front fenders, hood, deck lid, and aluminum inner fenders and bumpers. Based on the performance of the one-off A/FX Fairlane, campaigned by Tasca Ford's Bill Lawton, Bob Tasca pitched Special Vehicles Activities managers Jacque Passino and Frank "Zimmy" Zimmerman on building lightweight 427 Fairlanes.

Bob Tasca, an influential member of Ford's Drag Council, was successful. Ford contracted with Dearborn Steel Tubing to build one hundred 427 Fairlanes. DST Project Manager James "Hammer" Mason and SVA's Dick Brannan, Charlie Gray, Danny Jones, and Vern Tinsler were responsible for the build-out.

Working with NHRA's Super/Stock class weight break of 7.5 pounds per-cubic-inch, the 427 Fairlane had to come in at 3,202 pounds to be competitive. Fairlane 500s tagged for conversion were built without insulation, sound deadeners, seam sealers, carpeting, radio, heater, wheel covers, passenger side windshield wiper, sun visors, trunk mat, jack, spare tire, armrests, rear window cranks, and mirrors. To make the weight break, fiberglass front fenders, hoods, and aluminum bumpers were installed. Additional dietary components included Plexiglas side windows and backlight and Bostrom Econoline van bucket seats.

Thunderbolts were fitted with 427 High-Riser engines with cross-bolted mains, steel cranks, forged 13:1 pistons and heads with fully machined combustion chambers, and 2.72 x 1.34-inch intake and 1.86 x 1.30-inch exhaust ports. Originally developed for NASCAR competition, the big-block's 7,000-rpm valvetrain utilized lightweight 2.19-inch intake and 1.73-inch exhaust valves. All cars received tube headers and stock, single pipe exhaust systems.

In order to shoehorn a 427 into a Fairlane, inner fender panels and upper control arms and brackets had to be modified. Large, 6-inch diameter hoses connected to screened grille inlets and directed fresh air to a pair of Holley No. 4150 four-barrels on a tall aluminum manifold. A trunk-mounted 95-pound battery was installed to increase traction.

In 1964, Thunderbolts distinguished themselves on drag strips from coast to coast. Gas Ronda ran 120.16 miles per hour in 12.05 seconds for a class win at the NHRA Winternationals and won the NHRA Super/Stock World Championship. Butch Leal won Super/Stock at the NHRA Indy Nationals, turning 11.76 and 122.78 miles per hour.

Ronda also won Super/Stock (12.56 E.T.) and Eliminator (119.68 miles per hour in 12.08 seconds) at the *Hot Rod Magazine* Championships at Riverside Raceway. Another Drag Council member, Bill Lawton, in the Tasca Ford Thunderbolt, set both ends of the NHRA record, 126.05 miles per hour in 11.69 seconds, at a Division 1 points meet.

Dearborn Steel Tubing turned out almost turnkey Super/Stockers. Suspensions were beefed with two-leaf rear springs on the left side and three on the right to help offset the 427's incredible torque. Crafted from square tubing, Vern Tinsler's traction bars linked 9-inch Galaxie rears to crossmembers with driveshaft safety loops. Thunderbolts were delivered with NHRA-spec 7-inch cheater slicks, but racers were responsible for installing roll bars and tweaking engines.

Thunderbolts were built in two colors, Wimbledon White and Vintage Burgundy, and had four-speed and modified Lincoln C6 automatic transmissions. The first eleven went to Drag Council members in October 1963. Dearborn Steel Tubing didn't halt production after completing 100 T-Bolts in May 1964. An additional twenty-seven Fairlane Super/Stocks were built for dealers—the majority submitted DSOs directly to DST. They were not included in Ford sales data. Total production was 127.

After the 1964 season, many T-Bolt owners continued to race their cars and win in Modified Production. It's hard to argue with Dick Brannan, who feels "the Thunderbolt was one of the most successful Super/Stock cars ever built."

TOP: Bob Ford Inc. was originally owned by Henry Ford's nephew and was very active in Midwest drag racing. It was one of the three dealership Thunderbolts, running in A/MP against a '57 Ford at 1964 NHRA Indy Nationals.

MIDDLE: Len Richter testing the second-built T-Bolt, one of three $1.00 427 Fairlanes that went to Bob Ford in Dearborn. This photo is taken at the Ford test track after the T-Bolt was repainted Champagne Black & Gold. At an AHRA Championship meet, Richter won Mr. Stock Eliminator and set the S/S record at 126.76 miles per hour in 11.37 seconds. *Dennis Kolodziej*

BOTTOM RIGHT: The potent 427 High Riser engine came stock with air induction hoses feeding fresh air to dual Holleys from screened inlets in the grille. Of the first 100 T-Bolts built to qualify for NHRA S/S, this is one of the forty-one built with four-speed transmissions. *Dennis Kolodziej*

BOTTOM LEFT: This is the actual SVA Thunderbolt that served as a C-6 automatic transmission development car. I photographed it at the Dearborn Proving Ground during testing in 1964. Note the Ford World Headquarters is in background.

1965

One of two Riviera Gran Sports tested for *CARS* annual award. This was the East Coast Riv and the photo was taken in Forest Hill Gardens, New York. It boasted unmatched luxury, plus real GT performance and handling.

CHAPTER SEVEN

The more the merrier

The Motown beat goes on: new engines, new supercars, and new factory-built race cars.

Not long after having access to 1965 performance cars, I suggested to Mel Jacolow, editor of *CARS* magazine, that he change the name of the award "American Classic of the Year" he presented annually to carmakers. With production cars getting quicker and faster and carmakers targeting the burgeoning youth market, I felt we needed something more relevant. My suggestion was "Top Performance Car of the Year." It was not an easy sell. Shortly after agreeing to the name change and after we started test-driving suitable candidates, Jacolow abruptly resigned.

Five years after becoming editor of *Custom Rodder* and *CAR Speed and Style*, I was tapped to take over *CARS*. My first issue would be April 1965—our annual award issue. I hired Fred Mackerodt

The Z16 Chevelle SS396 was boxy and lacked GTO's visual appeal. Performance was outstanding and Chevrolet built just 200 coupes before the end of the 1965 model year.

as assistant editor. Later I was named the company's editorial director.

As part of a road and track test, Gordon Chittenden, *CARS* West Coast editor, had driven a new 425-cubic-inch, 360-horsepower Riviera Gran Sport from Los Angeles to GM's Proving Ground in Mesa, Arizona. The dual four-barrel Wildcat engine in the Riviera generated 465 lb-ft of torque.

He turned in a glowing report: "The luxury is apparent in around-town and highway driving. Performance shows up when you're on a twisting mountain road watching a sports car driver trying to out-corner you. And, on the first straight strip of road you blast through and leave him choking in the dust."

Under GM supervision, Chittenden clocked 92 miles per hour in 15.4 seconds, 0 to 60 miles per hour in low-to-mid-sevens and a top speed of 130 miles per hour. I had driven a Skylark Gran Sport powered by the 400-cubic-inch, 325-horsepower version of the 425. Both engines were old design, small-valve Nailhead V-8s that suffered from loss of breath at higher rpm.

The Skylark, like the Riviera, exhibited a wonderful combination of ride, handling, braking, and performance. All GS models were built on stiffer convertible model chassis with heavy-duty everything. The Skylark GS that I tested earlier at GM's Milford Proving Ground ran consistent

mid-fifteens at 86 to 88 miles per hour. Even though it was not a serious GTO competitor, I really liked the car. *NOTE: At the time I believed that the Riviera and Skylark tested were engineering-prepared cars and most likely quicker and faster than showroom stockers.*

At that point I decided to amend our honor to "Top Performance Car(s) of the Year" and presented the award to Buick General Manager Edward Rollert. I remember congratulating him on the full-page Skylark advertisement, tagging the GS-400 "A Howitzer with Windshield Wipers."

Seemingly overnight Pontiac, with its GTO, had created and then dominated a new performance car category—supercars. Targeting young enthusiasts in both age and mindset, Pontiac created a powerful, exciting intermediate-size car. It had all the right stuff either standard or optional: tri-power 389/348 engine, four-on-the-floor, heavy-duty suspension, metallic brakes, bucket seats, and Safe-T-Track rears.

Fortunately, the Tempest line was due for refreshed styling, and the GTO—still an option and not a distinct car line—benefitted from a new front end with vertically stacked headlamps. And it retained what had become an iconic option list.

Pontiac also upgraded the GTO's engines that were rated at 335 horsepower with single four-barrel and 360 with tri-power. Increased power was attributable to intake manifold and head modifications. The '65 GTO ushered in the first of what would be a mainstay of performance GTO models and options—Ram Air. On August 17, 1965, Pontiac dealers started selling a new air scoop package, No. 984716, for converting tri-power GTOs to fresh air induction. Priced at $70 retail, the do-it-yourself or dealer-installed Ram Air kit included a tub or fixture complete with gaskets, foam, and hardware that sealed stock air cleaners to the underside of the hood. Replacement trim was used when the decorative hood scoop was opened, allowing fresh air to flow to the carbs.

Chevrolet had been slow to bring a high-performance midsize car to market. Toward the end of the 1965 model year, the carmaker revealed the potent Z16 Chevelle Malibu SS396, powered by an all-new Mark IV 396 big-block. While somewhat boxy, it was the most powerful car in the supercar sweepstakes. But there was a problem. Chevrolet General Manager Bunkie Knudsen's foray into the market dominated by Pontiac was hardly noticed. Because of its late entry in August, production was limited to two hundred, plus a single convertible. Since the SS396 was built around a beefy convertible chassis fitted with big-car brakes and front and rear stabilizer bars, it would have been a simple matter to

produce convertibles. But time was not on Chevy's side.

There was a small Z16 press event at GM's Mesa Proving Ground in February 1965. The word was that the big-block coupe was fast, but visually paled by comparison to the GTO. Since so few were produced, only key dealers were given opportunities to place orders and Z16s sold out quickly. A number of GM executives drove Z16s as did celebrities such as Dan Blocker, Hoss Cartwright on TV's *Bonanza*. Chevrolet loaned Blocker a yellow Z16 coupe.

Performance feedback from Mesa indicated that the Chevrolet Engineering–prepared Z16 could sprint to 60 miles per hour in the low sixes with quarter-mile times of mid-high-fourteens at close to 100 miles per hour.

The Z16's all-new, big-block displaced 396 cubic inches and rated at 375 horsepower at 5,600 rpm and a whopping 420 lb-ft of torque at 3,600 rpm. It showcased a heavy-duty block, heads with canted valves, forged steel crank and rods, 11:1 pistons, and an aluminum intake manifold with a big Holley four-barrel. It was a one-year-only RPO L37 hydraulic-lifter engine unique to the Z16. Full-size Chevys could be optioned with 325- or 425-horsepower Mark IV engines. The death knell had sounded for the outdated 409 engines, yet 340- and 400-horsepower versions were still available.

Thanks to a new 400-cubic-inch four-barrel engine rated at 345 horsepower at 4,800 rpm and 440 lb-ft of torque at 3,200 rpm, the 4-4-2 suddenly gained status on the street. This engine was developed for use in the 4-4-2 and would go on to become a mainstay in Oldsmobile's high-performance portfolio. They also updated the model with high-profile ornamentation.

The really good stuff enhanced its appeal: high-performance police chassis and suspension, front and rear stabilizer bars, low-restriction exhausts, heavy-duty rear suspension arms and bushings, and optional heavy-duty manual steering. Oldsmobile's 4-4-2 was becoming a serious supercar, and Lansing sold 25,003 4-4-2s—more than eight times more than its predecessor.

Ford did not increase the size or output of the top Mustang engine option, the 289/271 small-block, but it did increase its

The all-new 396 Mark IV big-block marked Chevrolet's entry into the Supercar Sweepstakes. The 396/375 Z16 engine was a one-year-only, single-model engine with hydraulic cam and big Holley four-barrel. Future 396/375 engines came with solid-lifter valve trains.

appeal by adding a fastback model. Carroll Shelby took it one step further and converted stock 289/271 fastbacks into street and race GT350 Mustangs with Cobra bite. Even the 306-horsepower street models were race cars! The R-model B/Production Shelby put out 330 to 350 horsepower at 6,500 rpm. Shelby American won the B/Production Championship in five of the SCCA six regions. Jerry Titus drove No. 5R001 to win the American Road Race of Champions and SCCA National Championship.

On the quarter-mile, A/FX Mustangs, powered by 427 SOHC engines, won big in national events and helped Ford win NHRA's Manufacturers Award for the second year in a row. The first 427 A/FX Mustang built at Dearborn Steel Tubing went to Ford's Dick Brannan and I put it on the cover of the May 1965 issue of *Rodder and Super/Stock*.

Ford's midsize 289 Fairlane was still not ready for prime time. Completely restyled and reengineered, the full-size '65 Galaxie was Ford's street fighter. It could be optioned with 410-horsepower single four-barrel or 425-horsepower dual four-barrel 427 engines. The 1965½ production 427 Galaxie came with an upgraded side-oiler block fitted with a forged steel crank, high-rpm valvetrain, and lightweight hollow-stem valves and heads with machined combustion chambers. This was the same block used for 427 SOHC race engines.

The Galaxie had a 119-inch wheelbase and was a heavy car, yet it delivered impressive street performance. Some of my old test notes show that a stock 427/425 Galaxie with four-speed could sprint from 0 to 60 miles per hour in the fives if you could get the tires to hook up. On the drag strip, it was not unusual to run fifteens at around 95 miles per hour. When tuned and equipped with headers and sticky tires, times would drop into the fourteens.

Chrysler covered all bases catering to performance enthusiasts in 1965. New Dodge Coronets and Plymouth Belvederes could be ordered with 365-horsepower 426 Wedge engines with four-speed or TorqueFlite. Unlike the GTO and 4-4-2, Mopar middleweights were void of eye-catching decor. But they were strong enough to get the job done. Chrysler had planned to make a street version of the 426 Hemi available in midsize and selected full-size models. Only development vehicles were ever built.

Dodge and Plymouth carried over successful Super/Stock programs based on shorter wheelbase Code A-990

intermediates powered by 426 Hemis with aluminum heads and magnesium intake manifolds. Factory built with 60-percent lighter, acid-dipped steel front fenders, scooped hood, and doors, they were fitted with Corning lightweight side glass. Four-speed or automatic NHRA-legal Super/Stock race cars could be ordered at any authorized dealership. Dodge built 101 426 Hemi Coronets; Plymouth produced 102.

When building Hemis for Factory Experimental, wheelbase was shortened to 110 inches. The rear wheels were moved forward 15 inches and the front wheels by 10 inches, providing an incredible improvement in weight distribution. Each FX car was also treated to a special Plaza Fiberglass Manufacturing "diet," which included scooped hood, front bumper, front fenders and doors, trunk lid, and dashboard. Average weight loss was 80 pounds. Other weight reduction tricks included an 18-pound steel front K-member and Dart/Valiant front spindles and brakes for a 50-pound advantage.

Ford and Chrysler had invested millions in their stock car racing programs. Before the start of the 1965 NASCAR season, they butted heads with Bill France—and each other. Ford complained about Dodges and Plymouths running 426 Hemis and told NASCAR's France that they were planning on running the new 427 Single Overhead Cam (SOHC) engine. Chrysler's circuit racing guru, Ronnie Householder, told France if he allowed the SOHC engine, Chrysler would run a dual overhead cam engine (that it didn't even have!). That's when France kicked sand in Ford and Chrysler grilles.

France banned Chrysler's Hemi, Ford's Cammer, and 427 High-Riser Wedge since they were not available in any production cars. France came up with three new NASCAR classifications. The most important was Class I, allowing a minimum wheelbase of 119 inches and engine displacement to 430 cubic inches for Super Speedways only. Chrysler took its cars and went home. Ford stayed in since it had a full-size Galaxie with a medium-riser 427. And—it cleaned house!

Ford debuted the NASCAR-legit 427 Mid-Riser engine at Riverside and the first eight-place finishers were Fords and Mercurys. Dan Gurney won the *Motor Trend* Riverside 500 for the third straight time. Ford Galaxies won forty-eight out of fifty-five races, including the Daytona 500. Ford driver Ned Jarrett was NASCAR Grand National Champion.

It was a great time to be an automotive magazine editor!

TOP: When NASCAR banned the SOHC 427, Ford SVA had circuit-racing engines diverted to its drag racing program. Dick Brannan's Mustang fastback was the first 427 SOHC Mustang built. Originally fitted with a single-four-barrel NASCAR engine, it was updated with dual quads. *Dick Brannan Collection*

ABOVE: Six factory lightweight A/FX Comets with 650-horsepower 427 SOHC engines were built in 1965. One of these engines is in "Dyno Don" Nicolson's Comet, owned by Irwin Kroiz.

RIGHT: Shelby American converted 289/271 Mustang fastbacks into street and race GT 350s. They dominated SCCA B/Production competition and some ended up as drag cars. NHRA record-holder Gus Zuidema drove Harr Ford's Shelby Mustang and Cobra in NHRA Division 1.

TOP LEFT: Galaxies ordered with 427/425 big-blocks and built after January 1965 came with upgraded side-oiler engines with forged crank, machined heads, and high-rpm valvetrain. A potent motor for the street.

TOP RIGHT: Dodge made sure that nobody missed the 426 Hemi drag racing engine at the 1965 Chelsea Proving Ground press preview in June 1964. It was the first and only time in my career that a carmaker used a scantily clothed model at a press introduction. Not exactly PC, but it was effective.

BOTTOM RIGHT: The March 1965 issue of *CARS* broke the Dodge 426 Hemi Super/Stock story. The latest Hemi came with lightweight aluminum heads and magnesium intake manifold. These were turnkey race cars built on the production assembly line.

BOTTOM LEFT: Oldsmobile decided to get serious about supercars and upgraded its 4-4-2 with a new 400-inch four-barrel engine rated at 345 horsepower. With more exclusive ornamentation and real performance, the 4-4-2 gained traction in the youth market. *General Motors*

THE GOLDFISH THAT ATE MUSTANGS

Golden Commandos' small-block 273 Barracuda had a 90 percent win record—proving that less could be more.

Plymouth, with its '64 Barracuda, may have beaten Ford's Mustang fastback to the marketplace, but it barely dented Ford's ownership of the pony car market segment. Even with its Formula S Barracuda with 273/235 powertrain, too many enthusiasts viewed the Barracuda as simply a fastback Valiant. Plymouth was, unquestionably, the underdog, constantly playing catch-up with Ford. The Mustang had established the market segment and offered a proven solid-lifter 289/271-engine option. But Plymouth had a not-so-secret weapon: the Golden Commandos' *Goldfish*.

Plymouth's in-house drag-racing engineers—members of the Golden Commandos club—were tasked with building a race car to raise the performance profile of the Barracuda. With the 273/235 engine, the Barracuda fit right into NHRA's F/Stock class. Ray Kobe, a lubricants engineer and president of the club, assigned engine-building chores to dyno and tuning specialist Forrest Pitcock.

In June 1965 I spent a couple of hours with Forrest and the *Goldfish* at the Chelsea Proving Ground drag strip. He was evaluating engine modifications and I was working on a story for the November issue of *Hi-Performance CARS*. He graciously loaned me his helmet so I could make a few passes in the four-speed *Goldfish*. With its small-displacement, single-four-barrel engine and 4.89 gears, I shifted at a tick-under 6,000 rpm. It felt like a strong mid-fourteen-second car. Three months later, driver and transmission engineer John Dallafior won F/Stock at the NHRA Indy Nationals. He was a *little* quicker and faster than me—103.68 miles per hour in 13.47 seconds.

The Golden Commandos put the same level of effort into building the *Goldfish* as they did the club's Super/Stock and Factory Experimental Hemis. They removed approximately 150 pounds by acid-dipping the Barracuda's front fenders, hood, and doors and installing Lexan in place of the driver's side window. All body putty and sound-deadening materials had been deleted. In order to make NHRA class weight, the spare tire and divider between the rear seat back and trunk

LEFT: The Golden Commandos brought the *Goldfish* to the *CARS* Magazine S/S and FX Championships at Cecil County. They ran national record breaking times, including 111 miles per hour in 12.56 seconds. It was not class-legal at the time. This photo is taken on August 21, 1965.

RIGHT: The *Goldfish* interior in 1965, with Sun tach mounted on top of the dash. The radio was never installed and all sound deadeners and putty were removed. The front end was acid-dipped.

TOP: Bruce Lindstrom found the *Goldfish* rotting away in a cow pasture in 1999. It's been restored back to exactly how it ran in NHRA F/Stock and won its class at the Indy Nationals. *Gary Jean*

BOTTOM: The pro-built 273 small-block has original Formula S 273/235 valve covers, now fitted with a single Holley four-barrel. Engine output is 375 horsepower at 6,500 rpm and Lindstrom has the dyno sheets to prove it. *Gary Jean*

were filled with water. The "missing" 150 pounds reappeared strategically over the rear wheels to improve traction. Questionably legal, but not unusual!

After winning at Indy, the NHRA refused to allow the race car's 8³/₄-inch rear in stock classes. The Commandos continued to race at AHRA events and later converted the Barracuda to run in C/Modified Production. For C/MP, the engine received an Isky camshaft, Racer Brown valvetrain, and a pair

of Carter four-barrel carbs on an Edlebrock manifold. Dyno ratings were in excess of 375 horsepower—1.38 horsepower per cubic inch. Dallafior continued his winning ways, running over 108 miles per hour in the 12.90s.

At the 1965 *CARS* Magazine S/S and FX Championships at Cecil County Dragoway, Dallafior posted some incredible times in the C/MP *Goldfish*. His best time was an impressive 111 miles per hour in 12.56 seconds.

In 1966 Plymouth Engineering instructed the Golden Commandos to send the *Goldfish* to the crusher, a typical "final solution" for cars that were no longer competitive and illegal for sale to the public. It seemed like the end of the road for the little Barracuda with a 90 percent win record. Well . . . not exactly. Somehow it never made it to the crusher.

Fast-forward thirty-three years. In 1999, Kearney, Nebraska, Mopar enthusiast Bruce Lindstrom accidentally discovered *Goldfish* rotting in a cow pasture and he became its owner. It had 352 miles—racked up a quarter-mile at a time—on its odometer. Once authenticated by Ray Kobe, retired Chrysler engineer and Golden Commandos historian, Lindstrom started on the long road to bring it back to the way it looked and ran as a 1965 class-winning race car. Credit for most of the *Goldfish*'s restoration goes to Dr. Bud Smithson, who took it on as a class project at Seward County College Area Technical School in Liberal, Kansas. After showing the *Goldfish* at a number of Mopar-related shows and drag-strip reunions, Bruce Lindstrom was inducted into the Mopar Hall of Fame in 2013.

Fifty years after driving the *Goldfish* at the Chelsea Proving Ground, watching it post incredible times at the second-annual *CARS* race and win its class at the NHRA Nationals, I was reunited with the *Goldfish* in Sarasota, Florida. Bruce, the *Goldfish*, and I spent a day together at a Sarasota Café Racers event. I actually got a chance to ride shotgun with Bruce on a few ground-pounding 0-to-30-mile-per-hour blasts. Since it had no plates, I spent much of the time watching for cops. From the passenger's seat, it felt considerably stronger that it did on that summer day at Chelsea. The single four-barrel race engine in the "new-old" *Goldfish* had been dynoed at 375 horsepower at 6,500 rpm and 337 lb-ft of torque at 5,200 rpm. Bruce feels that he could squeeze a solid 20 to 25 more horsepower out of the 273-inch motor. I just wanted to take it to a drag strip!

DODGE'S HYBRID "STREET" HEMIS

Two vastly different Hemi-powered and streetable '65 Coronets broke cover a year before the 426 Street Hemi was announced—and I drove both of them.

Over decades, writers such as me have been responsible for penning confusing and sometimes inaccurate information about these two white '65 Dodge Coronets. The only thing they really had in common was a 426 Hemi engine. Other than coming off the same assembly line, they couldn't have been more different.

In June 1965 at the 1966 Press Preview at the Chelsea Proving Ground, I spotted a lone '65 Coronet 500 hardtop parked off to the side of 1966 pilot and prototype models. When it was time to drive cars, most media guys made beelines for next year's models. Something about the '65 Coronet piqued my interest. As I checked out the year-old model that nobody else cared about, the first thing I noticed was blackwall police tires on oversize wheels and, upon closer inspection, big front disc brakes.

A young engineer who parked it asked if I want to take it for a drive. Before I had a chance to find out what was under the hood, he said, "It's just a Street Hemi, one of the six original 1965 development cars. We kept it around after the 1965 program was canceled." In less time than it would take a Hemi to go from 0 to 60, I traded my camera bag for its keys.

While driving over to the long straight used by the Golden Commandos and Ramchargers for quarter-mile testing, he talked about the Mule's blueprinted 10.25:1 Street Hemi, beefed TorqueFlite transmission, 4.10 Sure-Grip gears, cop-car tires, and big brakes. An information card attached to the sun visor indicated 10.50:1 compression. He let me know that it had run consistent mid-thirteens at 100 to 102 miles per hour. At that point I completely forgot about the 1966 models I was there to drive.

Unfortunately, the clocks were not set up, but I had the concrete-paved drag strip to myself. My new best friend was a photography buff and happy to take photos with my camera while I played. What a deal! I made so many back-to-back runs the Hemi overheated and dumped coolant on the track. Once I got the Coronet to hook up, it was like a rocketship—and love at first shift! After the press preview—and because I was now known as the "great imposter" who drove Jim Thornton's *Candymatic* Max Wedge around New York City the year before—Dodge's "Moon" Mullins called. "How would you like to play David Pearson this time and drive his '65 Coronet Hemi?" he asked.

"I'm ready, but I seriously doubt that Bill France will get on board. Or that David and NASCAR team owner Cotton Owens would let me get within 25 feet of their Dodge Hemi."

"Not to worry," he said. "We own the car and it has license plates. Just keep it on the street since it doesn't have a roll cage. However, it's not his NASCAR racer. It's the car he drove on the Shell 4000 Trans-Canada Rally. We cleaned it up and took out a lot of rally equipment. But it still has the Hemi powertrain and all the good stuff between the rails."

With Chrysler out of NASCAR, David Pearson, like Richard Petty, looked to other racing venues. Petty campaigned

Not used to driving a rally car, especially a big Dodge powered by a streetable 426 Hemi, on challenging roads, NASCAR-charger Pearson got off-road even when he didn't want to.

a 426 Hemi Barracuda drag car and Pearson tried long-distance rallying in a Hemi Coronet. Petty ended up crashing the Barracuda and Pearson didn't do much better.

Having the opportunity to drive a Hemi—the only one on the street in 1965—ranked right up there with my *Candymatic* experience. Since '66 Street Hemis hadn't been built yet, I had the ultimate advantage of surprise. But there were problems. With 4.30 gears, hard shifting four-speed, metallic-faced clutch plate, and a Hemi under the hood, getting the power to the pavement took more talent than I had. Most of the time, it either stumbled or the tires went up in smoke.

The single four-barrel Hemi was a brute and it had a rough idle and low-rpm stumble. I brought it to Pacers Automotive in Oceanside, New York, the home of the *CARS* magazine–sponsored, NHRA record–holding, AA/A *Tasmanian Devil*. Tuned by Charlie Dodge and driven by George Snizek, it was Hemi powered. After sorting out timing and adjusting the Holley, George and I made some runs with the Coronet and his stock 283/270 '61 Corvette on Lawson Boulevard. George and I took turns driving, but the results were always the same. The Corvette *spanked* the Hemi! If we had more than an eighth-mile or so, I believe the Hemi would have trounced the Corvette.

While I never checked the Coronet's vin plate, it most likely was built as a radio and heater-delete WO-series Hemi race car. It had a plexiglass backlight and quarter windows. According to Dodge PR, Cotton Owens and Scott Harvey

TOP: A one-off 426 Hemi drag race motor, with lower compression, milder camshaft, and a big Holley four-barrel on an aluminum manifold powered David Pearson's Dodge. I had it tuned at Pacers Auto, but it was still a bear to drive on the street.

MIDDLE: One of the actual six 426 Street Hemi development mules, a well-trimmed '65 Dodge Coronet hardtop, being tested by the author on Chrysler's drag strip at the Chelsea Proving Grounds in June 1965. It was left over from the original Street Hemi program that was postponed one year.

BOTTOM: Pearson didn't want typical lightweight rally car buckets, but preferred the stock seat with improved padding and serious tube-steel bolsters. I found seating a pain for typical street use. Note the unique shoulder belts.

at Chrysler Engineering were involved. The blueprinted 426 Hemi race engine was detuned with 10.25:1 pistons and a milder camshaft and topped off with a single Holley four-barrel. The only Hemis with single Holleys were in circuit racing. The chassis was also modified to circuit racing specs. A 13-gallon Dodge Lancer auxiliary fuel tank was installed in front of the trunk-mounted battery. How it ever got through safety/tech inspection is anyone's guess.

Chrysler engineer and championship SCCA rally driver Scott Harvey was responsible for making it rally-ready. Extra lights, dash-mount timing equipment and, for some strange reason, a Plymouth-logo radio were added. Harvey was also prepping his Barracuda for the Shell 4000. He finished first in Class III, third overall, and won the SCCA National Championship.

The Shell 4000 covered 4,200 on-and-off-road miles from Montreal to Vancouver between April 24 and 30 in 1965. The Dodge press release issued after the event skirted the issue of how Pearson and the Hemi performed: "It took about 300 man hours to prepare the car. It took Pearson 100 driving hours—the length of the rally—to determine the durability of man and machine."

Pearson and Fred Browne, an experienced navigator, never actually finished the event. I'm not sure if they even made it past the first or second day. The Budd California Highway Patrol disc brakes failed and the speedometer broke. Pearson experienced a bunch of off-road mishaps trying to get the big Dodge to handle like a sports car. Pearson was quoted in Phil Murray's Shell 4000 Rally story in the June issue of *Canada Track & Traffic* magazine: "Ah'm not gonna bust mah keaster on this thing no more! I got off road, brakes failed, no heat in colder weather."

TOP: All of the rally instrumentation and roof-mount spotlight were removed before the Coronet was shipped to New York. Built as radio-heater delete race car, it was eventually converted into a Super/Stock. I found it to be somewhat of a disappointing ride on the street, but it did sound hairy and get a lot of looks. And, nobody ever asked me for a David Pearson autograph.

BOTTOM: Even though I never checked the rally car's VIN, I'm pretty sure it was built as a WO series race car. The scooped hood was standard issue on the drag cars; inboard Lucas Flamethrowers were part of Scott Harvey's rally prep at Chrysler Engineering.

Pearson's Hemi Coronet was eventually converted into a proper Super/Stock. Though it was ill suited for the street, a bear to drive, and not as fast as I would have liked, driving a one-of-a-kind, pro-built Hemi that had been driven by NASCAR champ David Pearson was one unforgettable experience.

1966

Chevy's SS396 was new for 1966, and offered the most performance possibilities of any GM supercar. However the 375-horsepower solid-lifter version was late to the party and under-promoted. A lack of traction plagued our 396/360 test car.

CHAPTER EIGHT

POWER TO THE PEOPLE

Chevrolet and Chrysler raise the performance bar with 427 Mark IV and 426 Street Hemi engines; Ford builds R-Code 427 Fairlanes for fifty-seven lucky buyers.

When carmakers announced their 1966 models in September 1965, it was like the muscle car floodgates had opened. Ford had already proven that its 1964–1965 marketing mantra—"Win On Sunday, Sell On Monday"— worked. For 1966 Chrysler, Ford, and General Motors unleashed their all-time hottest models and, in Ford's case, the most ambitious racing plans of any carmaker ever. It was nirvana for car enthusiasts and automotive magazine editors.

The April 1966 issue of *Hi-Performance CARS* carried annual award coverage. The Poly Red 426 Hemi Charger on the cover was tested at the Chrysler Proving Ground. Slick fastback styling set it off from other Mopar middleweights.

The biggest big news for 1966 was the 426 Dodge and Plymouth Street Hemi. After teasing us with on-again, off-again *streetable* 426 Hemi cars in 1965, the option was officially announced. Rated at 425 horsepower at 5,000 rpm and 490 lb-ft of torque at 4,000 rpm, the Street Hemi was, essentially, a detuned race Hemi with milder 276-degree solid-lifter camshaft, 10.25:1 compression, and dual inline Carter AFB four-barrel. It boasted the same valve and port size cast-iron race Hemi heads and added new cast-iron long-branch exhaust manifolds. Since race heads did not have provisions for exhaust heat crossover, heat was piped from an exhaust header to the intake manifold.

Early plans focused on making the 426 Street Hemi available in full-size models. I actually drove a prototype '65 Dodge 426 Hemi Polara in June 1964. I remember telling an engineer: "The only Hemi Polaras you'll sell will be to the California Highway Patrol and other law enforcement agencies!"

Mopar supercar enthusiasts, drag racers, and stock car racing fans rejoiced when the Street Hemi was announced. With the engine available as a production option, NASCAR's Bill France reversed his 1965 Hemi ban. On Sunday, February 27, 1966, Richard Petty won the Daytona 500 in his Petty Blue '66 Plymouth and David Pearson's Cotton Owens '66 Dodge placed third. Both were Hemi-powered.

We evaluated a number of candidates for *Hi-Performance CARS* magazine 1966 Top Performance Car of the Year honors. Citing Street Hemi availability and unique, four-place fastback styling, Managing Editor Fred Mackerodt and I chose the all-new Dodge Charger. "When you combine the 426 Street Hemi's impressive horsepower and torque with the engineered suspension and handling package, you end up with one of the most roadable middleweights in production."

We tested Poly Red and Poly Silver 426 Street Hemi and 383 four-barrel Chargers at the Chelsea Proving Ground and lived for a couple of weeks with a Poly Silver prototype Street Hemi with 383 badging. My personal favorites were the automatic Street Hemi and four-speed 383, rated at 330 horsepower. "The Street Hemi will propel a Charger to 60 mph in approximately 5 seconds and trip the quarter-mile clocks in the high-13s at speeds close to 108 mph," I wrote at the time.

In addition to its performance and styling, we really loved the Charger's interior: "There are four matching vinyl-covered contoured buckets, many yards of carpet and vinyl trim and the

Even though Chevrolet increased the size of its Mark IV big-block to 427 in full-size cars and Corvette, the biggest news of the year was the long-awaited 426 Street Hemi available in midsize Dodge and Plymouth models. This shot of me with a 426 Plymouth was taken at Chelsea Proving Ground in June 1965.

LEFT: Even though this '66 Olds 4-4-2 with L79 Tri-Carb 400 was a finalist for an annual award, its styling was still a little bland to do battle against the GTO. Olds did an excellent job of combining luxury, handling, and performance. Our tester was quicker than a 400/360 GTO.

RIGHT: The late introduction Charger came stock with the best interior in the industry. The beautifully laid-out instrument panel and four bucket seats influenced our choice for the annual performance car award.

neatest set of gauges we have ever laid our eyes on. With the rear seats folded flat, the rear armrest flipped over to pad the console and the storage panel dropped, it looks as though the Charger is a rolling billboard for a carpeting company! There's carpeting from the backs of the front buckets to the rear bumper. Surfing anybody?"

One of the finalists for *Top Performance Car* honors was Oldsmobile's 4-4-2: truly a supercar to be reckoned with. Engineers in Lansing had finally come up with a big-engined midsize car to compete seriously with Pontiac's GTO. Not long after revealing the latest 4-4-2 with four-barrel 400/350, they upped the ante with a late-arriving Tri-Carb version conservatively rated at 360 horsepower. It was Oldsmobile's first use of three-two-barrel induction since the legendary 1957–1958 371-cube J2 Rocket V-8s, rated at 300 and 312 horsepower, respectively.

We found that an L69-option Tri-Carb 4-4-2 with four-speed and 3.90 Anti-Spin gearing was quicker and faster than the 360-horsepower Tri-Power GTO we tested for March 1966 *Hi-Performance CARS.* GTO styling was refreshed in

1966 and it became a distinctive model series, no longer a Tempest option. The best time we ran with the GTO was 100 miles per hour in 14.50 seconds, compared with an L69 Olds' 13.80s and approximately 105 miles per hour.

Oldsmobile engineers in Lansing worked on the L79 W-30 engine project in late 1964 and 1965, and Tri-Carb packages first surfaced on '65 4-4-2 Mules. The Lansing Engineering facility was down the road from Demmer Tool & Die, a GM supplier. There was a lot of "information" sharing between Olds and Demmer drag-racing engineers. Demmer raced a Tri-Carb 4-4-2, *RECTIFIER-2*, and worked closely with Oldsmobile. In 1968 Demmer built the 455-inch Hurst Olds. Unlike GTO Tri-Power with vacuum-operated linkage opening the end two Rochester 2GC carburetors, the Oldsmobile L69 Tri-Carb utilized smoother, progressive mechanical linkage.

An Oldsmobile 4-4-2 performance brochure encouraged enthusiasts to not only buy a 4-4-2, but instead: "Turn it on. Tinker with it. Make it dance to your tune." "Exclusive on the 4-4-2 Tri-Carb. For peak breathing at the high end, just

ABOVE: Scott Davies has been running a real R-Code '66 Fairlane (left) for decades in a variety of NHRA classes with low and medium riser 427s. His best times are in the 10.3s. *Scott Davies*

BELOW LEFT: No longer running in NHRA B & C/Stock by 1968, NHRA Springnationals upgraded '66 Olds 4-4-2s with Tri-Carb successfully competed in Super Stock/F.

BELOW RIGHT: Bill "Grumpy" Jenkins won over Chevy fans with his red and white '66 Chevy II, powered by an optional L79 Corvette 327/350 small-block. He ran in mid-elevens, held a national record, and won Mr. Stock Eliminator at 1965 NHRA Winternationals.

One of the top competitors in C/Stock on the East Coast was this Bill Lagana–prepped (right) and Al McCormack–driven C/S '66 Comet. Bill and his brother Bob Lagana also campaigned a 427, tube-frame Comet match racer.

pull two bolts from the crossover valves on either side of the center carb, rotate the covers 90 degrees and bolt them back down," the brochure continued. Not great for cold starts, but perfect for taking advantage of cooler, denser air-fuel mixture for better performance.

With a choice of Anti-Spin gearing up to 3.90 and dealer-installed 4.11 or 4.33 gears, plus close or wide-ratio Hurst-shifted four-speeds, the Tri-carb 4-4-2 was a serious supercar. Taking it up a notch, it was available with a W-30 option that didn't change the factory power rating, but unquestionably improved quarter-mile performance. Key W-30 ingredients included a chromed Tri-Carb air cleaner with 4-inch hoses ducting fresh air from front bumper openings, a high-lift, 308-degree-duration camshaft, and relocation of the battery to the trunk. The majority of W-30 engines were in base model F-85 4-4-2 Club Coupes.

After teasing enthusiasts with a very late- and very limited-production Z16 Chevelle SS powered by a proprietary 396/375 Mark IV big-block, Chevrolet followed up with a newly styled '66 Chevelle SS396 with less horsepower. First introduced with base 396/325 and optional L34 396/360 hydraulic-cam motors, it was a while before they *quietly* offered the L78 396/375 solid-lifter powerhouse that enthusiasts craved. It appeared in March 1966 with little fanfare or marketing support.

Except for displacement and advertised horsepower, the 396/375 and 427/425 were very similar. The 427/425 Mark IVs in the full-size Chevy and Corvette and 396/375 had four-bolt-main blocks, 11:1 compression, .520-inch-lift solid cams, rectangular-port heads with 2.19-inch intake valves, and an aluminum intake manifold with a 780-cfm Holley four-barrel.

Chevelle SS396 models were trimmed to appeal to, and powered to impress, supercar shoppers. All SS396 Chevelles came with rear-frame reinforcements. We tested a 396/360 Chevelle with four-speed 3.73 Posi rear for the May 1966 *Hi-Performance CARS* and we were not that impressed. Our best 0 to 60 was 8.0 seconds and it couldn't do better than 91 miles per hour in 15.85 seconds on the track. Getting the power to the ground was a major problem. With sticky tires and 4.11s, high-low mid-fourteens would be in reach.

The sleeper in the Bow-Tie Brigade's portfolio was the Chevy II Nova SS, powered by one of the best all-around performance small-blocks, the Corvette-based L79 327/350 with single 585- to 600-cfm Holley four-barrel, high-performance hydraulic lifter cam and free-breathing heads. Small-block-powered Novas could run in the fourteens and deliver good fuel economy on the street.

Bill "Grumpy" Jenkins did a lot of winning in 409 and Z11 Chevys and Super/Stock Mopars, but really started building his Chevrolet fan base while racing his '66 L79 Chevy II *Grumpy's Toy* in 1965 and 1966. He put his small-block Nova into the elevens and was just about unbeatable in NHRA A/

Stock. At one point he set the 11.66-second national record. In 1966 his primary rival was header-manufacturer Jere Stahl and his Mopar Street Hemi. An NHRA national record holder and Mr. Stock Eliminator winner at the 1965 NHRA Winternationals, Jenkins had a legendary relationship with Chevrolet's Vince Piggins because of the 327/350 Nova.

In the youth-driven supercar market, Ford continued to play catch-up with GM's enormously popular GTO and Chevelle SS396. In 1966, Pontiac sold an incredible 96,946 GTOs. Dearborn's top entries were Fairlane GT and GTA and Comet Cyclone GT models with 390 cubic-inch big-blocks rated at 335 horsepower. They weren't quite there yet.

We tested a Fairlane GTA that had originally been built by Holman-Moody for a *Car & Driver* test. Powered by a blueprinted 315-horsepower 390 brought up to 335-plus horsepower specs, it also had extensive chassis upgrades. Most of the added parts carried Ford part numbers and could be ordered from any Ford dealership.

We reported on it in the April 1966 issue of *Hi-Performance CARS*. With 4.11 gears and a Detroit locker and Firestone Super Sport tires, our top time at the track was 99 miles per hour in 14.50 seconds and our best 0 to 60 mile-per-hour sprint was 7.1 seconds. "The only place our GTA really excelled was on the street. You can't hardly beat that long-stroke 390, Sportshift trans and 4.11 gears when it comes to stoplight hole-shooting!" we wrote.

To stay in the drag racing limelight, Ford contracted with suppliers Holman-Moody, Bud Moore, and Bill Stroppe to build 390 and 427 Stock and Super/Stock Comets and Fairlanes. Mid-year, Ford introduced a very limited-production 427 Fairlane, powered by a Medium-Riser R-Code side-oiler. Two prototype development cars were built in Ford's X-Garage under the direction of Dick Brannan and Vern Tinsler, key players in the 427 Thunderbolt program. R-Code 427 Fairlanes were shipped from Ford's Atlanta plant with dual-quad 425 horsepower engines. Engine compartments were then covered with scooped, lift-off Plaza Fiberglass hoods.

Ford built fifty-seven Wimbledon White 427 Fairlanes with four-speeds and 9-inch rears, thus meeting NHRA's fifty-vehicle minimum for Stock classes. Some 427/425 Fairlanes were $1 cars "sold" to factory racers, with the balance available from dealers. In 1966, a 427/425 Fairlane campaigned by Downing and Ryan Engineering in Rutherford, New Jersey, set the NHRA B/Stock National

Record at 11.42 seconds; 427 Fairlanes won A/Stock at the NHRA Springnationals and Super/Stock Nationals.

Ford's NASCAR and USAC standard-bearer Galaxie was face-lifted and available with 427/425 engine and four-speed options. A new, uplevel model, the 7-liter, was added to the full-size lineup. Powered by a hydraulic-lifter 428 rated at 345 horsepower at 4,800 rpm, it was available *only* with an upgraded C6 automatic. There was also a special Police Interceptor version with an aluminum four-barrel manifold, rated at 360 horsepower at 5,400 rpm.

Ford's ownership of the pony car market continued and the Shelby GT350, then available with a Paxton supercharger, further bolstered the Mustang's image. GT40 Mark IIs won the prestigious 24 Hours of Le Mans, a first for an American carmaker. Ford also won the 1966 International Manufacturers Championship, International Championship for Sports Cars, Division II, and the first SCCA Trans-Am Championship.

At the Indy 500, Ford four-cam 255-inch V-8s powered the first four place cars. Drag racing Mustangs, powered by 427 Wedge and SOHC engines, continued their winning ways.

For the 1966 model year, Ford outsold Chevrolet for the first time in five years. Together with Mercury, Ford sold in excess of 2.5 million vehicles. It was a great year for racing and car sales—and especially for car people.

DAY 1.5:
FROM SALT TO SUBURBIA

This '66 Plymouth 426 Street Hemi Satellite set the B/Production Flying Mile record of 156.35 miles per hour at the Bonneville Salt Flats. Then it got license plates and I used it for commuting to work in New York City.

Normally I wouldn't have paid much attention when land speed racer Bob Summers drove a '66 Plymouth to B/Production records at Bonneville in August 1965. Carmakers and racers had been contesting Production records at the Salt Flats for decades. However, what did pique my interest was that Street Hemi production hadn't started yet.

Bob Summers's pre-production '66 Plymouth 426 Street Hemi registered a top speed of 160.82 miles per hour, and set a USAC-FIA two-way Flying Mile record of 156.35 miles per hour. It also set the two-way Flying Kilometer record of 155.30

ABOVE: Bob Summers belted into the Street Hemi *Satellite* at Bonneville Salt Flats, a couple of months after Schorr drove it at Chelsea. In November, the Summers Brothers returned to the Salt with their *Goldenrod,* powered by four naturally aspirated 426 Hemis. On November 12, Summers ran 409.227 miles per hour, setting the piston-powered, wheel-driven land-speed record.

RIGHT: The multiple-personality Street Hemi cover of the March 1966 *Hi-Performance CARS*. The same issue carried four-speed 360-horsepower GTO and new OHC six Tempest road tests. Reader response and mail was overwhelmingly about the *Satellite.*

miles per hour. The B/Production records had been owned by factory Pontiacs prepared and driven by Mickey Thompson.

A couple of months after Summers set the records, I was joking with a Chrysler PR guy about their record-setting Street Hemi. "Give me a break. That Satellite is probably as stock as the Golden Commando's A/FX race car!"

He called my bluff: "That Satellite is so stock, you can check our USAC/FIA records and then drive it home. In fact, you can even keep it for a couple of weeks. Use it for commuting to Manhattan. Take it out to the track. Do whatever you want with it."

"Remember that gold Street Hemi Satellite you drove in June at Chelsea? Well, you'll be driving it again. Now it's white and has a four-speed instead of its original automatic."

A few months earlier I had driven a Citron Gold 426 Street Hemi Satellite hardtop at the 1966 Press Preview. It was equipped with TorqueFlite and 3.23 gears. I'm pretty sure it also had power steering. The white record-setting Satellite I picked up in November was the very same Citron Gold Satellite I had driven in June. Chipped paint revealed its original color and the side view mirror that was removed for Bonneville had been reinstalled. The power-assisted steering was replaced with quick-ratio manual steering.

Installing and removing the multi-point roll bar left scars on the gold vinyl seats. Because of its ultra-stiff ride and balky clutch that wouldn't allow aggressive shifting, I brought the Street Hemi to Pacers Automotive to have it checked out. Once up on a lift, we knew for sure this was the actual record holder. There were still traces of salt deposits and the A-833 four-speed was obviously installed post-production. Telltale saw marks on the floorboard and a cast-steel bellhousing revealed extensive modifications. The bellhousing casting

ABOVE: Bob Summers (left) looks on as the crew works on the rear end. The Dana 9¾-inch Sure-Grip rear was fitted with 2.93 gears for the record runs. After Bonneville, 3.54 gears were installed for the street.

RIGHT: The new optional 426 Street Hemi looked totally stock, but the Satellite's performance indicated that it was most likely blueprinted for Bonneville runs.

number, 2206044, and smaller 10½-inch clutch were traced to 1964–1965 factory race cars. All four-speed '66 Street Hemis came with 11-inch clutches and cast-iron bellhousings.

Charlie Dodge and George Snizek at Pacers tried lubricating the clutch, but to no avail. It was obvious that salt had taken its toll. They drilled-out the clutch cross-shaft, installed a lube fitting, and pumped it full of grease. There was nothing they could do about improving its brakes. When this car was built, front discs were not available. The standard 11-inch police car drum brakes with metallic linings left a lot to be desired.

The Satellite's front suspension had been lowered slightly and the sway bar was thicker than the production .94-inch bar. An 8-inch-wide steel "hat" protected the deep oil pan, much like a skid plate on a rally car. There were numerous suspension/drivetrain modifications, including welded-in steel torque boxes used to anchor the roll bar. The 2.93:1 Bonneville gears in the 9¾-inch Dana 60 Sure-Grip rear had been swapped with 3.54s.

After one week of daily commuting in rush hour traffic from suburban East Rockaway to Manhattan, I had enough of the Satellite's biceps-building steering and 6 to 7 miles per gallon consumption of Sunoco 260. Our Satellite's billboard lettering proved to be a magnet for cops and restricted my racing to Westhampton drag strip. With 7.75x14-inch Goodyear police tires, we started off running in the mid-fourteens at speeds around 105 miles per hour. By the end of the day, our best time was 108 miles per hour in 13.95 seconds.

Using our stopwatch, 0 to 60 sprints came in around 5.5 seconds. We were impressed considering its rear gearing and closed exhausts. Quarter-mile times were better than expected. I had little doubt that its engine had been "breathed on" before Bonneville.

Even with its steering and braking shortcomings and unquenchable thirst for Sunoco 260, it was really cool driving the Street Hemi Satellite before and after Bob Summers drove it into the USAC-FIA record books!

During our test drive, I stopped to check engine oil, necessitating lifting front and rear "hoods."

THERE'S NO SUBSTITUTE FOR CUBIC INCHES

Double your displacement—double your fun. Four-wheel-drive '66 Oldsmobile Toronado packs an 850-cubic-inch punch.

Whenever I visited Los Angeles in the 1960s and 1970s, I usually stopped at Grant Piston Rings to spend time with consummate hot rodders Grant and Richard "Dick" MacCoon. Their uncle, Gerald Grant, founded the company in 1922 and, in 1952 when he passed away, left the company to his two nephews.

During a visit in 1968, Grant MacCoon tossed me the keys to his Toronado and said, "It's got plenty of gas. Take it out with Dick for the day and have some fun."

I knew something wasn't right. What was so special about driving a used '66 Toronado—and why were there two key rings? When Dick and I got into the Toro, it was impossible to miss two ignition switches and enough extra gauges to monitor multiple engines. That's what was so special about Grant's Toronado —two engines!

It takes an incredible amount of engineering and fabrication to convert a single engine, front-wheel-drive car into a twin-engine car with selective front or four-wheel drive. I was beyond impressed that in-house techs were able to shoehorn a 425-inch Toronado V-8 and drivetrain into what had been the trunk without impacting rear seating or making major body modifications. Small unobtrusive scoops over the rear wheelwells directed cool air to the engine.

"I wanted a domestic, easy to maintain, reliable, luxury GT with ultimate performance and handling," MacCoon said. "And the only way I could get exactly what I wanted was build a twin-engine Toro. It was my idea. Our father, L.P. MacCoon, designed the car and company engineers and techs built it."

TOP: The dash is a dead giveaway to Toro's dual-engine powertrain. Note the dual ignition keys, instrumentation and single gas pedal that controls single or dual engine operation.

LEFT: The rear engine has its own drivetrain and rear-mount radiator. The engine is flanked by 13-gallon fuel tanks, replacing the stock tank. Dual fans keep the rear engine cool.

I started off running on the front engine and then stopped and put the gearshift lever in Neutral. Next I opened the hidden under-dash throttle valve, and twisted the second ignition key. The trunk-mounted 425-incher instantly came to life. Both engines and Hydramatics were synchronized via an electrical connection. The front unit governed shifts. With the rear engine off, its transmission can't be shifted. With both engines running and the shift lever in Drive, a solenoid shifts the rear transmission into Drive. A vacuum line connecting both engines balances shifts.

Initially, the single gas pedal threw me off. With both under-dash hydraulic valves in the "On" position, the single pedal controls both engines. When parking, you can switch both valves off and the gas pedal drops to the floor, preventing the car from being moved.

We spent an afternoon cruising through the LA foothills and made some freeway runs. With both engines engaged, we clocked 0 to 60 in seven seconds flat and cruised effortlessly at over 100 miles per hour. With 770-horsepower, four-wheel-drive, and full torsion bar suspension, ride and handling matched its performance. Stock Toronado rear leaf springs had been replaced with Toronado front torsion bars.

During the 1980s, Grant MacCoon's Twin-Toro was rumored to be at US Automobile Barretta in Munich, Germany. Over the last decade, it or a well-worn clone has surfaced in the United States. I feel lucky that I was able to drive the Twin-Toro when it was in its prime.

427 SOHC:
AN ENGINE IN SEARCH OF A CAR

Even though Ford officially announced a 427 SOHC Galaxie in 1966, it never happened. The engine that dominated a variety of drag racing classes, and was at the center of a highly publicized two-year battle between Dearborn and Daytona, remained an orphan.

The 427 SOHC single overhead camshaft engine was a sophisticated extension of the incredibly successful 427 big-block Ford introduced in 1963½. Upgraded over a couple of years, it distinguished itself in drag racing, NASCAR-USAC competition, and, in 1966, powered the winning GT40s at Le Mans.

Because the new 427 SOHC, nicknamed Cammer, utilized an almost identical production 427 side-oiler block with cross-bolted mains and forged crank and rods, development time for this multi-cam engine took a fraction of the time normally associated with new engines. In approximately three months, Ford engineers took the Cammer from computer to dyno testing. First shown in a '64 Galaxie Mule, the prototype SOHC engine, with a single four-barrel and 12:1 compression, generated 616 horsepower at 7,000 rpm and 515 lb-ft of torque at 3,800 rpm.

In order to convert from a traditional block-fitted single cam to one camshaft per cylinder bank, new heads were required. The cam-carrying 427 SOHC heads feature hemispherical-shaped combustion chambers, large valves, big ports, and a lightweight, beefy valvetrain without pushrods or lifters. A 6-foot double-link roller chain controls the camshafts and valvetrain operation that allowed the free-breathing big-block to safely make power up to 7,500 rpm.

In 1965 Ford's primary mission for developing the Cammer was to combat Chrysler's 426 Hemi on super speedways and then drag racing. The first engines were allotted to Holman-Moody for NASCAR. When Bill France deemed it, and the Hemi, illegal for 1965, SOHC engines were tagged for drag racing.

Bill France's rule changes regarding engine legality in 1965 followed in 1966 by multiple classes of cars with engine limitations caused Chrysler and Ford to threaten pullouts. After the Hemi engine was banned, Chrysler took its "toys" and went home. In 1966 it was Ford's turn. France allowed the Hemi, based on production 426 Street Hemis.

Since Ford's 427 Cammer was not available in production cars, France allowed the engine only if installed in a car with an approximate 450-pound-plus handicap. Ford would have to run 427 SOHC Galaxies against lighter Hemi Dodges and Plymouths. Ford wanted to run the SOHC engine in its new midsize Fairlane. France sweetened the pot by permitting Ford to equip 427 Wedge engines with a second four-barrel. Ford was still not happy.

While working on this book, I found a Ford press release dated March 4, 1966, announcing the availability of its 427 SOHC engine as a production option. It had been crafted in Dearborn—yet distributed by Ford's Southern PR office in Atlanta, Georgia. Distribution was limited to racing media

The 427 SOHC Galaxie is not the ideal car for a tight road course, but the Cammer just loves to rev and rev and make power. July 1966, handling course, Ford Dearborn Proving Ground.

ABOVE: The early prototype 427 SOHC had spark plugs located on the lower side of heads, later updated to top of heads to do away with lengthy plug wires. This Cammer was dressed as a NASCAR motor with single four-barrel and cowl-induction air cleaner. *Ford Motor Company*

LEFT: Gasser legend "Ohio George" Montgomery's AA/GS *Malco Gasser* Mustang was powered by a blown-injected Cammer. He had used a similar powertrain in his vintage Willys Gasser. He was a consistent AA/GS winner.

A potent 600-horsepower 427 Cammer looks like it belongs in the Fairlane's engine bay. The shock towers had to be modified and the master cylinder moved to shoehorn the engine in. A dual quad intake used in factory drag-racing cars tops off a rare engine. *Charlie Lillard*

and race-sanctioning organizations. I had never received it when I was editor of *Hi-Performance CARS*. In it, Donald N. Frey, company vice president and Ford Division general manager, stated:

> Ford Motor Company today announced that a street version of its 427 cubic-inch single overhead cam engine now is available as a production item. The 427 SOHC is available through Ford dealers in the Galaxie line at a premium cost of $995 above the current Ford high-performance engine. First to purchase one of the SOHC Galaxies was astronaut Gordon Cooper, who plans to use the car for drag racing.

The 427 SOHC engine has dominated Factory Experimental drag racing for the past two years. However, in December, NASCAR and USAC officials ruled the engine out of stock car competition because they felt it did not meet production requirements. At that time, officials of both groups said they would reconsider the single overhead cam engine when it went into production. In making the engine available to the public, we hope to qualify it for the stock car circuits.

Officially, Ford never built any 427 SOHC Galaxies. Unofficially, I knew of two built at Special Vehicles Activity's

ABOVE: Fun and games with Dan Gurney at Bud Moore's shop in 1966. The rare photo shows Dan found a use for one of the leftover 427 Cammer engines.

RIGHT: The see-through cam cover reveals a single cam layout head with beefy valvetrain and 6-foot roller chain. Without pushrods or lifters, the free-breathing Hemi Cammer safely makes power to 7,500 rpm.

X-Garage: a Wimbledon White hardtop driven by SVA chief Jack Passino and an Emberglo Galaxie that was loaned to Astronaut Gordon Cooper for promotional purposes.

On April 15, 1966, Henry Ford II announced that Ford was boycotting NASCAR and warned its contract drivers that if they attempted to run as independents or drive other make cars, they would be terminated.

In July 1966 I drove Passino's Galaxie Cammer on the Dearborn Proving Ground road course. I held the story, waiting for production confirmation that never came. I did finally write about it in the June 1967 issue of *Super/Stock & FX*. I found it a little clumsy on the tight road course, but the engine felt like it had an unlimited redline; it just revved and revved and made power. And it sounded great.

In August 1966, NASCAR announced its 1967 rules. They would allow Ford to compete with Fairlanes with 396-, 403-, and 427-cubic-inch Wedges with new Tunnel Port heads and manifolds. Henry Ford reversed his earlier decision, allowing contract teams to return to competition. Even with Ford's part-year boycott of NASCAR, Fords and Mercurys won twelve races.

The SOHC engine left its mark on the quarter-mile. Connie Kalitta was the first to use the SOHC engine in a Double A Fuel dragster. The first major win for a SOHC-powered dragster was at the 1966 NHRA World Championships in Tulsa, Oklahoma. Pete Robinson took Top Fuel Eliminator honors in his AA/FD.

In 1967, Kalitta hit the trifecta: Top Fuel Eliminator wins at the NHRA and AHRA Winternationals and NASCAR Winter Championships. "Dyno" Don Nicolson put his Comet into the low-sevens. The Cammer was a truly great engine without a strong enough business case to warrant production.

1967

Buick's Skylark GS-400 was updated with bold frontal styling and a modern 340-horsepower, 400-inch V-8; a great combination of luxury and performance.

supercars, pony cars & major muscle

Chevrolet and Pontiac were three years late to the pony car party, but the long-hood, short-deck Camaro and Firebird made up for lost time.

Suddenly, the pony car market was chock full of new style and power choices. Soon after the Camaro's public introduction, there appeared a potent 302-inch small-block in Z/28 trim and big-block 396 engines with up to 375 horsepower. Pontiac marketed its Firebird with a GTO-style options menu, offering various trim levels and high-performance overhead cam six and 326- and 400-inch V-8s.

Plymouth upped the ante with a redesigned and very slick Barracuda in fastback and notchback coupe and convertible body styles. Its wheelbase and overall length of 108 and 188 inches, respectively, were exactly the same as the new Camaro and Firebird. It was a little short of power, though. Engine choices included a 273/235 small-block and, for the first time, a 383/280 big-block.

Since the new Barracuda's engine compartment was configured for a small-block, the 383 had to be shoehorned in—and not without shortcomings. There was no room for free-flowing exhaust manifolds, power steering pump, or AC compressor. The "choked" 383 ended up being rated at 280 horsepower. We tested a one-off, pre-production 383 Barracuda with 3.55 gearing for the December 1966 issue of *Hi-Performance*

TOP: Bill Blanding launches his 396 Camaro during Super/Stock eliminations at the 1968 NHRA Springnationals. In the far lane is the Berry Ford big-block Mustang. The '67 Camaro was a consistent winner.

BOTTOM: A spy shot of a pre-production M-plate '67 Firebird convertible at Milford Proving Ground during high-speed testing in 1966.

CARS. We were not happy with the heavy manual steering. Our best time was 95 miles per hour in 15.2 seconds.

GM's F-body twins, the Camaro and the Firebird, represented the carmaker's first venture into Mustang territory. Slightly longer, wider, and lower than a Mustang, they introduced new levels of power. While Chevrolet and Pontiac shared a basic platform and much of the sheet metal, including front fenders, door skins, and rear quarters, power choices and options were brand-unique. Pontiac relied on a peaked hood, split front grille, and GTO-style taillights to set the Firebird apart. When it came to a rear suspension, GM engineers were penny-wise and pound-foolish. They utilized a less-than-desirable monoleaf rear suspension from the Chevy II parts bin.

After the Camaro's introduction, 350- and 375-horsepower 396 big-block engines were made available. On February 23, 1967, five months after the Camaro intro, Pontiac launched no less than five Firebird variants: Firebird, Firebird Sprint, Firebird 326, Firebird 326 HO, and Firebird 400. The Sprint was powered with a 215 four-barrel OHC six, while the 400-inch V-8 was rated at 325 horsepower. When fitted with functional Ram-Air and a hotter cam, horsepower rating remained the same.

Even though the Camaro and Firebird shared a common platform and some sheet metal, they looked and drove differently. When presenting the new Firebird, Pontiac took a page from the GTO playbook. Thanks to a number of performance, image, and comfort and convenience options, buyers could turn a Firebird into anything they wanted.

Fred Mackerodt, managing editor of *Hi-Performance CARS*, summed it up in his Firebird First Drive article in the March 1967 issue: "The Firebird and the Camaro are as much the same car as the GTO and Chevelle SS396 are the same."

GM's new pony cars were plagued with a serious problem. If you got the tires to hook up on initial acceleration, you could expect horrendous rear spring windup causing wheel hop. To help alleviate spring windup and unloading, Chevrolet added a torque arm on the right side that connected the axle to the frame. Pontiac added the same on automatic transmission cars, but four-speed cars received left and right rods. The only way to really stop wheel hop was to install aftermarket traction bars.

Chevrolet expanded its use of four-barrel big-block engines in 1967, offering 396/325 and 396/385 versions in full-size models and 396/350 and 396/375 engines in Camaros

ABOVE: The Baldwin-Motion Marina Blue SS427 Chevelle—built for Charlie Mason and still on the road—started out as one of only 612 SS396 models built in 1967 with 375 horsepower. Powered by an aluminum head 427, it ran 123 miles per hour in 11.50 seconds on slicks.

RIGHT: The Barracuda was beautifully restyled, received a 383 big-block, and made the cover of the December 1966 issue of *Hi-Performance CARS.* Lack of power steering, AC, and decent exhaust manifolds were big drawbacks.

and Chevelles. Divisions were prohibited from using tri-power on passenger car engines.

In the mid-1960s, Chevrolet spent as much time denying its involvement in racing as it did actually participating. In 1967, Vince Piggins had Roger Penske bring his Z/28 Trans-Am race car to the GM Proving Ground to sort out suspension issues.

GM's anti-racing policymakers must have been on vacation in April 1967 when Chevrolet slipped the L88 engine into the Corvette options list. Because of its 430-horsepower rating, which was five under the top 427/435, nobody noticed. Credit for the L88 went to Zora Arkus-Duntov. The 12.5 compression L88 could be nourished *only* with 103-octane gas. Goodies included a forged *everything* lower end, solid-lifter .540/.560-inch lift and 337/340 degrees duration cam, 850-cfm Holley on an open plenum chamber aluminum manifold, and big-valve aluminum heads. Advertised horsepower was 430 at 5,200 rpm, but actual dyno horsepower with headers and open pipes was closer to 550 to 560 at 6,400 rpm.

The L88 engine option cost $947.90, more than twice as much as the L71 tri-power 427/435. It was a racing engine and totally impractical for the street. Just twenty L88 Corvettes were sold. However, hundreds were sold as service engines to racers.

In my files I have a letter about L88 Corvette production from Joe Pike, Chevrolet Motor Division, and dated November 22, 1974. He had been Corvette National Sale Promotion Manager, started the National Council of Corvette Clubs, and was the first editor of *Corvette News.* He knew *everything* about the Corvette:

> *In reply to your letter of November 19, I do not have all the information available that you requested, but I can say that in the 1968 model year we built in production just 80 L88 Corvettes and just 98 in 1969.* **There were no L88 Corvettes built in 1967.** *The L71 427 rated at 435 horsepower was the top engine that year.*

> *Very Truly Yours, J. P. Pike, Assistant-Manager Merchandising Passenger Cars*

ABOVE: Pontiac's GTO lost its tri-power, but retained the same horsepower and performance thanks to new 400-inch Ram Air engine. Sales were down to 81,722 in 1967, but its domination of the supercar market continued. *General Motors*

LEFT: For an extra $2,000, you could get a Shelby GT500 with a real 427 side-oiler under the hood. Richter's Moss Green GT500, Vin No. 0289, was the first 427 Shelby built. *Kevin Suydam Collection*

Chevrolet did, in fact, build 20 1967 L88 Corvettes, 80 in 1968 and 116 not 98 in 1969.

When I chose the 390 Mustang for 1967 Top Performance Car of the Year honors in *Hi-Performance CARS*, the decision was based on driving the highest-performance 289-390 Mustangs for two days at Ford's Dearborn Proving Ground. I flogged the cars on the road course and skid pad, and ran a best quarter-mile time of 90 miles per hour in 15.2 seconds in a 390 convertible on the drag strip.

The only 390 Mustang available was a pre-production non-GT model with GT options, including four-speed and competition handling package. The four-barrel 390/320 was rated at 335 horsepower in the '66 Fairlane. With 10.5 compression, the 390 generated 320 horsepower at 4,800 rpm and 427 lb-ft of torque at 3,200 rpm. The first production big-block Mustang wasn't the quickest or fastest high-performance car available, but I felt it offered a unique combination of performance, ride, handling, and image.

Updated for 1967, the Mustang was available with GT Group disc brakes and handling package. Hardcore track-day enthusiasts could opt for the outstanding competition handling package. It consisted of 16.0:1 quick-ratio steering, 365 pounds-inch-rate front coil springs, 125 pounds-inch-rate rear leaf springs, 35mm adjustable Koni shocks, $^{15}/_{16}$-inch diameter front sway bar, and a 3.25 limited-slip rear. Some of these components were on the Mustangs that won the 1967 Trans-Am Championship.

If you wanted a hotter Mustang, Carroll Shelby had a GT500 powered by a dual-quad Police Interceptor 428/335. With headers and tuning, 400 horsepower was within reach. For an extra $2,000, approximately 45 percent of the price of a GT-500 with mandatory options, you could have a 427 rated at 390 horsepower. There were just two takers. A third GT500, powered by an alloy-head, medium-riser 427 engine, was not for sale. Dubbed *Super Snake*, it was used by Goodyear for high-speed tire evaluation and recorded a top speed of approximately 170 miles per hour and an average speed of 142 miles per hour for 500 miles.

Dodge and Plymouth freshened their midsize models for 1967 and increased high-performance options. The top-dog 426/425 Street Hemi was carried over and joined by a 440/375 Wedge that was ideally suited for the street and track. New 440 four-barrel models were much cheaper to buy, insure, and live with than Street Hemis. Mopar Hemi engines continued to distinguish themselves in competition.

TOP: We really liked the new 440/375 big-block, available in midsize Mopars. The '67 Dodge R/T was a magazine project. Pacers Automotive and Motion Performance did the work and we played. When stock, it ran 93.16 miles per hour in 15.13 seconds. With headers, Hurst shifter, dyno-tuning, 4.56 Sure-Grip gears, and 7-inch cheater slicks, the best run was 103.70 miles per hour in 13.60.

BOTTOM: One of the 390 Mustangs we tested at the Dearborn Proving Ground when evaluating 1967 cars for Top Performance Car of the Year. The ragtop is cooling down after making a number of runs, a with best time of 90 miles per hour in 15.2 seconds.

Richard Petty, driving the No. 43 Plymouth Hemi, won the 1967 NASCAR Grand National Championship.

With General Motors enforcing multiple-carburetion and power limitations for 1967, the B-O-P trio of supercars—Buick Skylark GS400, Oldsmobile 4-4-2, and Pontiac GTO—underwent subtle updates. In the final analysis, enthusiasts were not really shortchanged by GM's edict. Performance-minded engineers and marketers managed to deliver freshened and powerful industry-leading supercars.

Buick finally updated its Nailhead V-8 to modern standards and new 400/340 and 430/360 engines powered

Nick Smith was a consistent NHRA C/Stock winner in the Miami, Florida, area in this '67 Rambler. It was powered by a blueprinted 343/280, Z-Code Typhoon V-8. Nick ran consistent 12.20s at 107 miles per hour, and was Florida State champ. *Factory Lightweight Collection*

the 400-inch L78 engine—350 at 5,000 rpm. After Fred Mackerodt's test article appeared in the October 1967 issue, the W30 engine acquired an additional 10 horsepower—360 at 5,000 rpm.

On a W30 car, fresh air was directed to a sealed air cleaner via hoses to intakes on both sides of the grille. To make room for the hoses, the battery was relocated to the trunk. Mackerodt and Joe Oldham did quite well at the track, clicking off 6.6 second runs to 60 miles per hour and a best track time of 103 miles per hour in 14.10 seconds. It was quite impressive for a street-driven Olds. Unfortunately, 4.33 gearing severely limited highway cruising. We all came to the same conclusion about the 4-4-2, regardless of engine package. It consistently demonstrated the best overall ride and handling characteristics in the field.

the Skylark GS-400 and Riviera GS, respectively. The class-topping, luxurious Riviera Grand Sport, tested in the October 1967 issue of *Hi-Performance CARS,* clocked 0 to 60 in 8.6 seconds and 87 miles per hour in 16.10 seconds on the track. We put 1,000 miles on a Skylark GS-400 for a test in the June 1967 issue and found it to be, "the quietest, most luxurious performance package on the supercar market."

Other than 3.90 Positive Traction gearing not available at the time on automatic transmission cars, our stock automatic GS-400 sprinted to 60 miles per hour in 7.8 seconds and hit 90 miles per hour at 15.5 seconds at the track. Overall, it was a most impressive middleweight.

In 1967, we were able to drive two Hurst-shifted four-speed 4-4-2 Oldsmobiles—base L78 and W30. We brought the first 4-4-2, built prior to W30 production, to Motion Performance for dyno tuning. Prior to running at the track, Joel Rosen installed colder Champion J-10Y plugs, richened up the Quadrajet, and recurved the distributor for 35 degrees total advance. Factory-fitted with close-ratio four-speed and 3.91 Anti-Spin gears, our best times were 0 to 60 in 6.8 seconds and 100 miles per hour in 14.20 seconds. Our testing was covered in the April 1967 issue of *Hi-Performance CARS.*

The W30 4-4-2 was equipped with the cold air induction package, close-ratio four-speed, and 4.33 Anti-Spin gears. At the time the W30 engine had the same horsepower rating as

Like Oldsmobile, Pontiac lost its tri-power yet retained optional Ram-Air and the same horsepower ratings. A single four-barrel 400/360 Ram-Air GTO generated the same performance as a tri-power 389. For 1967, the GTO's exterior was facelifted and, for the first time, available with a great three-speed TurboHydramatic transmission. The car that invented the supercar was still the leader of the pack.

Not saddled with corporate engine restrictions, Ford and Lincoln-Mercury were free to utilize Ford's most powerful engines for its midsize models. Fairlanes were available with a W-Code single four-barrel 427/410 or R-Code dual-quad 427/425, while Comets offered just the 427/425. Because of 427 option costs—$1,200 for R-Code 427—very few were built. Total 427 Fairlane production was 230 and just 60 427/425 Comets were built. John Elliott set both ends of the national A/SA record and won the NHRA Division 3 Points Championship in the Sandy Elliott 427 Comet. Mario Andretti won the Daytona 500 in a 427 Fairlane.

And more power was on the horizon!

427 CAMARO:
THE THOMAS NICKEY AFFAIR

Within a couple of months after Chevrolet's September 1966 introduction of its all-new '67 Camaro, Nickey and Nickey/Thomas SS427 Camaros were on the road.

Bill Thomas Race Cars, of Anaheim, California, built 427 Camaros for California customers, while Nickey Chevrolet, Chicago, Illinois, covered the rest of the country. I drove Bill Thomas's first SS427 Camaro, built on a Bolero Red SS350 donor, around Orange County in early 1967. It retained its original 350 emblems and 1966 Illinois dealer tags.

My reason for visiting Bill Thomas was not to sample one of the Nickey 427 Camaros. I was working on stories about race-prepping fuel-injected Corvettes, improving the performance of Gen I and Gen II Rochester fuel injection and exhaust tuning. Bill Thomas was absolutely brilliant in those areas. His background included building and tuning road race and drag cars and creating the radical Chevy-powered Cheetah. In 1962 he tuned Hayden Proffitt's NHRA World Championship '62 Chevy 409 Bel Air.

When I was there, he was building big-engined cars with Bonneville-type rear gearing, which included 427 Camaros, for serious street racers who used LA and Orange County freeways as racetracks. He jokingly referred to them as "Freeway Freedom Fighters." The 427 Camaro he offered me was more suited for the quarter-mile than for freeway cruising. Basic Nickey/Thomas 427/425 Camaros were $3,711, while the prototype-demo Camaro I drove listed for approximately $4,300. In addition to the base 427/425 engine, four-speed, Posi, and standard factory equipment, Thomas added chromed Cragars, his own traction bars and headers, 4.88 rear gears, Cure-Ride shocks, and dual Carter AFB quads on a low-rise aluminum manifold. The

Early 427-engined Camaros from Nickey, Baldwin-Motion, and others usually had stock hoods and minimal exterior body mods based on availability of aftermarket parts. This first-built Nickey/Thomas Camaro started out as an SS350, as big-block models were not yet available. Chromed Cragars were a nice touch. The SS350 emblems were retained.

ABOVE: A simple NICKEY logo is the only hint of something big under the hood. Nickey-Chicago owner Stefano Bimbi reminded me that "4501" was on the all license plates used by Nickey Chevrolet, located at 4501 Irving Park Road in Chicago.

TOP: The BTRC 427 engine, with most unusual yellow-painted block and heads, was rated at 450 horsepower at 6,000 rpm. It was a blueprinted stock 425-horsepower engine with dual Carter AFB four-barrels. With 4.88 Posi gears, acceleration was breathtaking and cruising not that desirable.

LEFT: Bill Thomas designed and manufactured headers for big-block Camaros and used the Nickey/Thomas 427 Camaro to prototype them. They were the best headers for big-block Camaros on the market.

Thomas-tuned engine, with yellow-painted block and heads, was rated at 450 horsepower at 6,000 rpm. I found the rear gearing to be well suited for a drag strip, but not desirable for normal driving. At freeway cruising speeds, the engine revved around 5,000 rpm. On the bright side, stopwatch 0 to 60 blasts came in around five seconds. Thanks to Thomas's new traction bars and specially valved shocks, typical wheel hop was greatly reduced.

I recall thinking that a well-tuned big Holley four-barrel would have been a cheaper, less complex alternative to Thomas's dual Carter four-barrels. However, throttle response and launches from a dead stop were breathtaking. To make full use of the 427 engine's torque and Camaro's gearing, slicks were needed. BTRC's shop foreman, Warren Williams, and FI tuner, Pat LaFon, were involved in building the first Camaro and let me know it had run consistent 11.40s. I was very tempted to stay over for a couple of days to get a chance to run it at the track. Unfortunately, that did not happen. We ran some coverage of my day with the Nickey/Thomas 427 Camaro in the August 1967 issue of *SPEED and SUPERCAR* (formerly *SPEED and CUSTOM*).

ROYAL PONTIAC
GTO: BEWARE THE BOBCAT

Since the early 1960s, Royal Pontiac had been building and racing Pontiacs and selling modified Day Two Bobcats. In 1967, Royal worked with Jim Wangers and Pontiac PR to build a 360-horsepower Bobcat GTO for *Hi-Performance CARS*. I flew to Detroit, and drove the Bobcat back to New York.

One of Royal's most successful products was its performance-enhancing Bobcat Kit, used in the prep of our test car. The kit included compression-raising thin head gaskets, ignition advance kit, blocked heat riser intake manifold gaskets, rocker arm lug nuts to allow hydraulic lifters to be adjusted to full height, a Quadrajet modified accelerator pump, secondary rods and larger jets, J-10-Y Champion plugs, and Royal Bobcat emblems.

Schornack and Warren's engine had blueprinted heads with 65cc chambers, resulting in 11.4:1 compression. The engine's transistorized distributor was set for 44 degrees total

Thanks to Jim Wangers, Pontiac PR, and the speed merchants at Royal Pontiac, we got a full-on Bobcat instead of a stock Ram-Air GTO for testing in 1967. Once on home turf, we turned it over to Motion Performance for tuning.

advance at 2,500 rpm and a set of Doug's four-port headers were installed. Other modifications included a Turbo-Hydramatic transmission with special valve body and 1,500-rpm stall speed converter and a 3.90 Posi rear.

With headers hooked up to the stock exhausts and the tank topped off with Sunoco 260, I took Route 75 South to the Ohio Turnpike for the 900-mile break-in trek home. Cruising speeds of 50 to 80 miles per hour kept the freshly blueprinted engine at a maximum of 3,800 to 4,000 rpm and fuel consumption averaged almost 12 miles per gallon.

To baseline the Bobcat's performance, we ran it at Westhampton for "Time Only" with closed headers and street tires. The best we could do was just under 100 miles per hour in the fourteens.

Before spending serious track time, I brought it to Motion for dyno tuning. Running through the mufflers, Joel Rosen documented 180 rear wheel horsepower at approximately 4,000 rpm. He felt that some fine-tuning could bring the power up by a solid 10 percent. He redid the distributor, blocking vacuum for full centrifugal advance with 44 degrees total timing in by 2,000 rpm. Stock TVRS plug wires were replaced with burn-proof Packard 535 metal-core wires with Rajah Bakelite and steel plug connectors. A set of Motion Topcat Kit spacers was installed between the Quadrajet and manifold to isolate fuel from heat. These modifications brought the output up to 200 rear wheel horsepower.

AN OFFICIAL TIMED RUN AT

NEW YORK NATIONAL SPEEDWAY

CAR NO.	500
CLASS	A/S ①
E.T.	13.40 ☐ T
M.P.H.	108
W ⊘	☐ L Rd

34298B ELECTROWRITER SYSTEMS BY VICTOR COMPTOMETER CORPORATION 1116-2

CARS EDITOR MARTY SCHORR TAKES THE TROPHY AT N.Y. NATIONAL SPEEDWAY!

Marty Schorr and the *CARS* GTO that may be seen in your town!

We had a great time with the GTO on the street before having it lettered. Typical Day Two big-block Chevys and Mopars proved tough to beat, but a few Street Hemis did fall prey to our "plain-Jane" *Goat*! The modified TurboHydro shifted like a manual and, under full-throttle, shifted at 4,500 to 4,800 rpm. Thanks to the 1,500-rpm stall-speed converter, we usually idled off the line at around 1,100 to 1,200 rpm, and then nailed it.

Once Goodyear 8.50x14-inch, 7-inch-wide cheater slicks were installed, we changed our launch technique. With slicks pumped to 10 psi, we torque-loaded the powertrain at just under 1,500 rpm and floored it. Other trackside mods included disconnecting the power steering and installing "colder" J-61-Y Champions.

Our first trip to New York National netted us a best time of 108 miles per hour in 13.40. Running in A/Stock Formula 2 (A/S F-2), we waded through a field that included a new 396/375 Camaro. We lost the trophy to a '65 Z-16 Chevelle that ran 12.80/112 miles per hour.

The next time we ran New York National, they put our GTO in Super/Stock Showdown 3, and Rosen and I went though the entire SSS-3 field to win the Class at 104 miles per hour in 13.49 seconds. Then we nailed Super Stock Eliminator at 109 miles per hour in 13.40 seconds. We won a big trophy and $20 and ran within 6/10ths and 4 miles per hour of the national record. The trophy went to Pontiac and Rosen and I had a $20 victory dinner—still doable in 1967. Coverage of the Bobcat build and our racing exploits appeared in the September and October issues of *Hi-Performance CARS*.

TOP: We did most of our running at New York National, but did try E-Town once during an NHRA record meet. They wouldn't let us run for record or class based on alloy carburetor spacers. We made a couple of runs and then went to New York National. This shot was taken when we won SSS-3 class and eliminations. Our best time was 109 mph in 13.40.

MIDDLE: On this trip to the track, they put us in A/Stock Formula 3 and our best run was 108 miles per hour in 13.40, not good enough to beat a Z16 Chevelle for the class.

BOTTOM: Our publisher capitalized on our trophy winning and created this promotion piece for our distributors. After the photo, the trophy was shipped to Pontiac PR, where it was on display for a few months.

A base model Camaro with RPO Z/28 powered by the unique 302-inch small-block underrated at 290 horsepower. It was a late addition to the 1967 lineup. Its reason for being was to compete with Mustang on the Trans-Am circuit. *General Motors*

OPTION Z/28:
CHEVY BUILDS A BOY RACER

It was only an RPO code, but "Z/28" turned a 302-cubic-inch Camaro into a legend. And proved that less could be more.

It was Vince Piggins, Chevrolet Product promotions manager and keeper of its revolving backdoor, who conceived the Z/28 Camaro to battle Mustang on the Trans-Am circuit. Once approved by Pete Estes, Chevrolet general manager and GM vice president, he was given the green light to prototype a true four-place sports coupe. Estes had a rich performance car history at GM and was responsible for Pontiac's GTO, the industry's first supercar. Chevrolet's primary focus was beating the Mustang in high-profile Trans-Am racing and creating a halo for the nameplate and brand. It worked!

The prototype Z/28 was shown to Pete Estes on the road course at the Milford Proving Ground and later shown to the press. However, it was not a real Z/28. It had all the chassis mods, but under the hood was a 327 dressed as a 302. Estes was impressed and signed off on the project.

If Chevrolet had to develop a unique engine to race in the Trans-Am Series, the Z/28 Camaro would never have happened. The displacement limit imposed by the SCCA was 305 cubic inches and Chevrolet had only 327 and 350 engines available. Drag racers running in Junior Stock classes had been building small-displacement Chevy engines, using 327 blocks with 283 cranks, to come up with 302 cubic inches. Piggins knew that he could easily create a 302 small-block with low-development costs using off-the-shelf components to meet SCCA specs. He utilized a 4-inch bore 327/350 block fitted with a 3-inch stroke 283 crank.

The production solid-lifter 302 engine, available only in the Z/28 Camaro, was underrated at 290 horsepower at 5,800 rpm and 290 ft-lb of torque at 4,200 rpm. Dyno reports from Chevrolet Engineering indicated that a well-tuned 302 could generate closer to 350 to 375 horsepower, with a redline closer to 7,000 rpm.

Powered by a hot-rodder's dream engine designed for high-rpm performance, the Z/28 could not be equipped with air conditioning or automatic transmission. To ensure high-rpm reliability, the 302 engine was fitted with a forged steel crank, shot-peened forged steel rods, and forged aluminum 11:1 pistons with notched valve reliefs. For maximum

The first Z/28 Camaro, ordered by Hugh Heishman on December 13, was built on December 29 (first day of production) and raced at the first 1967 T/A race at Daytona on February 3. It did not finish. Craig Fisher posted the best finish in a Z/28: second. *Jon Mello*

performance at mid-to-high rpm, heads featured 2.02-inch intake and 1.60-inch exhaust valves and large ports.

Piggins went to the Corvette parts bin for a suitable camshaft and valvetrain for the 302. His choice was the No. 3849346 solid lifter cam with .485-inch lift and 346 degrees duration and matching valvetrain. These components had been used in 1964 to 1965 Sting Rays with 327/365 carburated and 327/375 fuel-injected engines. Intake chores were handled by an 800-cfm Holley double-pumper on a dual-plane aluminum manifold. Tuned headers and a cowl-induction air cleaner were optional and delivered in the Camaro's trunk for owner or dealer installation.

Because of the Z/28's late development and the timing of the first race of the 1967 Trans-Am Series, Piggins made the SCCA and FIA aware of its Trans-Am plans prior to the Camaro's introduction in September 1966. He prepared for the possibility of the Z/28 Camaro not meeting the SCCA's 1,000-car minimum for entry in the Trans-Am Series by applying for FIA homologation for two Camaros. He filed papers for the SS350 Camaro and Z/28 Camaro for Groups 1 and 2, respectively. In 1967 Chevrolet sold just 602 Z28s, but the 398-unit shortage was covered by SS350 sales of almost 30,000.

Z/28 Camaro production started on December 29, 1966 and the first sixteen were "tagged" for racing. They were built without radios, heaters, and sound-deadening materials, and were not intended for street use. The actual first Z/28 Camaro was ordered on December 13, 1966, by Hugh Heishman at Aero Chevrolet, Alexandria, Virginia, and built sixteen days later.

A Penske-Sunoco Z/28 Camaro, driven by Mark Donohue, finished third for championship honors. It would all change the following year when the Penske/Donohue juggernaut won the first of two consecutive championships. And a legend was born.

LEFT: The engine in the first Z/28 is fitted with factory RPO Z/28-2 cowl-induction plenum air cleaner and RPO Z/28-3 tuned exhaust headers. The headers and air cleaner were supplied loose for dealer or buyer installation. *Jon Mello*

BOTTOM: Roger Penske's Sunoco Z/28, driven by Mark Donohue, won T/A Series races at Marlboro, Massachusetts; Las Vegas, Nevada; and Kent, Washington, and finished third in the championship. It was the fourteenth Z/28 built and its body was acid-dipped to reduce weight, then braced with a NASCAR-style roll cage. *M. M. "Mike" Matune Jr.*

1968

The hottest GM supercar for 1968 was the SS396 Chevelle rated at 375 horsepower. This is a Baldwin-Motion 427/450-horsepower version with functional scooped hood with tach, mags, and mid-series Corvette side exhausts.

CHAPTER TEN

SOMETHING FOR EVERYONE!

Motown unleashes an unprecedented barrage of sizzling supercars and potent pony cars—starting at $2,900. You could even order a turnkey 10-second Super/Stock at your friendly Dodge or Plymouth dealer.

Pontiac's GTO created and dominated the supercar marketplace in 1964 and, in 1968, was downsized and restyled. GM's successful supercar formula that started it all showcased 115-inch wheelbase, two-door coupes with large displacement engines and unique trim and badging. Downsizing reduced wheelbase to a sportier, more appealing 112 inches. With the reduction in wheelbase and overall length came all-new long-hood, short deck, Coke bottle styling. Restyling set the Skylark GS-400, Chevelle SS396, Pontiac GTO, and Oldsmobile 4-4-2 apart from each other and from crosstown competition.

Each nameplate carried distinctive styling cues and proprietary engines with price points related to the division's status in the marketplace. The Buick Skylark GS-400 was the most expensive and luxurious, while Chevrolet's powerful Chevelle SS396, the least expensive, appealed to a huge fan base. In keeping with tradition, Pontiac offered great performance and the widest range of options. Oldsmobile did the best job of combining image with performance, ride, and handling. GM had the marketplace covered.

The Skylark GS-400 came with a 400-inch engine rated at 340 horsepower at 5,000 rpm and 440 lb-ft of torque at 3,200. The 10.25 compression engine was available with GM's excellent TH-400 automatic or a Hurst-shifted four-speed. Known only to Buick engineers, dealers involved in drag racing, a small group of racers, and the NHRA, the first of Buick's Stage series of ultra-performance engines surfaced in 1968. It was never advertised. Dubbed the Stage II 400, it was rated at a very conservative 350 horsepower and fitted with 11:1 pistons, .455/480-inch lift, 340/360-degree duration camshaft, and special heads. There was no Stage I. Buick filed specs for this engine with the NHRA, listing it as

a Heavy-Duty Stage II option on Skylarks. It is unclear how many, if any, Stage II GS-400s were factory built. My guess is that Buick dealers who participated in drag racing may have built a few.

With new styling, shorter-wheelbase chassis, and 400-inch engine, the Cutlass-bodied 4-4-2 celebrated the coming of age of one of the best-packaged supercars of the era. No longer an option, the 4-4-2 was a full-fledged model available in Sport Coupe, Holiday, and convertible body styles. Standard 4-4-2 engines were 400/325 or 400/350 with TH400 automatic or Hurst-shifted four-speed, respectively. Unlike the previous Force-Air Induction 4-4-2, hoses now brought fresh air to the Quadrajet from 13-inch-wide under-bumper scoops. The battery did not have to be relocated to the trunk.

Although still displacing 400 cubic inches, the new engine had a small 3.87-inch bore and 4.25-inch stroke, utilizing a crank from a 455-inch engine. The long-stroke, high-torque engine delivered improved emissions and performance.

For those craving maximum performance, the W30 Force-Air Induction 400/360 engine with second-design .475-inch lift, 328-degree duration camshaft was optional. W30 engines

Joel Rosen making test runs after dyno tuning, on Sunrise Highway. Olds PR alerted us to GM Legal finding out about us racing with GM M license plates, so we replaced them with New York dealer plates. They still took the car back.

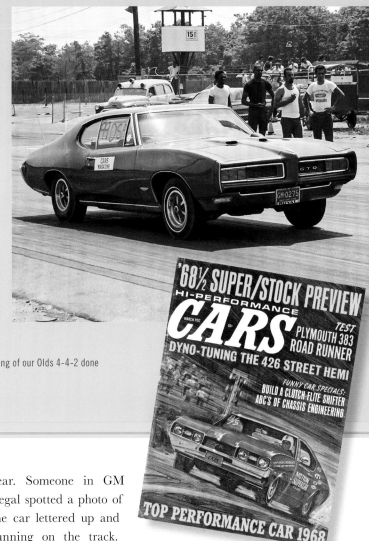

TOP LEFT: Testing the new slick fastback 390 Torino at Riverside Raceway in July 1967. At the time of its introduction, the 428 CJ engine was not available. The streamlined Torino excelled as a NASCAR stocker.

TOP RIGHT: Testing one of the forty-seven-built '68 1/2 Ram Air II GTOs with TH400 automatic transmission at Westhampton. This one was ever rarer, as it was a Royal Pontiac Bobcat GTO. Times were consistent mid-thirteens running DS/A. Yes, we did get a call from GM Legal about the GM license plates!

BOTTOM RIGHT: Our 1968 annual Top Performance Car of the Year issue featured a rendering of our Olds 4-4-2 done prior to having a finished car. It actually ran in D/Stock, and was Nocturne Blue.

were built using specially selected short blocks with select-fit crank and rod assemblies. Specially ported heads and a high-rpm valvetrain, with maximum power coming in at 5,400 rpm, made it ideal for drag racing. Available with automatic or manual transmissions and 4.33 gears, the W30 Olds was actually a lot hotter than the advertised specs. You could opt for 3.42, 3.91, or 4.66 gears.

As appealing as a W30 was, many enthusiasts were put off by the lack of power brakes. The .475-inch lift Gen II cam with 108 degrees overlap produced a shortage of engine vacuum that was needed for boosting brakes. I drove a W30 test car for a couple of days and couldn't wait to return it. Stopping a car as big as an Olds 4-4-2 with non-power-assist brakes took an enormous amount of pressure. I was surprised that dealers sold 1,915 of them.

Hi-Performance CARS named the '68 Olds 4-4-2 Top Performance Car of the Year, and partnered with Motion and Oldsmobile on an NHRA D/Stock 4-4-2. Primarily a local race car, we ran consistent twelves and had a lot of fun. But our racing plans ended abruptly halfway through the model year. Someone in GM Legal spotted a photo of the car lettered up and running on the track. They noticed its GM manufacturer license plates and traced the registration to Oldsmobile Public Relations. Before we knew what was happening, a transporter arrived and took our 4-4-2 away!

Midway through the model year, Pontiac released an optional 400-inch Ram Air II engine for GTO and Firebird applications. There were conflicting power ratings for this engine of 365, 366, and 370, depending on the release date and source. We covered the first 1968$\frac{1}{2}$ Ram-Air GTO Bobcat, undergoing testing at Miami Dragway. The story, written by Roger Huntington, appeared in the July issue of *Hi-Performance CARS*.

Drag-prepped by Royal Pontiac and driven by Milt Schornack, it posted times in the high-twelves at more than 110 miles per hour on 7-inch cheater slicks.

We borrowed a Verdoro Green '68 GTO Bobcat powered by a Ram Air II engine from Royal Pontiac. We had it

The pricier Dodge Coronet R/T hardtop could be had with Wedge or Hemi engines and a full range of options. This is a Hemi we tested for *Speed and Supercar* magazine, edited by Fred Mackerodt.

dyno-tuned, and ran it on the street and at Westhampton. The engine had the new, round-port heads with 65cc chambers, special exhaust manifolds and .475/.480-inch lift, 308/320-degree duration cam, and valvetrain. It was very responsive at low- and mid-range on the street and we posted consistent mid-thirteen-second times.

In its quest to attract young, budget-minded enthusiasts, Plymouth packed power and status into its base midsize Belvedere I and created the Road Runner. With an MSRP of approximately $2,900, the Road Runner had a special hood with raised, non-functional scoops, unique badging, and a 335-horsepower 383 with 440 engine heads, intake manifold, exhaust manifolds and a 450/.465-inch lift, and .268/.284-degree duration cam. Chrysler's beefy four-speed was standard.

To support Plymouth's bargain pricing, the Road Runner's spartan interior was more taxi than supercar. If you wanted traditional comfort, convenience, and enthusiast options, you could expect an MSRP on a par with supercars such as the 350/325 Olds W31 Cutlass. A well-equipped Road Runner with a 426 Street Hemi, updated with a new oil pan windage tray and 284-degree cam, could cost around $4,000.

Boosted by *Looney Toons* and *Merry Melodies'* Wile E. Coyote and *Road Runner*–themed advertising—and even a "beep-beep" horn—the Road Runner was an instant success. It was well received as a mass-market supercar, exceeding all sales estimates and finishing the model year with sales in excess of 44,000. Of that, Plymouth sold 1,009—a record number of Street Hemi models.

Dodge followed suit with a catchy Super Bee model based on its midsize Coronet and priced at approximately $3,000. It did not catch on as well and dealers sold less than 20 percent of Road Runner sales. Both models offered the same levels of performance. We tested a dyno-tuned 383/335 Super Bee in the October 1968 issue of *Speed and SUPERCAR* and recorded a best quarter-mile time of 99 miles per hour in 14.60 seconds. Average times of stock 383 Road Runners and Super Bees were in the 15.0s with trap speeds of 95 miles per hour.

Total Performance was alive and well in Dearborn. With racing enthusiast Bunkie Knudsen (who was newly poached from GM) at the helm of Ford Division, its investment in high-performance road cars and support of racing appeared to have no limit. One of Knudsen's favorite expressions was: "Build what we race and race what we build."

The big product news was availability of 427/390 and 428/335 Mustangs, Torinos, Mercury Cougars, and Cyclones. First came the 427, available only in early-build cars with automatic transmissions. A total of 357 GT-E 7.0-liter Cougars were built with 427/390 engines and C-6 automatic transmissions. There were some 427 Mustangs, Fairlanes, and Cyclones, but no records exist of any being sold to the public. Those cars were primarily R&D vehicles driven by engineers at the proving ground—and loaned to executives over weekends.

Ford's street fighter was the mid-year 428 Cobra Jet Mustang, with Toploader four-speed manual or beefed C-6 automatic transmission. The CJ powertrain option was available in coupe, convertible, and fastback Sportsroof models. Cobra Jet Mustangs swept Super/Stock Class and Eliminator titles at the NHRA Winternationals.

Streamlined fastback Ford Torinos and Mercury Cyclones, powered by the latest 427 Tunnel Port motors, dominated stock car racing competition in 1968. David Pearson nailed down his second NASCAR Championship, winning sixteen races in Holman-Moody Torinos. Ford won NASCAR, USAC, and ARCA championships.

Even with new 302-cubic-inch small-block with single and twin four-barrel carburetors, Ford and Shelby's Trans-Am effort for 1968 could not stop Chevrolet's dynamic duo—Roger Penske and Mark Donohue. They swept the series in a Sunoco Blue Z/28 Camaro and gave Chevrolet the Trans-Am Championship in 1968.

Compared with the Big Three, American Motors was at a major disadvantage when competing for a piece of the performance pie. AMC didn't have the hardware or the budget to challenge established nameplates on the track or in

The first 1968½ Ram Air II GTO during Royal Pontiac testing at Miami Dragway. Milt Schornack ran high-twelves on 7-inch cheater slicks.

Grant Industries and AMC were involved in this unique '68 Rebel SST fuel-burning Funny Car. Driven by Hayden Proffitt, it had a Logghe chassis and blown-and-injected AMC engine. This was its last match race event, at Puerto Rico International Raceway in 1969, before being retired.

the marketplace. Things changed in 1968 when AMC burst on the scene with the long-hood, short-deck 390 Javelin, followed by a mid-year 390 AMX two-seater.

AMC's new pony car had the displacement, but not the power, to run with the big doggies—Camaro, Firebird, and Mustang. Mustang had the 428 CJ motor and 396 Camaros and 400 Firebirds were upgraded and suspensions improved to solve traction problems. They were tough to beat.

Javelin's optional 390 engine was rated at 315 horsepower at 4,600 rpm and an impressive 425 lb-ft of torque at 3,200 rpm. While it fell short in horsepower, the Javelin offered some advantages over the established nameplates. Typically, pony cars had 108-inch wheelbase platforms and overall lengths of approximately 185 inches. For adults, rear seat room was almost non-existent and trunks offered little storage. In keeping with the sporty look was a tight cockpit. The Javelin had a 1-inch-longer wheelbase, and was a solid

4 inches longer. That translated into a roomier interior and a trunk that held something bigger than a backpack. The two-seat 1968½ AMX was a shortened Javelin with 390-engine availability and 12 inches less wheelbase and overall length.

In 1968, AMC's Performance Activities Department supported drag racers and teams competing in Stock, Super/Stock, and Funny Car classes. They were also involved in Trans-Am road racing and sponsored the Rambler-powered Navarro Engineering Special at the Indy 500. AMC Dealers were encouraged to sponsor Javelin clubs, market high-performance parts, and get involved with enthusiasts at grassroots drag racing and road rally events.

Growing factory participation in racing fueled a seemingly endless bragging rights and horsepower race. Never before had enthusiasts been faced with so many choices when shopping for their perfect performance car.

ABOVE: AMC made its presence known in drag racing circles after introducing the 390 Javelin (far lane) and the two-seat AMX iteration (foreground). AMC had a factory race parts program, along with cash contingency awards. Very competitive dealer-sponsored E/Stocks at E-Town.

BELOW: "Grumpy" Jenkins was a force to be reckoned with in SS/C competition. The *Toy IV* was a 396/375 '68 Camaro. He worked closely with Vince Piggins at Chevrolet.

455 HURST-OLDS:
LANSING'S EXECUTIVE EXPRESS

Conceived by Hurst's Jack "Doc" Watson as personal transportation for George Hurst, Oldsmobile turned his one-off concept into a supercar legend.

Some of the brightest engineering minds in the industry created the only GM midsize car powered by a rules-bending 455-inch engine. In 1968, GM policy still limited the displacement of engines in midsize models to 400 cubic inches. However, corporate policymakers turned a blind eye to Oldsmobile's rogue 455-inch Cutlass.

Available in any color as long as it was Peruvian Silver Metallic with Ebony Black stripes and deck lid, the '68 Hurst-Olds delivered uncompromising road performance and sub-fourteen-second quarter-mile times. It was an uplevel 4-4-2 boasting outstanding packaging of horsepower, torque, ride, handling, and performance.

The engines chosen for Hurst-Olds production utilized 455 Toronado short blocks with either W30 Force-Air Induction heads and valvetrain on non-AC W45 cars or basic 400-inch 4-4-2 heads and valvetrain on W46 models with AC. Both engines had the same "advertised" power—390 horsepower at 5,000 rpm and 500 lb-ft of torque at 3,600 rpm. Transmission choices included close or wide-ratio four speeds or modified TM400 automatic with Hurst dual-gate shifter.

Even though I attended Doc Watson's Hurst-Olds press briefing in Detroit and was friendly with Oldsmobile engineers responsible for creating the production car, I didn't know the car's actual backstory until years later. According to Oldsmobile, the project was greenlighted by GM because Demmer Tool & Die would build it as a Hurst-Olds. That's the story most editors went with. But there were a lot of gray areas.

GM divisions were prohibited from putting larger-than-400-inch engines in midsize cars, so credit for the complete build was attributed to Demmer. That was not the case. The 455 engines were actually put into 4-4-2s on the Olds assembly line and then brought down the road to Demmer for final assembly. Oldsmobile signed off on the cars and they were shipped with other models to Oldsmobile dealers.

Oldsmobile contracted for 500 cars, a nice round number that signifies limited production—necessary with a car that,

One of fifty-six Hurst-Olds Sport coupes built out of 515 total production. Hurst Performance used custom convertibles for promotions at auto shows and major track events in 1968. *General Motors*

according to GM, shouldn't have existed. The Hurst-Olds was so well received by dealers that the number was raised to 515—56 Sport Coupes and 459 Holiday hardtops. Before the official launch date, Story Oldsmobile in Lansing sold almost a dozen. More than 2,500 orders were placed, but only 515 filled. When ordering a Hurst-Olds, a purchaser had to sign authorization releases allowing Demmer Tool & Die to perform the Hurst conversion.

The Oldsmobile engineers responsible for turning the Hurst concept into a production reality were John Beltz, Ted Lucas, Dale Smith, and Bob Stemple. Beltz was later promoted to general manger and a GM vice president and Bob Stemple climbed the ladder all the way to the top— to GM chairman. They were friends of John Demmer who, with his son, drag raced 4-4-2s and purchased two Hurst-Olds.

Only a very small percentage of Hurst-Olds were built with four-speeds because the modified three-speed TM400 automatic was so well suited for handling the engine's ground-pounding torque. Magazine testers recorded ETs as low as 13.70s and 13.80s with speeds of 102 miles per hour. With slicks, a well-tuned Hurst-Olds could break into the twelves. It's no wonder they sold out so quickly and became supercar icons.

TOP: Stopping off for some Sunoco 260 during an evaluation drive. Note the price of gas and location, next to car guy hangout, Ted's Drive Inn on Woodward Avenue in Bloomfield Hills, Michigan.

BOTTOM: Forced-air induction hoses did not require relocating the battery to the trunk. Fresh air is picked up from 13-inch under-bumper scoops. The air cleaner has an Oldsmobile Rocket 455 ID.

A-BODY HEMIS:
THE KILLER BEES

With help from Hurst Performance, Plymouth and Dodge added purpose-built 426 Hemi Super/Stock race cars to its 1968 product lines.

In mid-May 1968, a drag racer and old friend of mine, Charlie Castaldo, hitched a trailer to his luxurious Dodge Monaco station wagon at his home in Scarsdale, New York, for a 650-mile trip to Madison Heights, Michigan. The purpose of this trip was to take delivery of one of eighty Hemi-Darts built at Hurst Performance. A loyal Dodge enthusiast, Charlie passed on buying one of the seventy 426 Barracudas in favor of a boxier Dart.

After Charlie had Speedwin race-prep the Hemi for SS/B, he ran sub-eleven-second ETs and joined other 426 Barracuda and Dart owners in the mid-ten-second club. These limited-production Super/Stocks dominated NHRA SS/B and SS/BA. There was a fleet of Hemi Mopars competing for SS/B honors at the 1968 NHRA Springnationals, including

Charlie- and Dodge-sponsored Dick Landy and Plymouth's Sox & Martin. When the smoke cleared, Ronnie Sox took the gold. Later at the NHRA Indy Nationals, Arlen Vanke, driving a SS/B Hemi Barracuda, beat Wally Booth's SS/E '68 Camaro to win Super/Stock Eliminator.

For racers only, 426 Barracuda and Dart Super/Stocks, Code B029 and L023, respectively, came with 500-horsepower Hemis and were built without heaters, body sealers and deadeners, silencing pads, outside mirrors, right side seat belts, and body paint. Other than a choice of four-speed or automatic transmission, no optional equipment was available. Sold without warranties, these cars did not conform to Federal Motor Vehicle Safety Standards and could not be legally used on the road.

In 1968 at the Chelsea Proving Ground, I asked Chrysler engineer Tom Hoover about the new 426 Hemi Barracuda and Dart. His first response was: "They will be as close to race-ready as anything that has ever rolled out of an assembly plant."

A founding member of the Ramchargers, a key player in the creation of Max Wedge race cars, and considered the godfather of the 426 Street Hemi, Hoover added: "It's the strongest package to come out of Motown for production drag purposes so far."

In order to bring weight down, hoods and front fenders were replaced with Plaza Fiberglass panels and door skins were acid-dipped. Front bumpers were lighter than stock. Special Chemcor .080-inch thick glass was used, back seats were deleted, and heavy batteries were trunk-mounted. Lightweight Bostrom Dodge van bucket seats were fitted using lightweight alloy hardware.

All retail sale Hemi Darts and Barracudas were fitted with cast-iron 426 Hemi engines with 12.5 compression, stock Street Hemi camshafts, and dual Holley four-barrel carbs on Chrysler's *signature* cross-ram manifold. Some cars were delivered with aluminum intake manifolds, others with magnesium manifolds. In some cases, magnesium manifolds were shipped to owners whose cars had the aluminum intake. Hooker supplied the headers.

Hoover stated: "We would have liked to deliver SS/B cars with race cam and a

Ronnie Sox on his way to winning Super/Stock Eliminator at the 1968 NHRA Spring Nationals. The Sox & Martin Hemi Barracuda won NHRA, AHRA, and *CARS* magazine events. The top running Tritak & Morgan SS/E station wagon is in the far lane.

TOP: Charlie Castaldo checks out the 426 Hemi engine in his Dart at Hurst Performance before loading the Super/Stock on his trailer and towing back to New York. The engine was blueprinted before the car was ready for the track.

BOTTOM: 383 Barracudas and Darts were donor cars, delivered in primer with fiberglass front ends and lightened doors and front bumpers. Charlie and his Dart are ready for the trip back home. Finished Super/Stocks waiting for transport lurk in the background.

deep oil pan, but they presented drivability and shipping issues. They had to be drivable since shippers and dealership personnel would handle them. Each car was fitted with a large sign attached to the windshield stating, 'THIS SUPER STOCK VEHICLE IS TO BE SHIPPED ON THE BOTTOM LEVEL ONLY OF ALL TRUCK AND RAIL TRANSPORTATION.' We encouraged racers to pick up their vehicles at Hurst, if possible."

The concept of Chrysler building Hemi Barracudas and Darts for NHRA Super/Stock first surfaced at a meeting in late 1967 between product planning engineer Dick Maxwell,

Tom Hoover, and Bob Tarozzi. Initially proposed for SS/A, plans changed when NHRA revamped class rules. The cars then fit perfectly into SS/B with its formula of 6.00 to 6.99 pounds-per-horsepower. Engines were rated at 500 horsepower and race-ready cars would weigh approximately 3,000 pounds. After this program, Maxwell became manager of performance activities, eventually retiring as the head of all corporate racing programs.

According to Hoover, the Hemi Super/Stock program was not a formal corporate design/engineering project. "Lead engineer Bob Tarozzi, drag racing mechanics Dan Knapp, Larry Knowlton, and John Bauman and I collaborated and made use of lab specialists and engineering departments only to work on special problems," he said.

In 1969, Charlie Castaldo, running in the mid-tens, rolled his car while making a pass at E-Town. He quickly replaced his SS/B Dart with an SS/BA Dart, and went on to win the 1969 *Super/Stock* magazine nationals. In 1969, many of the A-body Hemis were reclassified for SS/A, and continued winning.

428 COBRA JET:
KING OF THE ROAD

Tasca Ford's "King of the Road" KR-8 Mustang was the inspiration for the 428 CJ Mustang that rewrote the 1968 Super/Stock record book.

Bob Tasca of Tasca Ford, working with driver Bill Lawton and head wrench John Healey, built his own Cobra Jet Mustang powered by a 428 engine and presented it to Ford. His one-off 428 engine had a Police Interceptor block and aluminum intake manifold with a 735-cfm Holley, 390 GT cam and valvetrain, 427 low-riser heads, and 428 and 390 GT exhaust manifolds. He felt that Ford didn't have a suitable Mustang to compete with the new Camaro, which could be optioned with a 396/375 solid-lifter big-block. He had built a Mustang that would give any stock Camaro nightmares. Tasca's KR-8 Concept was well received in Dearborn, and became the inspiration and guidelines for the production 428 CJ Mustang.

Prior to the Cobra Jet Mustang and Fairlane public introduction as a 1968½ model on April 1, 1968, Ford built fifty-four Wimbledon White 428 CJ Mustang fastbacks—

TOP: Al Joniec, on his way to beating Hubie Platt to win SS/E at the 1968 NHRA Winternationals. His best time was 120.6 miles per hour in 11.49 seconds and he also won Super/Stock Eliminator, launching a successful year of CJ Mustang competition. *Ford Motor Company*

BELOW LEFT: Ford drag team member Hubie Platt also successfully campaigned a new fastback 428 CJ Torino in SS/F. He ran 11.90s at the 1968 *CARS* Super/Stock meet at Cecil County.

BELOW RIGHT: The NHRA's Wally Parks congratulates Al Joniec for winning Super/Stock class and Eliminator at 1968 Winternationals. *Ford Motor Company*

twenty specifically for drag racing. Tasca Ford received ten CJs and approximately ten were assigned to Dick Brannan's group at Ford Special Vehicles Activity. A select group was prepared by Holman-Moody-Stroppe, of Long Beach, California, for Ford Drag Team drivers for C/SA, SS/E, and SS/EA competition at the AHRA Winternationals on January 28 and the NHRA Winternationals at Pomona on February 2 through 4.

Jerry Harvey, Al Joniec, Don Nicholson, Hubert Platt, and Gas Ronda raced six cars at the high-profile winter events. They were not successful at the AHRA race, but dominated the NHRA Winternationals. Four of the six CJs made it to their respective class finals and Al Joniec, driving the Rice-Holman SS/E Cobra Jet, Vin No. 5050, beat teammate Hubert "Georgia Shaker" Platt's CJ to win SS/E. He ran 120.6 miles per hour in 11.49 seconds. Next, he beat Dave Wren's Plymouth for Super/Stock Eliminator. Joniec created the "halo" for Ford's public introduction of the 428 CJ Mustang, Fairlane, and Cougar.

During the 1968 NHRA season, Cobra Jet Mustangs proved difficult to beat. Don Nicholson, driving the Dick Brannan Ford Mustang, consistently ran low-elevens at speeds up to 125 miles per hour. Barrie Poole, in the Sandy Elliott Team CJ Mustang, set the record in Canada at 11.87 seconds. He later ran in the 11.30s on tracks in the United States. Hubert Platt also set a number of records with his CJ during 1968.

Although the Cobra Jet Mustang was a mid-year '68$\frac{1}{2}$ model, a total of 1,299 CJs, including thirty-four convertibles, were produced. Street performance was outstanding and the Mustang made a comeback after having sand kicked in its grille by big-block Camaros. Ford underrated the production 428 CJ at 335 horsepower, primarily to qualify it for reasonably normal insurance rates. Insurance companies were having a field day surcharging customers based on engine displacement and horsepower that negatively affected performance car sales. They were unsuccessful, however, in under-rating the CJ to gain an advantage in AHRA and NHRA classifications.

One of the most important Cobra Jet Mustangs, Vin No. 5050. It is one of twenty built without seam sealers and sound-deadening materials specifically for SS/E, and it is still around. *Ford Lightweight Collection*

When you opted for the 428 CJ on a new Mustang, it was packaged along with a special hood with a fiberglass ram-air scoop, integrated fresh-air-induction air cleaner, and beefed suspension. Optional 9-inch limited-slip rears with 3.91 or 4.30 gearing were available. Mustang transmission choices included four-speed Toploader manual or three-speed automatic. Fairlane CJs could be ordered only with automatic transmission.

Cobra Jet option costs, over a base V-8, were reasonable considering the engine was truly underrated at 335 horsepower and 440 lb-ft of torque at 5,400 rpm. The CJ engine package added $420.96 to a Mustang and $306.27 to a Fairlane. The Cougar GT-E was a late arrival to the Cobra Jet "party" and just thirty-seven were built.

In 1968 we found it difficult to evaluate Cobra Jet performance because it was a midyear intro and not that many were around for testing before we started driving 1969s. There were a couple of factory track-prepped, street-driven 428 CJs in circulation, a Mustang and Cougar GT-E, and they were turning 103 to 106 miles per hour in the 13.20s to 13.60s.

Thanks to Rhode Island Ford dealer Bob Tasca, who had Henry Ford II and Lee Iacocca on his speed dial, and his one-off KR-8, the Cobra Jet was born.

CARS PROJECT:
390 SUPER JAVELIN

With support from American Motors' manager of performance activities, Carl Chakmakian, and our friends at LAB Engineering, Motion Performance, and Pacers Automotive, we transformed a stock Javelin into a Super Javelin. It turned out so well that I bought it.

I test drove a 390 Javelin at a press preview and really liked it. It wasn't a rocketship, for sure, but it had potential. Thanks to a larger-than-traditional pony car cockpit, it had plenty of room for my 6-foot-2 frame. Its biggest engine option was the 390/315 with mild hydraulic-lifter cam and a small Carter AFB. But it did boast a very strong lower end thanks to forged steel rods and a five-main-bearing forged crank. Talking with AMC engineers confirmed that 400 horsepower was within reach without a lot of work. I was hooked.

We discussed the possibility of building a *Hi-Performance CARS* project Javelin with AMC public relations and they responded by sending me a new car order form. I chose a Matador Red Javelin SST with red interior, black vinyl roof, 390 engine, automatic, 3.15 Twin-Grip gears, and AMX suspension with top-mount traction bars.

Our Javelin was a very early-build 390 car, so the engine was not fitted with the standard chrome dress-up kit. Since we planned on changing valve covers and air cleaner anyway, it didn't matter. What did matter was that it didn't run that well. Once on Motion's Clayton dyno and hooked up to a Sun 1020 scope, Joel Rosen discovered that four plug wires were crossed up. With the stock Javelin running right, the engine produced 170 rear-wheel horsepower at approximately 5,000 rpm.

With a 170-horsepower baseline, Rosen modified the stock Carter AFB by drilling out the secondary jets .002-inch. He installed a set of aluminum spacer plates between the carb and manifold to ward off fuel percolation and vapor lock. The distributor was re-curved for total advance of 35 degrees in by 2,500 rpm and M/P-Mallory 7,500-rpm points were installed. A high-flow air cleaner replaced the big silenced air cleaner and Champion N-10-Y plugs were installed. Back on the dyno we saw an increase of 20 rear-wheel horsepower—190 at 5,000 rpm. The total cost for dyno tuning and parts was $55.43.

Over at Pacers Automotive, Jardine headers were installed and outside exhausts were fabricated using custom Douglass 50-inch piggyback mufflers covered with mid-series Corvette finned aluminum exhaust covers. Sun gauges were fitted in the dash and a Sun tach was mounted on the steering column.

The stock wheel was replaced with a sporty Grant wood wheel. Stock wheels and tires were swapped for chromed S/S Cragars with Goodyear F-Series Wide-Tread GT tires.

Prior to internal engine modifications, Motion made some intake and ignition upgrades. An Edelbrock 180-degree aluminum intake manifold with a stock Holley R-3310-AAS four-barrel replaced the factory Carter AFB setup. The 780- to 800-cfm automatic choke Holley, standard on the 425-horsepower Corvette, was used with stock jetting. To ensure fuel supply at the top end, an M/P dual electric fuel pump was added.

The ignition system was upgraded with an M/P Mallory Super-Spark full-centrifugal-advance dual-point distributor,

The major exterior transformation included a '68 AMX grille and hood with flush keylocks and black paint. The work was done by Herb Gary of Gary's Auto Body, in Sea Cliff, New York. Black paint made the Javelin look longer and lower, and turned heads.

TOP LEFT: Lee Bandrow at Lab Engineering, cc'ng the 390 heads. He cleaned up the ports, and installed lighter Chevy 2.02/1.60-inch valves. He also dialed in an AMC .470-inch lift, 302-degree duration cam. The redline increased by approximately 750 rpm.

TOP RIGHT: Joel Rosen tuned our Javelin on a Clayton dyno with a Sun 1020 scope. With minor intake and ignition mods and headers, we picked up 20 rear wheel horsepower over stock—190 versus 170.

RIGHT: We upgraded the Javelin's interior with a Grant three-spoke wood steering wheel, Sun Super tach, and matching Sun gauges fitted into the speaker panel in the center of the dash.

BOTTOM: A fully dressed 390 engine with Edelbrock intake, Holley 780- to 800-cfm four-barrel, and Mallory ignition prior to internal cam and head modifications. It registered 220 rear wheel horsepower at 5,000 rpm.

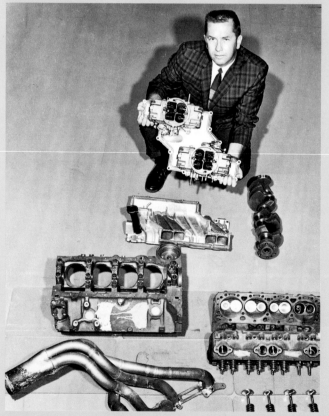

TOP: A rare photo of a cross-ram-equipped development '68 Z/28 with cowl-induction plenum air cleaner and headers during testing in 1967 at GM's Milford Proving Ground. The parts are prototype.

LEFT: If Chevrolet wasn't involved with racing, then how come GM engineer Bill Howell, Vince Piggins's right hand man, is displaying factory Z/28 competition parts taken off a Proving Ground mule? This photo was taken for a story in *Hi-Performance CARS*.

ABOVE: Motion's Tony Morgan checks out factory headers that were shipped with a '68 Rallye Green Z/28 test car. Headers were a must regardless of intake system as stock exhaust manifolds were terribly restrictive.

Baldwin Chevrolet's Z/28 with cross-ram and headers waits to get on the Clayton dyno's rollers at Motion. The car running on the dyno is an SS-427 Chevelle. During 1968 and 1969, headers, ignition work, and desmogging were the most popular mods to increase Z/28 street performance.

Mark II coil, and Ramcharger burn-proof wires with Rajah plug clips. Total timing was dialed in at 36 degrees by 2,000 rpm. Back on the chassis dyno after bolt-on mods, the Javelin generated 210 horsepower at 4,700 rpm and 220 at 5,000 rpm.

We consulted with Lee Bandrow and Bob Hall at LAB Engine Specialties of Lindenhurst, New York, about taking the 390 engine to the next level. Since spirited street driving was the mission, Lee's plan was to change the camshaft and valvetrain and performance-prep the heads. Since the stock heads had 2.02-inch intake and 1.62-inch exhaust valves, Lee replaced them with super-light, hard-chromed, and swirl-polished high-performance Chevy/Corvette small-block $2.02/1.60$-inch valves. The approximately 15-ounce-lighter valvetrain translated to an additional 750 to 1,000 *free* rpm. Heads were port-matched and machined for 51cc chambers and the stock cam was replaced with an AMC .477-inch lift and 302-degree duration cam and kit. Twin-Grip 3.90 gears, M/P Cure-Ride shocks, and weld-on traction bars were also installed.

After the project wrapped up and I owned the Javelin, Rosen and I played around with a variety of tuning mods, eventually getting the rear wheel horsepower up over 275. It could hold its own against big-block pony cars, but not 396/375 Camaros. But that was within reach!

1968-'69 Z/28 CAMARO:
THE BEAT GOES ON

The Z/28 Camaro was born to race, and in 1968, its second year, it gave Chevrolet its first of two consecutive Trans-Am championships. It became the poster car for successfully marketing roadable editions of a winning race car.

The 1968 and 1969 Z/28 Camaros were many things to many people. To Roger Penske and Mark Donohue, who soundly trounced the competition on the Trans-Am circuit, it was a thoroughbred sports-racing car. To drag racer Dave Strickler, winner of the International Hot Rod Association (IHRA) Super/Stock World Championship, it was an incredibly quick quarter-miler.

To tens of thousands of Z/28 buyers, it was all of the above plus an instantly recognized road rocket. The Gen I Z/28 was powered by an underrated 290-horsepower 302 engine that, professionally tuned and equipped with free-flow exhausts, could produce close to 1.2 horsepower-per-cubic-inch: 348 horsepower.

TOP: The Penske/Donohue '68 Z/28 at Laguna Seca. The lightened acid-dipped body necessitated a NASCAR-type roll cage to increase structural integrity. The Traco 305-inch-engined Camaro won ten of thirteen Trans-Am races, and brought Chevrolet its first of two consecutive T/A Championships. *M. M. "Mike" Matune Jr.*

BOTTOM: High-profile Super/Stock drag racer Dave Strickler was tough to beat in NHRA SS/F with his *Old Reliable* '68 Camaro Z/28. He ran high-elevens, and finished off the 1968 season by winning the IHRA world championship.

Because of its small 302-cubic-inch displacement, achieved by fitting a 350 block with a 327 crankshaft, the Z/28 Camaro engine needed de-smogging, headers, and ignition work for strong street performance. The Z/28 was born and bred to compete in the Trans-Am Series with engines limited to 305 cubic inches. Since serious Z/28 racers had pro builders such as Traco blueprint motors and add multi carbs and headers, they cared little about stock engine power. However, typical purchasers of new 1968 and 1969 Z/28s did care because street performance and occasional trips down the quarter-mile were all-important.

"We had a constant stream of Z/28 customers at Motion Performance for header installations, ignition modifications, and dyno tuning," said Motion's Joel Rosen. "They all had one thing in common. They loved their cars but felt that power was severely limited by factory exhaust manifolds and smog control tuning. Many wanted the same modifications that we performed on many new Z/28s sold by Baldwin Chevrolet."

The 1968 and 1969 Z/28s had many subtle differences, but power remained the same even though options varied slightly. Starting in 1968, Camaros with twelve-bolt rears and SS, Z/28, and HP models were built with multi-leaf rear springs to limit spring windup and axle tramp/wheel hop under maximum acceleration. All 1968 and 1969 Z/28s were built with four-leaf springs, while five-leaf springs were selected for other HP models. The basic '69 Camaro RPO

Z/28 was announced on September 26, 1968, and packaging and pricing details changed five times during the model run—October 1968 and January, April, September, and November 1969. The option price range was $458.15 to $522.40.

Chevrolet sold just 602 Z/28 Camaros in 1967. Thanks to racing tie-in advertising and marketing, sales hit 7,199 in 1968. Between the successes of the Roger Penske/Mark Donohue Trans-Am racing team and continuation of '69 Camaro production until the end of the calendar year, Z/28 sales skyrocketed to 20,302.

During 1968 to 1969, Vince Piggins's Product Promotion group at Chevrolet Engineering continued to support the Trans-Am racing effort. Under the guise of "Heavy-Duty Parts for Off-Highway Use Only," they developed an aluminum, dual-quad, cross-ram intake manifold with 600-cfm Holleys, cowl-induction plenum air cleaner, and tuned headers. They were incorporated into the homologation specs supplied to the FIA for international road racing. The JL8 four-wheel disc brake package came later.

Engineered for competition, these parts offered very little advantage for street use. The intake manifold did not have heat crossover and there were no chokes, making it impractical for normal rod use, especially in cold weather. The intake package was most effective in the 5,000- to 7,000-rpm range. If optioned on a new car order, Cross-Ram intake manifold, plenum air cleaner, and exhaust headers were boxed and shipped with the car to the dealer.

Specifically created for Trans-Am racing, Chevrolet's first Camaro four-wheel disc brakes appeared in March 1968 as over-the-counter parts. It was not until February 1969 that four-wheel-power disc brakes were listed as RPO JL8 on new car order forms. Priced at approximately $500, it was a short-lived option, because of cost and supplier problems. There were few takers, and after 206 orders were filled, the RPO was dropped in May 1969.

During '69 Camaro production, a ZL2 cowl induction hood was added as an $80 option. It allowed a stock single four-barrel engine to take in fresh air from the base of the windshield via a functional scoop inlet. For racing, a fiberglass version was available that mated to the cross-ram intake, thus doing away with the cowl induction plenum air cleaner.

The Penske-Donohue Sunoco Blue 1968 and 1969 Z/28 Camaros had a major impact on Z/28 sales. In 1968 Donohue won ten of thirteen Trans-Am races and the championship. Faced with an even stronger assault by Ford,

Donohue managed to win six of twelve races and the second championship for Chevrolet.

But did the production Z/28 Camaro live up to the image created by its outstanding track performance? Did it deliver on Chevrolet's advertising hype —"*Closest thing to a Corvette yet*" and "*Z/28—We've Got a Mean Streak*"?

I thought it came pretty damn close. I got in as much Z/28 seat time as possible during tests that we ran in *Hi-Performance CARS*. To me, the Z/28 represented the best of both worlds—high-revving sports car and potent performance car. You could order quick-ratio manual steering and four-wheel power disc brakes if you were going to track it. The small-block engine responded so well to minor mods. It was a shift-it-yourself, pure street fighter without power-robbing frills. No air conditioning. No automatic transmission. No excuses!

Except for a stone-stock '69 Camaro Z/28, the two other 1968 and 1969 models I drove were dyno-tuned at Motion after being fitted with cross-ram intake with factory cowl induction plenum air cleaner, headers, and traction bars. The white-striped Rallye Green '68 had 4.10 Posi gears and it sprinted to 60 miles per hour in 5.8 seconds and covered the quarter-mile in 13.75 to 13.80s at 105 to 107 miles per hour. In addition to engine modifications, the black-striped '69 Daytona Yellow tester had aftermarket wheels, D80 rear spoiler, and a hood tach. It was equipped with 4.56 Posi gears and traction bars, and ran a best 0 to 60 time of 5.5 seconds. At the track it clocked 106 miles per hour in 13.30 seconds.

A factory stock single four-barrel '69 Camaro Z/28 with 4.10 gears ran consistent 14.30s and 14.40s at trap speeds a tick over 100 miles per hour. While nothing looked as sexy as a 302 engine with cross-ram induction, there was a price to pay. Our modified Z/28s cost in excess of $4,000.

Ford met the Z/28 challenge on the street in mid-1969 with the Boss 302 Mustang, also powered by an underrated 290-horsepower 302. Larry Shinoda, who designed the Camaro's ZL2 hood while at GM, was responsible for Boss 302 branding and graphics when he moved to Ford with Bunkie Knudsen. The Boss 302 Mustangs, like Chevy's Z/28, could not be ordered with automatic transmission or air conditioning. A late entry in 1969, Ford sold just 1,628 Boss 302s.

A brand new Camaro arrived in 1970 and the historic Chevrolet-Ford bragging rights feud continued on racetracks and the street.

1969

Motion's Joel Rosen checks out our 426 Street Hemi Charger 500 before we took it to the track. The plain Jane look was an attempt at streamlining, along with a fastback backlight, but it did little for sales. On stock tires, the best we could do was 104 miles per hour in 14.35 seconds.

CHAPTER ELEVEN

WiLD in the Streets

The New Year brought race cars with license plates, winged warriors with NASCAR cred, and maximum muscle to dealers.

Choosing the right car was a daunting task. So we published the first road test guide to everything hot: *SUPERCARS ANNUAL '69.*

Produced by Joe Oldham and Fred Mackerodt, *SUPERCARS ANNUAL '69* contained twenty-nine road tests of supercars, pony cars, luxury supercars, and the "Don't Fits." It was the first publication devoted exclusively to evaluations of new, high-performance cars.

Choosing the recipient of our annual "Top Performance Car of the Year" award proved to be difficult and so we changed it to "Top Performance Manufacturer of the Year." Based on Ford's overwhelming array of performance cars and its commitment to racing, I presented our 1969 award to Ford Division General Manager John Naughton. "The Division deserves the award for its attitudes toward, and achievements

in, the high-performance field. In addition, for its great new engines, drag racing options, specialty cars, and continued support of racing."

For 1969, Ford unleashed a torrent of powerful pony cars, supercars, and unique models created for NASCAR. Mustangs were restyled and lengthened 4 inches. The SportsRoof Mach I could be ordered with the beefy 428/335 Super Cobra Jet engine, breathing through a shaker hood scoop. A new Drag Pack option included an oil cooler and a 9-inch rear with 3.91 Traction-Lok or 4.30 Detroit Locker gears. Later, the SCJ was rated at 360 horsepower.

When Bunkie Knudsen left GM and joined Ford as president in early 1968, he lost little time in demonstrating his passion for racing. He fast-tracked the Boss 302 and Boss 429 Mustang programs for 1969½ launches. With exterior graphics designed by ex-GM stylist Larry Shinoda, the Boss 302, like the Z/28 Camaro, was not available with AC or automatic transmission. With billboard graphics, rear wing, backlight louvers, huge front spoiler, and suspension designed by Ford engineers working at Kar-Kraft, it was a formidable Z/28 competitor.

Under the Boss 302's hood rested a new 302-inch small-block with four-bolt mains and forged steel rods and crank, underrated at 290 horsepower at 5,800 rpm. It provided a showcase for new Cleveland canted-valve, big-port heads, and high-rise aluminum intake with a manually choked 780-cfm Holley. A factory-installed rev-limiter, set at 6,150 rpm, kept the solid-lifter engine from self-destructing due to over-revving. A well-tuned Boss 302 Mustang with 3.91 Traction-Lok gears ran 95 to 98 miles per hour in the low-mid-fourteens, with 0 to 60 times in the low-sevens.

If he wanted to beat Mopar Hemis on superspeedways, Knudsen knew that Ford needed a new engine for its wind-cheating Torino Talladega and Cyclone Spoiler. And, in order to get it homologated for NASCAR, the engine had to be available in a production car. Enter the Boss 429, with

TOP: One of the 3,675 Indy 500 Camaro Pace Car replicas ended up at Automobile Barretta in Munich, Germany. Photographed by the author at Circuit Zolder in Belgium on the grid to pace an SCCI Corvette race.

ABOVE LEFT: Ford's response to the popular Road Runner was the fastback Torino Cobra, a $3,200 supercar that came with standard 428/335 Cobra Jet power and four-speed.

ABOVE RIGHT: The first road-test guide to the hottest muscle cars on the market was published by *Hi-Performance CARS* magazine in 1969. It was also the first newsstand magazine devoted exclusively to pony cars and supercars.

a unique 385-Series "dry deck" block, oversize aluminum heads with staggered valves, and crescent-shaped, Hemi combustion chambers. It was a pure racing engine designed and built by Ford and made available to the public in a Boss 429 Mustang.

Knowing that there was no business case for building Boss 429 Mustangs and that Ford would lose money on every one, Knudsen nevertheless pushed it through. The Boss 429 engine was homologated for NASCAR and David Pearson drove his H-M Torino to eleven wins and the NASCAR championship. Richard Petty won ten races in his Boss 429 Torino, and finished second to Pearson.

Boss 429 Mustangs couldn't be built on an assembly line, so SportRoof Mustangs were converted at Kar-Kraft. The first Boss 429 Mustang, Job #1, was completed on January 15, 1969, at Kar-Kraft's Brighton, Michigan, facility under the watchful eyes of Roy Lunn, godfather of Ford's GT40. In order to market the Boss 429, its engine was detuned using a small carburetor, mild cam, and restrictive exhausts for a 375-horsepower rating at 5,200 rpm. Torque was a ground-pounding 450 lb-ft at 3,400 rpm. All Boss 429 Mustangs were equipped with manual, driver-controlled Ram-Air induction.

Joe Oldham tested the fifth of 857 Boss 429s built, for the September 1969 issue of *Hi-Performance CARS*. Factory test cars were not available outside of Dearborn, so Oldham borrowed one with an MSRP of $4,937.51 from Berry Ford, Paramus, New Jersey. Berry techs re-jetted the Holley, re-curved the distributor, and added traction bars.

Even though Oldham was able to run a best time of 107.50 miles per hour in 13.34 seconds and 0 to 60 in 6.6 seconds, he expected more from this 429-inch Mustang. Without any tuning or traction bars, Boss 429 Mustangs ran 14.10s at around 103 miles per hour.

Chevrolet had the market covered with the Z/28 and SS and RS Camaros with solid-lifter, 396/375 big-blocks. Hot 396s were also available in Chevelles and Novas. Even though Ford's Boss 302 Mustang was a very competitive road racer, the Penske/Donohue Z/28 Camaro nailed down its second consecutive Trans-Am Championship.

Bright colors, a wing, and unique trim set the GTO Judge off from basic GTOs. Powertrains were shared, including the updated Ram Air IV rated at 366 horsepower. Jim Wangers championed the Judge concept.

Chevrolet had a very effective backdoor approach to ensuring its performance image. The process was called COPO (Central Office Production Order) and it allowed for the building of non-standard cars. Dating back to the late-1940s, it was initiated to accept low-volume orders from fleet operators, law enforcement agencies, and even taxi companies. A COPO number could cover a special paint color or interior trim, unique-duty suspension, or even a racecar! Some 1969 examples include the following: COPO 9560 ZL1 Camaro, COPO 9561 427 Camaro, and COPO 9562 427 Chevelle. Vince Piggins was a master at working the COPO system and getting senior management to sign off on some of the wildest performance cars of the era.

Chevy dealer and successful road racer Don Yenko worked with Piggins to get a few hundred 427/425 Camaros and Chevelles built. Yenko had a great relationship with Piggins and Duntov and first tested the waters in 1968 by ordering seventy 396/375 Camaros with specific options under COPO 9737, Yenko Sportscar Package. Almost all were re-powered with 427 engines.

In 1969, Yenko dealers sold 198 COPO 427 Camaros and 99 COPO 427 Chevelles, re-badged with SYC trim. Other dealers around the country did the same. Baldwin Chevrolet

A special Dan Gurney road edition of the streamlined Cyclone twin of the Boss 429 Torino Talladega that dominated NASCAR undergoes development at the Dearborn Proving Ground. *Ford Motor Company*

did sell some COPO Camaros. All its Baldwin-Motion 427 and 454 Camaros, Chevelles, and Novas were re-powered and built to order at Motion. COPO cars flew under the radar, and were not supported by advertising, marketing, or PR.

Piggins also proposed building one hundred street versions of a milder ZL1 Camaro under COPO 9567. It didn't get past the Pilot-build stage. Working with R. E. Marshall in the Passenger Car Styling Group, the one-off ZL1 street Camaro was ordered on March 24, 1969. Its MSRP was to be $8,581.60 for four-speed and $8,676.60 for automatic versions. The Tuxedo Black COPO 9567 ZL1 Camaro was shown to the press at Milford Proving Ground in the summer of 1969. It was a dynamite car, but its pricing would have made it a tough sell.

Dodge and Plymouth carried over most of their high-performance models and 340, 383, 440, and 426 Street Hemi engines. For increased durability on drag strips, A33 Track Pack and A34 Super Track Pack options with 9¾-inch Dana Sure-Grip rears were available for four-speed high-performance cars without AC.

The highest-profile Dodges were the low-volume '69½ Charger Daytona and Super Bee. The winged Daytona was the first stocker to be clocked at over 200 miles per hour on superspeedways. It also set Flying Mile records at Bonneville. The Super Bee, with new tri-power 440/390 and 426/425 Street Hemi powertrains and built from the midsize Coronet platform, was Dodge's response to specialty supercars such as the GTO Judge. Like with the streamlined Charger 500 and Charger Daytona, Creative Industries in Detroit also helped manufacture the Super Bee.

Pontiac started the supercar revolution in 1964 and, thanks to John DeLorean, created one of the industry's top performance car engineering-styling-marketing teams. When GTO sales started to slip, DeLorean formed a committee charged with creating GTO and Firebird concepts that would broaden the appeal of Pontiac's enthusiast nameplates. Committee members included Herb Adams, Bill Collins, Ben Harrison, and Jim Wangers, a drag racer and marketing powerhouse from Pontiac's advertising agency. Once the GTO Judge concept was locked in, stylist Jeff Young joined the group to create the Trans-Am. Both the Judge and the Trans-Am boosted Pontiac's presence in the performance car marketplace.

The Judge was a high-impact GTO with a wing and proprietary graphics and trim. The Trans-Am received a

RIGHT: Boss 429 engines were built at Ford's Lima, Ohio, plant and then shipped to Kar-Kraft for Boss 429 Mustang conversions. The Hemi engine had incredible racing potential and Boss 429 Mustangs were built to allow the engine to be homologated for NASCAR. *Ford Motor Company*

BELOW: This unique Torino was built by Holman-Moody-Stroppe for Bobby Unser to drive in the Pike's Peak race. A Boss 429 engine, built by Smokey Yunick, powers it. And it's hooked up to a Ford-developed C-6 drag racing automatic with 4,000-rpm stall speed converter. Unser set the Pike's Peak record in this car and held it for seven years. *Charlie Gray*

similar treatment. Contrary to popular belief, the Trans-Am was not created to homologate a Firebird for SCCA Trans-Am racing. It was Pontiac's upscale answer to the Z/28 Camaro, complete with potent Ram Air 400 power and a great suspension. It evolved from the 1968 PFST (Pontiac Firebird Sprint Turismo) Firebird Concept, championed by suspension engineer Bill Collins. It was powered by a Ram Air 400 and previewed the new Trans-Am's suspension.

To ensure Pontiac's appeal, the 1968$\frac{1}{2}$ Ram Air engine was updated and marketed as the new Ram Air IV option. Round exhaust-port heads increased breathing and 1.65 rocker arms allowed .520-inch cam lift. Horsepower remained the same: 366 at 5,400 rpm.

While Pontiac and Jim Wangers were busy hyping the GTO Judge, Lansing's Dr. Frankenstein–like *Dr. Oldsmobile* was the front man for its 1969 W-Machines, the 400/360 W-30 4-4-2 and the 350/325 W-31 Cutlass. They were essentially carryover cars. Oldsmobile continued building the cold-air induction 455-inch Hurst-Olds, rated at 380 horsepower.

We took delivery of a prepared winged H/O with 3.91 gears from Oldsmobile Engineering, and Joe Oldham, assistant editor Ephraim "Wolf" Schwartz, and I headed down to Cecil County Drag-O-Way in Maryland for some fun and games. Track owner Al Procopio was a friend and hosted our annual races. With Schwartz running the "tree," Oldham and I had our way with the automatic H/O. Best times of the day were impressive—0 to 60 miles per hour in 6.1 seconds and 101 miles per hour in the 13.90s.

Buick continued to market outstanding performance cars, but unlike its corporate siblings, without much fanfare. It didn't have a Jim Wangers or a *Dr. Oldsmobile*, but the manufacturer did have great engine engineers such as Dennis Manners and powerful Stage I and II engines. Stage I GS 400 Skylarks were advertised at 360 horsepower with

It didn't get much better than this for me at a press event: Riding with Zora Duntov in his '68 Corvette L88 convertible powered by a ZL1 engine and driving the one-off 350/360 Nova prototyped for the '70 Yenko Deuce. Zora's 'Vette weighed 2,900 pounds, ran the quarter in 12.10s at over 115 miles per hour, and sprinted to 60 miles per hour in the low 4s. Priceless!

The small line at the 1970 Chevy press preview at Milford Proving Ground waiting to drive the one-off ZL1-powered COPO 9567 street Camaro. Journalists who were there to drive 1970 models paid little attention to the "old" '69 Camaro. They did not know how unique this car was. It was the pilot car for a proposed 100-car build that never happened.

fresh air induction, available with four-speed or automatic. We tested one with automatic and 3.91 gears prepared by Buick Engineering in Detroit for the July 1969 issue, Stage I GS400: The Adult Supercar. "We collected a box full of time slips, with ets ranging from 15.00 to 14.80. Top end speeds averaged between 100 and 103 mph," we wrote.

The 1969 Stage II package was strictly for drag racing and available only as a dealer-installed option. Major components included a special high-lift cam, 11:1 TRW forged pistons, either a Rochester Quadrajet or 850 Holley, Mickey Thompson headers, and 4.78 gears. Most Stage II packages ended up in dealer-sponsored drag cars.

Every carmaker was vying for bragging rights on the road and track. Some more than others, but all had some skin in the game. Ford was the dominant force in racing, claiming a Daytona 500 win and NASCAR championship, an Indy 500 win, a fourth consecutive GT40 win at Le Mans, and 295 land-speed records at Bonneville. The winds of change were blowing, and future performance car and racing budgets were in jeopardy.

ZL1: ZORA'S LIGHT ONE

Before there was a COPO ZL1 Camaro and a RPO ZL1 Corvette in 1969, Zora Duntov's all-aluminum Mark IV program had already generated lightweight engines for Can-Am racing.

It all started with alloy 427 engines with Gen I L88 heads, tested by Jim Hall in his Chaparrel 2G. To make these, two aluminum Mark IV blocks were cast from heat-treated Reynolds 356 and 390 alloys. Before the ZL1 engine was available internally, aluminum Mark IV blocks cast from Reynolds 390 aluminum and open-chamber heads were available to Can-Am teams. Depending on bore and stroke combinations, Can-Am blocks could displace 430, 465, 494, or 509 cubic inches.

Chevrolet-powered cars dominated Can-Am racing. From 1968 through 1971, Bruce McLaren and Denny Hulme drove a variety of McLaren M8s powered by injected aluminum big-blocks to championship honors. Porsche 917s briefly interrupted Chevrolet's dominance of the series in 1972 and 1973.

Although Duntov championed aluminum heads and lightweight engines for the Corvette, the first production use of the ZL1 was in the 1969 COPO 9560 Camaro. Credit for the ZL1 Camaro goes to Vince Piggins, working with dealer Fred Gibb and drag racer Dick Harrell. They were looking to build a Camaro for NHRA Super/Stock to beat Mopar Hemis. Gibb agreed to order fifty, paving the way for COPO status. The COPO category was designed so that lots of fifty, one hundred, or more cars could be special built for specific applications.

Gibb ordered fifty, and other dealers chimed in with nineteen additional orders, which brought the total to sixty-nine. Some were built as four-speeds and some with automatic transmissions. At the time, dealers thought that Chevrolet was absorbing much of the development costs associated with the ZL1 Camaro. They assumed the option price was under $500. That didn't happen. The first ones were finished in mid-December in 1968. But strangely, the RPO ZL1 Corvette had midyear 1969 availability.

Because of price, ZL1 Camaros did not fly off the lot. Gibb tried, to no avail, to get Chevrolet to reduce the invoice price. The sixty-fifth ZL1 Camaro, Vin No. 643779, had an MSRP of $7,356.15. It was outrageously expensive, since a base Camaro started at $2,727. A ZL1 Corvette with some options was an almost $11,000 car. For street and occasional racing use, a 396/375 Camaro or 427/435 Corvette made much more sense.

The actual performance of ZL1 Camaros ran the gamut from mid-fourteens to low-thirteens, with trap speeds ranging from 100 to over 130 miles per hour. Magazine road tests were of tuned stock ZL1s and prepared cars with big slicks. Production stock ZL1s were not particularly great street performers because they had restrictive single exhaust systems, smog tuning, and tires that easily went up in smoke at the slightest provocation.

This is the third ZL1 Camaro race car built and it was shipped to Berger Chevrolet. The Daytona Yellow ZL1 with M22 four-speed was photographed in 1969 for *Hi-Performance CARS*. Only two Daytona Yellow ZL1s were built.

For decades, Chevrolet has supported its original ZL1 Corvette production/sale number: two. As you might expect, two examples have been showcased in enthusiast print and online magazines for years. Talking with Ken Kayser, a retired GM engineer who started his career at the Tonawanda plant in 1968 and in 1991 became Mark IV Business Unit manager, revealed that, most likely, more than two were built.

"We produced one hundred eighty-four complete ZL1 engines, hand-built in what Duntov used to call 'surgically clean' rooms. The 427 ZL1 engines had aluminum blocks; open-chamber, big-valve heads; and open plenum intake manifolds, cast by the Winters Foundry in Detroit," he said. "A total of sixty-nine were shipped for Camaros and seven shipped to St. Louis for Corvette installations. The balance was kept in inventory. Two were installed in 1969 Corvettes and the balance temporarily quarantined. Those five engines were not returned to Tonawanda."

Zora Duntov's "Lightweight One" remains an important part of Chevrolet's performance and racing heritage.

TOP LEFT: Chevrolet Engineering built a prototype ZL1 display engine with Corvette air cleaner and headers for the *Hot Rod* December 1968 cover shoot. *General Motors*

TOP RIGHT: COPO 9567 had a milder 11:1 compression ZL1 supplied by Tonawanda. Here, oil is being checked after some full-throttle runs at the proving ground. The Camaro was originally built with 396/375 power.

BOTTOM: The rarest of all ZL1 Camaros, pilot-build Tuxedo Black COPO 9567 at the Milford Proving Ground for the long-lead press preview. Proposed as a 100-car build as the ultimate street Camaro by Vince Piggins, it sported ZL1 badging, an oversize front spoiler, and hood pins. It was not approved for production.

CHARGER DAYTONA:
IT'S ALL ABOUT THE AERO

The only reason Dodge built the Charger Daytona was to be more competitive in stock car racing. It had little to do with competing with Pontiac's GTO Judge and Buick's GSX or dominating the top tier of the supercar marketplace. It was, however, the first 200-mile-per-hour supercar.

Chrysler engineers, led by Special Vehicles Manager Bob Rodger, approached the Daytona project with a laser focus and shared the power of a singular vision: to cheat the wind. They knew that aerodynamic styling could improve a race car's performance, stability, fuel consumption, and safety. The team included Special Vehicle Engineer George Wallace, Race Car Aerodynamicist Gary Romberg, and Chelsea Proving Ground High-Performance Supervisor Bill McNulty. They created the Charger Daytona that set 200-plus mile-per-hour speed records at Bonneville and Talladega, and never failed to attract a crowd on the street. It was the polar opposite of a stealth supercar.

Dodge wanted to build 500 or more Daytonas to satisfy NASCAR. The manufacturer cut it close with a total of 503, all but seventy powered by single-four-barrel 440/375 Wedge engines. Those seventy were fitted with 426/425 Street Hemis. A Daytona delivered similar road and drag strip performance as a Charger R/T. However, on superspeedways and the Bonneville Salt Flats in 1969 and 1970, race-prepped Daytonas excelled and set track and land-speed records. That's where aerodynamics made the difference.

Chrysler was not structured to produce low-volume specialty cars. It contracted with Creative Industries in Detroit to handle conversions and final assembly of '69½ Daytonas. A supplier to the industry since the 1950s, Creative Industries had previously converted 392 stock Dodge Chargers into streamlined fastback Charger 500s.

Bobby Isaac's K&K Insurance Special on the high-banked Chrysler test track. Note the unique wing, front nose, three hood pins, and more streamlined air extractor scoops. Isaac set more than twenty land-speed records at Bonneville, including Flying Mile at 216.946 miles per hour.

TOP: No passerby could resist doing a double take, including this dude who appeared to be more interested in checking his do!

BOTTOM: It took me a while to get used to the giant wing that followed me everywhere I drove. Driving an M-plated preproduction Daytona on the street was a major thrill and I never crossed paths with another one.

I made a number of trips to Chrysler's Chelsea Proving Ground in 1969, where I drove prototype Daytonas and witnessed high-speed testing of both street and NASCAR variants. The track-tested prototypes and production versions had only subtle differences. One red-trimmed white prototype had three NASCAR hood pins instead of two and an obvious lack of front fender air extraction scoops. At the test track, some had seen NASCAR Daytonas driven by Bobby Isaac and Buddy Baker. Baker clocked 235 miles per hour at Chelsea in a NASCAR mule. At a later date and in the same car, Charlie Glotzbach hit 240.

I rode shotgun with Bob Rodger in a white prototype Daytona, cruising at 100 to 120 miles per hour. It was rock steady. Obviously the aero styling and monster rear wing were working, and I let him know. "That's how it's supposed to be," remarked Chrysler's head of special vehicles. "The front end design pierces the air lower and lets less air get underneath the car. The less air you have passing under the car, the better the performance and stability. At speeds of seventy miles per hour and higher, aerodynamics is the most important single influence on performance. It affects a car's speed, acceleration, handling characteristics, and even fuel economy. The combination of an adjustable rear wing and frontal streamlining is responsible for an up to a 15-percent decrease in fuel consumption."

Rodger encouraged me to drive a Daytona on New York's mean streets and experience real-world conditions. "There's a Pilot-build, black-trimmed Hemi Orange Daytona with a 440 engine with your name on it here at Chelsea," he said. "We can ship it to Moon Mullins at the Dodge News Bureau in Manhattan and you can have it for a couple of weeks." I just nodded because I couldn't get YES out quickly enough!

I had a fantastic two-week adventure with the Daytona. Since I didn't expect its performance to differ much from that of a similarly equipped Charger, I never took it to the track. Its ability to attract people, when parked, and turn heads, while on the road, exceeded all possible expectations. Since very few were at dealerships and even fewer on public roads, it felt like I was running a Dodge Focus Group when I parked it.

At legal speeds, the aerodynamics and big wing were little more than window dressing. Parking was a major problem because you couldn't really see where the unprotected bumperless front end started. To get feedback from enthusiasts as well as the general public, I parked it at a high-traffic speed shop and in front of Nathan's hot dog heaven in Oceanside, New York, on a Saturday afternoon. The responses were almost evenly divided between love and hate. Here are some of the comments that appeared in "Dodge's Flying Machine," an article in the November 1969 issue of *Hi-Performance CARS*:

"If Dodge tries to sell that thing, they'll be laughed
  out of business."
"Hey Batman, does it fly?"
"They gotta be kidding. Who would buy such an
  ugly boat with a clothes dryer on the back?"
"Wow. It's the grooviest—like a beautiful trip. I
  gotta get one."
"Boss, man. You really know where it's at!"

Dodge's aerodynamic Charger Daytona turned out to be an incredibly successful race car, as well as an iconic road warrior. Bobby Allison, Buddy Baker, and Bobby Isaac were key players in Dodge's NASCAR effort that paid off with approximately twenty Grand National wins in 1969. In September, Bobby Isaac drove the K&K Insurance Hemi Daytona to more than twenty land-speed records at the Bonneville Salt Flats, including 216.946 miles per hour in the Flying Mile. Mickey Thompson held the previous record in this class, 188.173 miles per hour.

Dodge teams were still racing Daytonas in NASCAR in 1970, and on March 24, Buddy Baker set the official world closed course and lap records—200.447 miles per hour—in his Daytona race car at Talladega. At one point Baker was clocked at over 220 miles per hour. After the win, NASCAR's Bill France comment to Baker was: "Congratulations, Buddy, for being the fastest man on any speedway."

Did setting records and winning on Sunday sell Charger Daytonas on Monday? Not exactly. Dealers placed more

When I first saw a Charger Daytona at a press event at Chelsea, I made a lot of disparaging comments about its exaggerated wing. When I arrived home after a week testing cars, there was this photo from Dodge PR waiting for me. That's PR guy Tony Weis (right) and me holding my aluminum camera case. It hung in my office for years.

I was walking around the engineering buildings at Chelsea and shot this early iteration of Bobby's Isaac's No. 71 NASCAR Daytona driving back from the test track. Note the flat-top front fenders and stock door trim.

than two thousand orders for Daytonas before the first car was built. They saw it as being more than just another hot car. To them, it represented an inexpensive marketing tool for increasing showroom traffic. Shoppers did not exactly beat a path to Dodge dealers to buy over-the-top Daytonas. Dealers displaying new Daytonas did, however, report increased performance car sales.

The Charger Daytona looked fast on the street and was fast where it counted—on super speedways and the Bonneville Salt Flats.

RAM-AIR V GTO:
THE MYTH & THE MAGIC

Like Chevrolet's ZL1 Corvette and Buick's Stage II Gran Sports, Pontiac's Tunnel Port Ram Air V has been the subject of urban legends for decades.

According to Tom Nell, a special projects engineer at Pontiac in 1971, "Pontiac's Ram Air V or Mark V was the first Pontiac engine since the 1963 Super-Duty 421 to be developed around the concept of performance and durability, outside the realm of normal usage."

Many of the same high-performance engineers responsible for the 1969½ Ram Air IV 400 were also involved in the design and development of the Ram Air V. They took a page from Ford's 427 drag and NASCAR playbook, resulting in all-new maximum flow Tunnel-Port heads with huge round intake ports. The Ram Air V lineup included 303-, 366-, and 400-inch iterations for SCCA, NASCAR, and street and drag racing, respectively. At the time, there was also talk about a possible 428 version. But unlike the Ram Air IV, the Ram Air V never became a regular production option.

I expressed an interest in testing a '69½ GTO after learning that Jim Wangers had convinced Pontiac to install a pre-production 366-horsepower Ram Air IV engine in a new GTO. This engine had new heads, 1.65:1 rocker arms, aluminum intake manifold, and high-lift cam. Jim let me know that Pontiac was also supplying a prototype Ram Air V 400 engine for comparison testing. The good news got even better.

The '69½ GTO was delivered to Royal Pontiac, where Milt Schornack and Dave Warren converted it to Bobcat specs, and added headers and a Schiefer clutch. After some local racing, the GTO was shipped to Florida for testing at Miami Dragway. With open headers and 8.50x14 cheater slicks, it ran a best time of 109.52 miles per hour in 12.62 seconds. With closed pipes and street tires, it ran 108.42 miles per hour in 13.42 seconds. Impressive indeed!

Pontiac's 400-inch Ram Air V engine featured a reinforced four-bolt main block, forged steel crank and rods, forged 10.75 pistons, solid-lifter cam, big-valve heads, aluminum intake manifold with a Holley 800-cfm four-barrel, and tuned cast-iron exhaust manifolds. Pontiac planned on rating the engine at 375 horsepower, even though dyno tests were closer to 500.

After testing the Ram Air IV GTO, the Royal crew swapped engines. After a few burnouts and warmup passes, it was obvious that the RA V produced considerably more horsepower, as it easily overwhelmed the slicks. On its first full-throttle run, driver John Kosmala backed off after hearing a knocking sound. The engine was a well-worn prototype with many hours of dyno testing under load and it experienced a bearing failure. That was the end of testing, but not the end of the Ram Air V GTO. In 1970, the rebuilt original RA V engine was re-installed by Royal and the GTO clocked consistent 11.70s at Detroit Dragway.

The Ram Air V program was put on the back burner, and

TOP: Pontiac did not build any GTOs with Ram Air V Tunnel-Port engines. But this Crystal Turquoise '69 GTO, built with a Ram Air IV 400 in October 1968, was sanctioned by Pontiac to receive a Ram Air V engine at Royal Pontiac. It survives complete with original Ram Air V engine and *Hi-Performance CARS* signage, and is owned by Rita and Bill Schultz.

RIGHT: One of the warm-up runs of the Ram Air V GTO at Miami Dragway. The tunnel port motor easily overwhelmed the 9-inch slicks. After tests, Jim Wangers purchased it. *Bill Schultz Collection*

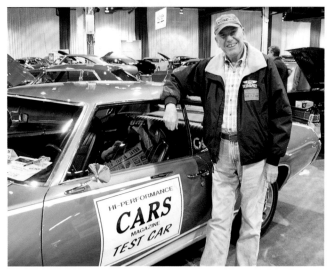

TOP: Milt Schornack makes final adjustments before John Kosmala does a full-throttle run. Bearing failure ended this test session. In 1970, this GTO with rebuilt Ram Air V engine ran consistent 11:70s at Detroit Dragway. *Bill Schultz Collection*

BOTTOM: Author Marty Schorr is reunited at MCACN 2010 with a one-off Ram Air V GTO magazine test car more than forty years after article was published. *Bill Schultz Collection*

well into the 1970s, complete engines and components were still available. It has been estimated that a couple of dozen RA V 303 engines and a considerably larger number of 400s were assembled. While some Pontiac dealers did install RA V engines in new GTOs and Firebirds, there are no records of assembly line installations. Some are still running today in sedan racing and on drag strips. The magic has survived.

454 CAMARO:
RAREST OF THE RARE

Built at the end of November 1969 and months past the typical model year cutoff, this Baldwin-Motion Camaro was one of just a few fitted with 454 engines. And, it may be the only one built for new car delivery with an LS7.

In late October 1969, Ray Dotterer drove from Lamar, Pennsylvania, to Baldwin, New York, to meet Joel Rosen at Motion Performance. The only thing on his mind was ordering *the* hottest Gen I Baldwin-Motion Camaro. He knew it might be difficult to get an order placed for a 1969 model so late in the year. Chevrolet had continued building Gen I Camaros past the typical model year cutoff in anticipation of a late-arriving, all-new Camaro. He wasn't interested in waiting for a 1970 model.

He optioned-out his dream '69 Camaro SS, Daytona Yellow with black stripes and Phase III 427 powertrain, only to be told by Rosen that Motion was no longer building 427 Camaros. While Dotterer was still in shock, Rosen added, "If you want the hottest Baldwin-Motion Camaro, let's change that order to 454 instead of 427." Before the ink had dried, he gave Rosen a $2,500 deposit check.

Once spy photos and details on the '70 Camaro leaked out, Baldwin Chevrolet placed very few orders for '69 Camaros. Ray Dotterer's 396/375 Camaro was built at the Norwood, Ohio, assembly plant at the end of production in late November 1969. Rosen's plan was to replace the 396 with a 454 LS7, rated at 460 horsepower and listed as optional on new '70 Corvettes. He ordered a replacement service engine through Baldwin Chevrolet. The option was cancelled before any LS7 Corvettes were built.

Factory-rated at 460 horsepower when listed on early Corvette order forms, the ultra-high-compression LS7 actually put out in excess of 525 horsepower and close to 600 lb-ft of torque. The open-chamber aluminum heads with hi-rise aluminum intake manifold were cast at the Winters Foundry, in Canton, Ohio, a GM supplier of high-performance alloy engine components. Before the LS7 was installed in Dotterer's Camaro, its camshaft was swapped for a Phase III replacement. The engine was mated to an M-22 rock crusher four-speed, sending power to a 4.88 Posi twelve-bolt rear.

ABOVE: Baldwin-Motion big-block Camaros are rare collectibles; this one is the most potent and rarest of all B-M Gen I Camaros. An LS7 454 with open chamber aluminum heads powers it. Its MSRP was $6,193.90. *Legendary Motorcar Collection*

BELOW LEFT: Even though the 454-inch LS7 engine was never installed in '70 Corvettes, a replacement engine was used by Joel Rosen for just a couple of late-production Baldwin-Motion '69 Camaros. Gen II aluminum L88 heads and a 850 Holley with signature Fly-Eye air cleaner top off the 454. *Legendary Motorcar Collection*

BELOW RIGHT: A simple Chevy 454 engine ID badging is worked into the hockey stick striping, letting anyone pulling up next to it at a traffic light know: "Don't mess with me!" *Legendary Motorcar Collection*

To get that stealth look, Rosen kept exterior mods to a minimum, and used rally wheels instead of mags. He even kept the hockey stick black stripe. The spoiler is a factory D80 used on Z/28s. It's sound and fury has to be experienced to be believed. *Legendary Motorcar Collection*

The suspension features signature Baldwin-Motion shocks and traction bars.

Ray Dotterer did buy the hottest Camaro available, but he also got one of the rarest. It's estimated that Baldwin-Motion built just two or three Gen I 454 Camaros and this could be the only one powered by an LS7. He couldn't have chosen a hotter ride for trolling for trouble. That's why Baldwin Chevrolet's Dave Bean wrote on the LS7 Camaro's invoice, "This is a race car—no warranty on power train."

OLDSMOBILE ROCKET SCIENCE

Instead of typically talking about new models at a press conference for the 1969 Detroit Auto Show, John Beltz, Oldsmobile general manager, spoke about the latest in maximum efficiency and performance engines. These lightweight multicarb, four-cam, and even Hemi engines were being developed for future production engine research.

Between 1969 and 1970, Oldsmobile Engineering was responsible for creating powerful ultra-efficient 350- to 455-cubic-inch V-8 engines rated up to 700 horsepower. Some were naturally aspirated and fitted with single Quadrajet four-barrel or Weber carburetors; others were fuel-injected and turbocharged. Most had aluminum blocks and heads. It was hard to imagine that these engines were anything other than veiled attempts at building pure racing engines, but they actually were. Oldsmobile engineering used these engines as prototypes for developing lighter, more fuel-efficient and "cleaner" production engines.

The mildest of the group was an all-aluminum 350 small-block, displacing 389 cubic inches and utilizing dual-throat Weber 48IDA carburetors. The alloy 389-inch engine ended up in a Cutlass that was driven to the C/Production record at the Bonneville Salt Flats in 1968. A friend and editor at *Hot Rod*, Lee Kelley, drove a factory-supplied Cutlass 169.133 miles per hour to set the record. Apparently during impound, SCTA officials never detected that the engine was an all-aluminum prototype.

The engine in Lee Kelley's record-setter was a one-off, rated at close to 500 horsepower and built in Lansing by Dave Maurer, a special projects engineer. At Bonneville, the Cutlass was crewed by Maurer along with racing legends Ak Miller, Jack Lufkin, and Ed Iskenderian.

One of the most interesting engines was the 455-inch W-43 Hemi. There were cast-iron and aluminum iterations with four-valve, Hemi chamber heads. The W-43 engine could be easily converted to chain- or gear-driven overhead camshafts. Fitted with a single Quadrajet, it produced in excess of 500 horsepower at 6,500 rpm. The aluminum version weighed 75 pounds less than the current production 455 engine. This engine found its way into mule cars tested at the Milford Proving Ground.

The same team responsible for the W-43 Hemi also produced the OW-43, a racing-only, four-cam 455 tested with four Weber carburetors and fuel injection with 3-inch ram stacks. The OW-43 was developed at the same time Chevrolet Engineering was working on the ZL1 for Corvette and Camaro applications and Can-Am racing. The OW-43 was tested in a Can-Am race car but never used in competition.

Based on the same bore-stroke configuration of a production 455, the OW-43 had heads and block with steel

TOP: The four-cam OW-43 engine was primarily a racing concept, built with aluminum block and heads and tested with both Weber carburetion and Lucas direct-port fuel injection. The fuel-injected iteration produced the most power: 700 horsepower at 6,800 rpm. *General Motors*

BOTTOM LEFT: The W-43 Hemi with a cast-iron four-bolt-main block was a streetable engine and tested in a 4-4-2. There was also a four-cam version done for competition. The four cams were driven through a train of ten-spur gears in a cast-aluminum housing bolted to the front of the block. *General Motors*

BOTTOM RIGHT: Oldsmobile supplied some 455-inch fuel-injected and turbocharged engines for Can-Am racing in the early years. This is the 1970 aluminum head and block version with injection and a pair of turbos. Output was around 700 horsepower. *General Motors*

cylinder liners cast from Reynolds 356-T-6 heat-treated aluminum. With a redline of just under 8,500 rpm, it produced 600 horsepower at 6,000 rpm and 700 horsepower at 6,800 rpm. The DOHC prototype had Forged-True 12.20:1 pistons, Carillo billet steel rods, and a forged steel crank. It weighed 50 pounds less than a production 455.

Oldsmobile engines displacing 389 to 455 cubic inches had powered Can-Am Series cars, such as the Bob McKee–built *Cro-Sal* racers in 1967. The highest output Can-Am Olds was an all-aluminum, single-cam 455 with injection and twin turbochargers. It generated 659 horsepower at 6,250 rpm and 554 lb-ft of torque at 6,200 rpm.

Decades later, lightweight, fuel-efficient, and high-output OHC engines found their way into production Oldsmobiles. Thanks, John Beltz!

STING LIKE A [SUPER] BEE

Dodge got its supercar act together with an aggressive, midyear Super Bee with a venomous sting.

Dodge's highest-profile enthusiast offerings were the low-volume '69½ Charger Daytona and Super Bee. The winged Daytona was the first stocker to clock over 200 miles per hour on superspeedways and set Flying Mile records at Bonneville.

Built off the midsize Coronet platform, the Super Bee was packaged for testosterone-infused enthusiasts. Like with the streamlined Charger 500 and Charger Daytona, Detroit's Creative Industries handled final assembly of Dodge's in-your-face Super Bee. With its liftoff, scooped fiberglass hood, tri-power 440 Wedge, beefy Dana 60 rear end, status graphics, taut suspension, and "electric" colors, the Super Bee was not just another poseur.

On February 19, Creative received the first one hundred 383 Coronets for Code A12 conversions to 440/390 Super Bees. Our *Hi-Performance CARS* tester was from the first conversions. Later, 440 engines were installed at the Chrysler assembly plant. There was also a Code A12 Road Runner,

TOP: There's no mistaking a Bahama Yellow '69½ Super Bee with matte-black scooped hood and black graphics for any other car, but it did lack the latest Coke-bottle styling of the period. Our tester had a base price of $3,138 and an MSRP of $4,234. It was as close as any carmaker came to offering a Day Two supercar on Day One.

BOTTOM: This interior was super functional with a three-spoke wheel and basic instrumentation with clock vying for space with tach. The T-handle Hurst shifter was part of the four-speed package. The bench seat kept costs down.

Stock tires leave a lot to be desired for max traction, although rear suspension mods work well on the street. Coming off the line without setting off a smokescreen takes some restraint.

powered by the same engine and fitted with a matte-black finish, lift-off fiberglass hood.

We tested a '69½ Super Bee in the September 1969 issue of *HPC*. Its powerplant was the new 10.5:1 compression 440 Six-Pack engine rated at 390 horsepower at 4,700 rpm and 490 lb-ft of torque at 3,200 rpm. A stout performance engine, it boasted forged pistons and rods, a high-lift 276/292-degree-duration cam with 54 degrees overlap, tuned cast-iron exhaust manifolds, and low restriction duals. Air conditioning, power front disc brakes, and cruise control were not available.

Early A12 conversion engines utilized Edelbrock aluminum tri-power manifolds engineered and designed by Chrysler. Once the 440/390 became an RPO on other models, Chrysler cast the six-barrel manifolds. When the vacuum-activated end carbs opened, total airflow for the three Holley two-barrels was an impressive 1,000 cfm.

Totally stock with a 3.55 Sure-Grip Dana 60 rear, our four-speed Super Bee recorded average 0 to 60 times of 6.6 seconds and track times of 99 to 100 miles per hour in the 14.60s to 14.80s. Our best time was 100 miles per hour in 14.65 seconds, shifting at approximately 5,500 rpm.

Chrysler engineers paid a lot of attention to the Super Bee's handling and traction qualities. Front 0.92-inch torsion bars were used, as well as a 0.94-inch sway bar. Left-side rear springs received five leafs, plus two half leafs, and the right-side springs had six leafs. Handling was excellent, but its manual drum brakes left a lot to be desired.

The scooped fiberglass hood looked fantastic, but also presented problems. There was a security issue since only four hood pins held it in place. Checking the oil became a two-person job, and the scoop provided easy entry for water when driving in the rain. Unlike fiberglass Corvettes with ignition shielding to ward off radio interference, the Super Bee lacked protective shielding. As a result, its exhaust sounded much better than its radio.

Although packing 35 horsepower less than the 426 Street Hemi, the tri-power 440 was a more flexible street engine with incredible torque. It was a lot easier to live with and I found it a better street performance engine. I would have preferred that our tester had a TorqueFlite rather than clunky four-speed. Either way, the Super Bee had the sting Dodge needed to score with serious enthusiasts.

1970

Powered by a Ram-Air 400/366 with four-speed and 3.90 rear, our loaded GTO Judge had an MSRP of $5,000. The 400/366 option cost approximately $100 more than 455/360.

CHAPTER TWELVE

Magnum Force From Motown

The new year ushered in bigger, more powerful engines; new specialty supercars; and a plethora of pony cars. But the future of the performance car phenomenon was not bright.

In many ways, 1970 was the storm before the calm. The war in Southeast Asia continued casting a pall over a much-divided country and thinning the ranks of young enthusiasts. Carmakers' racing budgets were being drastically cut and engineering resources reassigned to prepare for restrictive emissions and safety legislation. And pony car sales had been plummeting and would register new lows at the end of the model year.

Yet Motown launched its most aggressive ever portfolio of power. With the industry working on two to three-year product development cycles, there was no stopping the performance products scheduled to go public. In some cases, such as the new F-body Camaro and Firebird and E-body Challenger and Barracuda, they had been in the works for more than two years. They represented huge tooling expenses and GM and Chrysler's only route to staying competitive in what had been a scalding hot market.

Eagerly awaited, the all-new '70 Camaro and Firebird had been hyped by auto writers because of anticipated platform, engineering, and styling changes. They did not disappoint. But there were production problems. When we evaluated 1970 GM cars in June 1969 at the Milford Proving Ground, the only Camaros and Firebirds were carryover 1969 models. There was little interest in driving "old" cars and a lot of journalists missed the '69 Camaro prototype for a proposed limited-production street ZL1. To make the ZL1 race engine drivable, they modified the open plenum chamber intake manifold by welding in a restrictor plate and re-jetting the carburetor.

While Chevrolet design studios took the lead role in Gen-1 Camaro and Firebird styling, that was not the case with the Gen-II 1970 models. This time around, and before he moved to Chevrolet, Pontiac General Manager John DeLorean

lobbied to have Pontiac studios take the lead. He loved Italian styling—and his $12,000 Maserati Ghibli. And he wasn't shy about letting Pontiac designers know that: "I want the new Firebird to be a $3,000 Ghibli."

Two very talented designers, Hank Haga and Bill Porter, were, respectively, the studio chiefs for Chevrolet and Pontiac. There was a lot of competition and political intrigue over what they would come up with, but the end result was two outstanding pony cars with very different personalities and styling. Both incorporated European-influenced styling cues.

Built on a new 108-inch unibody platform, the long-hood, short-deck Gen-II Camaro and Firebird were longer, wider, and lower than their predecessors. Suspensions were seriously upgraded and ride and handling improved. They made the competition look old. The road-hugging, low-stance fastback Camaro and Firebird had distinctive looks and powertrains in keeping with each division's marketing philosophies.

I interviewed Bill Mitchell, GM Design VP, for a Corvette article, shortly before he retired in 1977. He extolled the virtues of the Gen II F-Car: "It's a designer's design and one of the best and most successful designs of my career." That

Inside the Norwood, Ohio, F-body assembly plant as the first Trans Am was coming down the line. Note the line of Camaros, both built at Norwood and Van Nuys, California, plants. *General Motors*

ABOVE: Chevrolet offered the most powerful GM supercar in 1970. The SS454 Chevelle with 454/450 LS6 engine had few peers. The F41 special suspension with rear sway bar and chassis beefing made the difference. If you opted for ZL2, you got a functional cowl-induction hood.

LEFT: Laying down some tracks at GM Proving Ground when testing a new 455-inch GTO pilot car. This was a very well-prepared factory car that was quicker and faster than it should've been. The new 455/360 pumped out 500 lb-ft of torque at just 2,700 rpm.

was high praise indeed, considering the landmark cars styled on his watch, which included the '49 Caddy, the 1955 through '57 Chevys, the '63 Riviera, and a variety of Corvettes.

Zora Duntov actually had some influence over the Trans Am's dashboard. He had commented to John Shettler, Pontiac Interior Design Studio chief, "the TA is a true 'driver's car' and deserved instrumentation to match." The results were wall-to-wall gauges on an engine-turned, aluminum instrument panel.

Both the new Camaro and Firebird experienced delays in bringing them to market. The reasons behind the delays were multifold. In addition to John DeLorean flexing his muscles,

there were parts delays from Fisher Body and glitches switching from Lordstown to Norwood assembly plants in 1969. The new Corvette was also delayed, primarily because of serious quality problems.

Chevrolet planted a potent 350/360 LT1 engine in the new Z/28. Thanks to a .030-inch bore increase, the new 396/350 and 396/375 big-blocks actually displaced 402 cubic inches. Neither 396/375 nor 350/360 solid-lifter engines were available with AC, but could be ordered with automatic transmissions.

Chevrolet showed us the new Camaro at a special drive program at Ontario Motor Speedway. We drove small- and

ABOVE: Ford's max-image supercar was a hefty 429 CJ and SCJ Torino Cobra, shown here with backlight louvers like those on Boss Mustangs. There was also a rare "stripper" Falcon version, ideally suited for drag racing. *Ford Motor Company*

BELOW LEFT: You could order your Hemi-Cuda or Challenger with the popular N96 shaker hood scoop, which hides the dual Carter quads. Street performance was much improved based on a new hydraulic lifter camshaft and valvetrain. I always thought the underhood billboard "Shaker" label was pretty hokey!

BELOW RIGHT: The heavy 4-4-2 fit into lower stock classes and did quite well. Olds Engineer Dale Smith kept factory-sponsored racers in engines and parts, and had complete specifications for blueprinting a 455-inch engine for NHRA competition.

After Joel Rosen backed our Hemi-Cuda test car off the Clayton dyno and went out on Sunrise Highway, another one passed him! Both guys got on it and I managed to get one shot before Mr. Motion freight-trained the interloper and blew his doors off.

big-block models, but Chevy was really pushing its Z/28. It did impress. The new LT1 was a strong, flexible engine, much better suited for street performance than its 302-inch predecessor. The Z/28 Camaro was the best balanced and most fun to drive, especially on the slalom course.

Pontiac's Firebird came in a variety of flavors, from a base Firebird and luxurious Espirit to high-performance Formula and Trans Am variants. Two excellent 400-cubic-inch engines, L74 Ram Air III rated at 335 horsepower and the range-topping LS1 Ram Air IV at 345 horsepower, could be had with stick or automatic. Out of 3,196 Trans Ams built, just 88 had Ram Air IV engines under their shaker hoods. In addition to power, Pontiac engineers concentrated their efforts on sporty car suspension tuning. The class-leading, head-turning Trans Am had a menacing, purposeful look that said, "Don't Mess With Me." One of the best Trans Am advertising tag lines was "Gauges that gauge, Spoilers that spoil and Scoops that scoop."

Because it was a midyear model and they were preparing 1971 models for media drives, we had limited access to road test cars. Royal Pontiac supplied the new Firebirds we drove, so we knew they would run better than showroom stock models. We drove a 330-horsepower Formula 400 with automatic and 3.07 gears. It clocked mid-six-second 0 to 60 sprints, and covered the quarter-mile in the high-fourteens, low-fifteens at 98 to 99 miles per hour.

The real treat was a new, blue-striped, Polar White Trans Am—one of just twenty-nine that would be built with a 400/345 Ram Air IV engine and four-speed. Gearing was a just-right 3.73. It looked fantastic and handled beautifully, and we almost broke into the 13s, running 14.2s at 101 to 103 miles per hour. Available only in two colors, a new Trans Am could also be ordered in Lucerne Blue with white stripes.

Dodge and Plymouth beat Chevrolet and Pontiac to the marketplace with clean-sheet Challengers and Barracudas. An impressive menu of 318 and 340 small-blocks, three 383 and two 440 big-blocks, and the 426 Street Hemi wowed enthusiasts. Buyers had a choice of close- and wide-ratio four-speeds or excellent TorqueFlite automatic and $8^{3}/_{4}$-inch or $9^{3}/_{4}$-inch Dana Sure-Grip rears. Whatever your appetite for performance, a slick new Challenger and Barracuda coupe or convertible could be tailored to your taste.

Twins under the skin, they were built on new E-body architecture utilizing A- and B-body components. But, there were differences. The Barracuda was built on a 108-inch wheelbase platform, while the Challenger had a 110-inch wheelbase. Both offered the same powertrain choices and very similar performance, although the Challenger was a little more luxurious.

Late in 1969, Joe Oldham and I spent road and track time with a bright red, early-build Hemi-Cuda convertible. With TorqueFlite and 4.10 Sure-Grip gears, it was reasonably quick, fast, and handled well. It had a slight transmission fluid leak and really was not a great car.

Oldham tested it first for *Speed and Supercar*. On its first run at E-Town, the transmission cooler line blew, dumping fluid all over the track. It went back to the dealer that prepped it, Rockville Centre Dodge, and then Joe tried again. The best he could muster was 97 miles per hour in 14.30 seconds—certainly not impressive for a 425-horsepower pony car. And it still leaked transmission fluid!

Back it went to the dealer, where a friend and drag racing tech, Al Kirschenbaum, re-curved the distributor, bumped up timing, re-jetted the carbs, and installed colder plugs. Waking up the Street Hemi worked and, with Al tuning and Joe driving, they recorded a best time of 103 miles per hour in 13.80s.

While quarter-mile times impressed and street performance improved thanks to the new 292/292-degree duration hydraulic-lifter cam with 68 degrees overlap, Oldham was never thrilled with the car. "Our test Barracuda convertible rattled so badly we actually questioned the need

for a convertible in the line," he said. The following year Chrysler announced that it was dropping Barracuda and Challenger convertibles at the end of the model year.

When I picked up the Hemi-Cuda, it still had a small transmission leak. The Hemi engine was quieter and low-end street performance was noticeably better than in the past. But I didn't like it any better than Joe.

While I liked the Barracuda's look, ride, handling, and performance, I was put off by poor quality. Ill-fitting plastic interior panels squeaked whenever you went over irregular road surfaces, negatively impacting the driving experience. I didn't much care for the new steering column either. "Chrysler's new ugly steering column looks like a refugee from a concertina factory," we wrote.

In the May 1970 issue of *Hi-Performance CARS*, we reported on the red Hemi-Cuda convertible. I had it dyno-tuned at Motion before taking it to the track. With stickier-than-stock rear tires and a driver with Funny Car experience, performance was right on the money. "Three trips through the traps netted us the following time slips: 13.40/105.10, 13.45/105.00 and 13.50/103.70," we wrote. "Our best 0 to 60 was 5.6 seconds."

Years later we would learn how rare and valuable that car was. They produced only fourteen Hemi-Cuda convertibles in 1970. One of nine automatics, our test vehicle was the actual first one built and the only red convertible with a red interior. It's currently in a major collection, worth mega millions.

Dodge and Plymouth were also well represented in the specialty supercar market with 383, 440, and 426 Street Hemi–powered Coronet R/T, Super Bee, GTX, and Road Runner. Plymouth filled the void left when Dodge ended production of the "aero" '69½ Charger Daytona. Plymouth's Superbird was a Road Runner with a wing and a nose job. Also produced by Creative

I snapped this shot of the Sox & Martin Pro Stock Hemi-Cuda at the Chrysler Proving Ground. It was powered by a Jake King–built 426 with twin-plug heads and ignition and topped with a Weiand tunnel ram intake with a pair of Holley dominators. Ronnie ran in the mid- to high-nines, and won a number of major national NHRA events.

Boss 429 Mustangs were built at Kar-Kraft and upgraded for 1970 with the addition of a solid-lifter cam and valvetrain. We drove this Boss 429 with 3.91 gears at the Dearborn Proving Ground. With disconnected air pump and tuning, we clocked 109 miles per hour in 12.80 seconds.

Industries, the Daytona-influenced Superbird proved to be a complex build. It required Dodge Coronet front fenders and hood to work with the steel nose cone. The Superbird's tall, raked wing was proprietary. To meet NASCAR requirements, Plymouth built 1,935 of them.

Designed to cheat the wind on superspeedways, Superbirds and carryover Daytona Chargers dominated NASCAR. Pete Hamilton drove his Hemi Superbird to wins at Daytona, Atlanta, and Talladega 500s and, together with Richard Petty, gave Plymouth twenty-one wins. Dodge clinched the manufacturers' title and Bobby Isaac won the drivers' championship.

Drag racing saw a major sea change in 1970. Plymouth's Ronnie Sox and Buddy Martin joined forces with other Super/Stock greats, including "Grumpy" Jenkins, Dave Strickler, and "Dyno Don" Nicholson, to lobby the NHRA for new heads-up competition class rules. This led to the birth of Pro Stock racing. The Sox & Martin Hemi Barracuda, fitted with new twin-plug heads with dual ignition, led all qualifiers at the NHRA Winternationals, the first major event to showcase Pro Stock racing. He lost to Jenkins in the final round.

Sox & Martin won at the Springnationals, followed by wins at the World Finals and the first NHRA Supernationals. Dick Landy's Hemi Challenger won the Summernationals and Herb McCandless won the Indy Nationals in the S&M Hemi Duster. Sox & Martin also raced a Hemi Superbird in C/MP.

General Motors finally dropped its 400-inch engine displacement limit for midsize cars. The Chevelle SS454 championed the assault with an optional 454/450, giving the LS6 Chevelle pavement-pounding power. Few cars, other than Mopar Street Hemis and Buick Stage I Skylarks, could hold their own against the popular Chevelle SS. All three cars, especially when tuned and fitted with headers, were capable of delivering low-to-mid-thirteens at 105- to 107-mile-per-hour terminal speeds.

Pontiac started it all with the GTO in 1964 and was still an image leader, thanks to a winged Judge and 400- and 455-inch engines. The hottest engine option was the 400-inch Ram Air IV, rated at 370 horsepower at 5,500 rpm in the GTO.

We tested two GTOs, a Ram Air 400/366 Judge for the July 1970 issue of *Hi-Performance CARS* and a 455/360 for *SUPERCARS '70½*, both with Hurst-shifted four-speeds and 3.90 rears. Pontiac supplied both GTOs and we suspected that the 455/360 had been massaged. Our best time with the 400/366 Judge was 100 miles per hour in 14.45 seconds and 0 to 60 miles per hour in 6.6 seconds. The 455/360 GTO was a Milford Proving Ground vehicle, and ran 103 miles per hour in 13.90 seconds. It was quicker to 60 miles per hour, taking just 6.1 seconds. I wanted to buy that one.

Oldsmobile, like Buick, offered serious supercars that were also luxurious road warriors. Its suspension packages were spot-on for delivering maximum handling without

a harsh, unpleasant ride. Oldsmobile had a very active revolving backdoor, often manned by engineer Dale Smith, for supplying drag and road racers with what they needed. Smith also distributed blueprinting and tuning specs for running a W30 Olds 4-4-2 in NHRA Stock classes.

I was a big fan of the '69 Hurst-Olds, the only GM midsize coupe that came with a 455-inch engine. For 1970, the biggest, baddest W30 Force-Air 455/370 was an RPO for the 4-4-2. When covering the hottest Olds in *SUPERCAR '70½*, I wrote: "Dr. Oldsmobile has done it again. Not only has he come back on the scene with out-of-sight 'W' machines, but he's knocked Hurst out of the box as well. He's put it to *Shifty George from Valley Forge* by coming out with 455-inch Supercars."

Olds Engineering focused on improving the new W30's breathing. Heads featured 2.07-/1.63-inch valves, actuated by a .475-inch lift, 328-degree duration cam with 108 degrees overlap. A performance-calibrated Quadrajet, on

The Cougar Eliminator could be had with big- and small-block motors, but one of my favorites was the Boss 302. This is not a California emissions model, but we did drive it at OCIR. With the stock engine, 6,150-rpm Autolite shutoff, Hurst-shifted four-speed, and a 4.30 noisy Detroit locker rear, it had too much gear for both road and track. I would have preferred 3.91 Traction-Lok gearing.

TOP: While I was driving 1971 AMC models at MIS in July 1970, I snuck into Roger Penske's garage. I managed to get one shot of Mark Donohue's Trans-Am Javelin before they threw me out. AMC nailed second place in the championship and set the tone for domination in 1971 and 1972.

ABOVE: Sox & Martin accounted for 75 percent of Mopar wins in Pro Stock in the 1970 and 1971 seasons. The team also campaigned this Hemi Superbird, driven by Dave McCandless, in C/MP. It was on the cover of *Hi-Performance CARS* for September 1971.

RIGHT: The fresh air–fed Boss 429 engine was designed for racing and had been extremely successful in both drag and NASCAR. Not so much on the street.

an aluminum intake manifold and sealed to the functionally scooped fiberglass hood, kept the big-block nourished.

The gold 4-4-2 we tested in *SUPERCAR '70½* was from Dale Smith's fleet. A W30 455/370 engine generating 500 lb-ft of torque at 3,600 rpm powered it. It was quick, fast, and, we suspected, not showroom stock. With automatic and 3.91 gears, our best quarter-mile time was 105 miles per hour in 13.70 seconds and quickest 0 to 60 was 6.6 seconds.

For the May 1970 issue of *Hi-Performance CARS*, our team tested a production 4-4-2 with a slightly different drivetrain. Also automatic, it had 3.42 gears and the very cool W27 aluminum differential carrier and cover. It represented an approximate 22-pound weight savings and was a $157.98 option. After learning the cost, our test driver commented: "I'd pocket the $157.98 and go on a 22-pound diet!"

Finished in brilliant yellow with red stripes, our 4-4-2 was noticeably slower than the gold car. Our best times were 98 miles per hour in 14.30 seconds at the track and 7.5 seconds sprinting to 60 miles per hour. With a great Rally Sports suspension, beefy sway bars, and variable-ratio power steering, the 4-4-2 was a great road car.

Ford refreshed Mustang styling as well as its powertrain portfolio. The Mach1 SportsRoof, available with a standard 351 and optional 351/300, 428/335 Cobra, and 428/335 Cobra Jet Ram Air, was the top image model. High-performance 351 engines received canted-valve Cleveland heads. Boss 302 and Boss 429 Mustangs were carried over and the Boss 429 updated with a solid-lifter valvetrain. Mustangs with 428 engines could be ordered with optional Drag Packs with either 3.91 Traction-Lok gears or 4.30 Detroit Locker gears. Drag Pack engines were also equipped with engine oil coolers and beefed lower end components.

The big news was a new SportsRoof Torino Cobra with matte black hood, shaker scoop, and standard 429/360 Cobra V-8. It had a 1.9-inch wider tread, 1.2-inch lower roofline, and a radical 57.5-degree windshield slope angle. Options included a Super Cobra Jet 429/370 with Drag Pack, oil cooler, and 780-cfm Holley carb. Some cars carried a 375-horsepower rating.

Bill Stroppe, about to clean the windshield of one of his Boss 302 Trans Am Mustangs, pitting at Bridgehampton on June 21, 1970. With Shelby and Ford out of the series, Stroppe relied on Parnelli Jones and George Follmer to get the job done. And they did, winning the series and giving Ford its third Manufacturers' title.
Ford Motor Company

With patriotic tape and paint treatment and a 390 four-barrel engine, the Rebel Machine was much more show than go. The car looked so much better in solid colors, although this was the launch edition. Much ado about nothing!

We drove a prepared Torino Cobra and covered it in the *SUPERCARS '70½* issue. It had a Super Cobra Jet engine, four-speed, and 4.30 Detroit Locker and, with a 117-inch wheelbase, was considerably larger than GM's midsize coupes. We saw some 13.30s with trap speeds in the 103- to 106-mile-per-hour range.

When we were evaluating new models for *Hi-Performance CARS* "Top Performance Car of the Year" honors, the Mercury 429 CJ Spoiler really impressed us and got the nod. It delivered true supercar performance and road-holding qualities, plus luxury appointments. It shared powertrain options with the Torino Cobra. The brand's upscale Cougar Eliminator was available with choice of Boss 302, 351, and 428 CJ power.

After the 1969 season, Carroll Shelby retired from the Shelby Mustang and Ford racing programs. That left Bud Moore flying Ford's banner in Trans-Am. Moore campaigned three Boss 302 Mustangs. Two were 1970 models and one a re-skinned 1969 race car, initially prepared by Kar-Kraft and driven by George Follmer and Parnelli Jones. He also still had his leftover '69 Mustangs and received Shelby's '69 Mustangs, all converted to look like 1970 models.

Even with restrictive budgets and incredible competition, Bud Moore's Mustangs outperformed the field. Parnelli Jones won at Laguna Seca, Lime Rock, Mid-Ohio, Kent, and Riverside, and Follmer took Louden. Ford won

its third manufacturers' championship and Jones was named Trans-Am champion.

AMC's representation in the supercar sweepstakes was a limited-build Rebel Machine. Produced by Hurst, the boxy cars were powered by upgraded Ram Air 390/340 engines with four-speeds and 3.54 rears. Rebel Machine advertising had some great copy and one sentence in particular summed up the car's performance: "It is not as fast on the getaway as a 427 Corvette, or a Hemi, but it is faster than a Volkswagen, a slow freight train, and your old man's Cadillac." I couldn't have said it better.

While we were celebrating Motown's heavy metal onslaught, engineers were well on their way to certifying lower compression, less powerful, and cleaner engines for 1971. That did not bode well for the future of performance cars. The party was winding down.

BUICK GS: SPEAK SOFTLY & CARRY A BIG STICK

Certainly not in keeping with Buick's traditional image, the Stage I GS-455 Skylark catapulted the Flint automaker into the heat of the battle for supercar supremacy.

The Skylark GS-455, in 360-horsepower Stage I trim, was the industry's first "adult" supercar. It was a powerful, high-quality, well-balanced midsize coupe (or convertible) with superb ride and handling qualities. Yet it was almost *invisible* compared with competitive offerings such as the SS Chevelle, GTO, Road Runner, or Cobra Jet Torino. Tasteful GS Stage I fender emblems were the Gran Sport's only status badging.

"Quiet" is the best way to describe the Stage I GS-455's appearance, but not its performance. Having driven GS Buicks, including Stage I Skylarks, at GM's Milford Proving Ground since the first Riviera GS in 1965, I was a believer. No carmaker did a better job of matching chassis/suspension tuning to powertrains than Buick. Once Buick started building Skylarks with 455-inch engines in 1970, they became players in the highly competitive supercar sweepstakes.

Buick dealers did not have a lot of experience selling performance cars to young people. Because Skylark Gran Sports were premium-priced and void of scoops, stripes, and wings, they didn't appeal to enthusiasts who wanted to make a statement. However, that all changed on February 9, 1970, when Buick announced the GSX, "Another Light-Your-Fire Car from Buick." Featuring a bold front spoiler, beautifully integrated rear spoiler, distinctive striping and graphics, badging and paint treatment, and a black hood with faired-in tachometer, a production Saturn Yellow GSX broke cover on February 10 at the Chicago Auto Show.

Also available in Apollo White with contrasting black trim, the GSX, with standard or Stage I 455 powertrains, was Flint's first attempt at targeting enthusiasts who were considering a GTO Judge or other high-profile car. Like Pontiac's GTO-based Judge, the GSX was a loaded Skylark GS-455 customized to appeal to enthusiasts who wanted their car to turn heads. It certainly was not for anyone looking for a stealth street racer.

A late entry in the marketplace, the GSX did not appear in 1970 model catalogs, and was not well promoted by Buick dealers. With deliveries starting in March 1970, total GSX sales hit just 678. A base GSX carried an MSPR of $3,283.

For the 1970 model year, GM lifted its self-imposed 400-inch midsize model displacement ban, allowing Chevrolet to market a 454/450 Mark IV big-block Chevelle. Buick, Oldsmobile, and Pontiac offered 455-inch Skylarks, 4-4-2s, and GTOs. Once magazines started road testing new models, it was obvious that 360-horsepower Stage I GS-455 Skylarks were delivering performance numbers equal to, or better than, cars powered by higher output engines.

The Stage I GS-455 engine was rated at 360 horsepower at 4,600 rpm and an unrivaled 510 lb-ft of torque at 2,800 rpm. It was obviously suspect that there was only a 10 horsepower difference between standard and Stage I engines. When you opted for Stage 1, the 10.5:1 engine was fitted with a re-jetted and modified Quadrajet four-barrel with fresh air induction, high-performance valvetrain; .490-inch-lift, 326/348-degree-duration camshaft; and new heads with $^{2.12}/_{1.75}$-inch valves. If you chose an automatic transmission, it was a beefed TH-400 with a 2.48 first gear.

Based on advertised 360-horsepower rating, the Stage I GS-455 Skylark was quicker and faster than it should've been. As you can tell by the tire tracks, we had a ball with this Stage 1 Skylark.

TOP: With Rallye ride control suspension with front and rear sway bars, reinforced upper control arms, and chassis beefing, this M-plated Stage I Skylark was a ball to drive on GM's ride and handling loop.

BOTTOM: Laying down tracks during GM's 1970 press program at Milford Proving Ground. We had to be careful not to melt the Polyglas GT tires! The beefed TM 400 automatic had 2.48 first gear, high-rpm shift points.

The Stage I engine was a $113.75 option on the $4,932 non-air-conditioned automatic GSX that Joe Oldham tested. The *Electric Banana* was featured in the October 1970 issue of *Hi-Performance CARS*. He obviously liked it: "Buick's GSX was the best handling Supercar we had driven at the time. Over the road with the windows up, the Stage I GSX was silent despite the 455 cubes throbbing under the hood."

Back in the day, it was not unusual for carmakers to keep the lid on horsepower ratings. Insurance companies had a field day raising rates on high-performance cars, especially for young owners. The higher the horsepower, the higher the rates. While all eyes were on horsepower, insurance companies paid little attention to torque ratings, which are the key to actual performance. The Stage I had the highest torque rating, at 510 lb-ft, of any performance engine in 1970 and held that honor for a number of years. Prior to the 1970 Winternationals, the NHRA rated the Stage I Skylark engine at 400 horsepower.

Magazine road tests from that period revealed a wide range of performance times, indicating that all test cars were not created equal. When I tested a pre-production Stage I GS-455 Skylark for *SUPERCARS '70½* in June 1969, it was an automatic with 3.64 Posi rear. My best quarter-mile time was 102 miles per hour in 14.10 seconds. Oldham tested a GSX, same specs as my Skylark, at E-Town and posted a best time of 103 miles per hour in 14.0 seconds. He recorded a 0- to 60-mile-per-hour sprint in 6.2 seconds. "It was quick. I can remember blowing off the likes of GTOs and 442s in informal runs late at night on deserted stretches of road," he said.

Some West Coast magazines tested Stage I Skylarks that were considerably quicker and faster than the ones we tested. More than one magazine tested a GS that had been professionally tuned. It ran 13.30s at over 105 miles per hour. Some of the Stage I test cars based in Los Angeles received special attention at Reynolds Buick in West Covina. Reynolds was the home of the record-setting Kenne-Bell Buicks, prepped by Jim Bell and driven by the legendary Lennie "Pop" Kennedy.

Buick's Stage I Skylark GS-455 was the surprise hit of 1970. It was quick. It was fast. It delivered premium performance for those who understood the advantages of speaking softly and carrying a big stick. Joe Oldham said it all in his GSX road test: "No question, the Stage I Buick is one of the quickest, best running musclecars of all time. It may also be the best handling."

Lennie "Pop" Kennedy drove the Reynolds-sponsored Kenne-Bell Stage I Skylark. Totally stock, it ran 13.9s at 101 miles per hour. With Stage II motor and slicks, shown here, the automatic GS-455 ran 10.70s at 127 miles per hour.

STAGE II GSX:
BUICK'S PHANTOM SUPERCAR

A one-off 500-horsepower GSX showcased Buick's Stage II engine program. It had the potential to dominate the supercar field . . . and then it disappeared.

Much has been written over the years about the legendary 1968 through 1970 Stage II Skylarks built for drag racing using dealer-available parts. In 1969, Buick built two complete Stage II GS-455 Skylarks under the direction of Staff Project Engineer Dennis "Denny" Manners. One was for internal development use and the other, a '70 GSX, was designated for road and track exposure. The development car was a dark green '69 Skylark GS-400 used first for the 1969 Stage II program and then fitted with a Stage II 455 engine. Buick was considering an off-road-only Stage II Engine option for 1971 Skylarks.

Manners sent an inter-departmental memo dated April 1, 1970, and titled "STAGE II ENGINE OPTION" to his boss, J. E. "Jack" DeCou, with copies to sales, marketing, and public relations executives. In it, Manners outlined Stage II program details: "Per request of the Sales Department, the Stage II engine will not be offered as an RPO for 1971 and will continue to be a dealer-installed package. Engineering GSX #4085, equipped with a Stage II engine and four-speed, will be loaned to the PR Department for exposure in the Los Angeles zone. In addition, Stage II components will be furnished to Reynolds Buick for evaluation in their automatic GS-455 racecar. Engineering will release the Stage II cylinder head, 11-to-1 forged pistons and rings as service parts for 1970."

The original 500-horsepower Stage II engine package included new 15-percent-increase high-flow heads with Stage I valves and enlarged ports, a 455-/480-inch-lift, 340-/360-degree-duration camshaft, TRW 11:1 forged pistons, and proprietary Kustom Equipment $2\frac{1}{8}$-inch headers with 36-inch collectors. When blueprinting a Stage II engine and cc'ing the heads, you could achieve a final compression ratio of 12:1. An 850-cfm Holley double-pumper and Edelbrock B4B aluminum manifold were included. Because of head casting problems, less than one hundred sets were released.

Powertrain group in 1996, "An engineer missed a shift while testing the GSX and put a rod through the side of the block. We disassembled and scrapped the GSX, saving only the scooped hood and handmade GSX emblem. My '69 Skylark Stage II development car was also scrapped."

Manners had also prototyped a 455-inch Tunnel Port engine. Strictly for drag racing, the TP engine included an extra-heavy-duty four-bolt main block and heads with huge, round intake ports. Some heads and a half-dozen blocks were produced before the curtain came down on drag racing programs at Buick. One Skylark is currently racing with a TP 455 and it runs in the nines.

TOP: The prototype Stage II GSX, engineering No. 4085, with handmade GSX emblem and unique chrome lettering on its functionally scooped hood. Note the MFG license plate while on loan in Los Angeles in 1970.

BOTTOM: A rare photo of the 500-horsepower Stage II engine with Holley intake. Note the non-power brakes and unique ram-induction air cleaner that works with 4-inch-tall hood scoop. It idled at 1,000 rpm.

While on loan in LA, it was fitted with 4.78 gears, Hurst shifter, Lakewood scattershield, racing clutch, Delco air shocks, and 10-inch slicks. It ran in the elevens at close to 120 miles per hour.

"The Stage II engine was never intended to be a street engine. It was engineered for drag racing, to run with open exhausts. It did not develop enough vacuum for power brakes," Manners said.

The Stage II GSX was returned to Buick. According to Manners, who retired as assistant chief engineer in GM's

CHALLENGER T/A & AAR 'CUDA:
SIX-PACK TO GO

Created to battle Z/28 Camaros and Boss 302 Mustangs on the road and track, 340-inch Challenger T/As and AAR 'Cudas proved that less could be more.

Dodge and Plymouth had been involved in SCCA competitive events since the early- to mid-1960s, before the pony car explosion and factory participation in Trans-Am racing. SCCA's 1970 Trans-Am rules allowed carmakers to destroke production engines to meet the series' 305-cube limit. Chrysler responded with the Challenger T/A and AAR 'Cuda.

Chrysler involvement in SCCA rallying and racing in 1964 through 1965 laid the groundwork for its Trans-Am efforts. In 1964 and 1965, Chrysler engineer Scott Harvey won the SCCA Rally Championships while driving a Valiant. In 1964 he finished third in class at the Monte Carlo Rally, and won the SCCA Central Division Road Racing Championship. He continued his winning ways with a Barracuda in 1965.

Group 44's Dodge Dart, campaigned by Bob Tullius and Tony Adamowicz, was a surprise entry in the 1966 Trans-Am Series. It garnered a first at Marlboro and a second at Sebring. Plymouth also participated in the first year of the series with Barracudas driven by Scott Harvey and Bruce Jennings.

The '70 Challenger T/A and AAR 'Cuda were powered by a new 10.5:1 tri-power 340, underrated at 290 horsepower

The scooped fiberglass hood on the T/A is forerunner of the one used later on Pro Stock race cars. The T/A and AAR pony cars had a great stance, with E60 tires up front and G60s at the rear.

Challengers had a 110-inch wheelbase and overall length of 191 inches, while shorter, 'Cudas had a 108-inch wheelbase and overall length of almost 187 inches.

While much of AAR and T/A trim differs from that of standard E-body Mopars, it's the engine that truly defines these cars. Special 340 engines were based on a new beefy block cast with increased webbing to allow for four-bolt mains like those used in destroked race engines. The new heads offered increased breathing, thanks to smoother intake ports. Port-matched intake and exhaust manifolds ensured breathing at high rpm.

Production features included an Edelbrock aluminum manifold with three Holley two-barrels and low-restriction throaty duals with side-exit exhausts. The .430-/.425-inch lift hydraulic cam and relocated pushrods, special rockers, and Hemi valve springs made 5,500-rpm shift points possible.

The engine in our magazine test T/A was great. "It was amazingly responsive and was right there up to six-grand. Unfortunately, the T/A's *Mickey Mouse* tach took a while to catch up to the high-revving engine!" we reported.

Chrysler engineer and Ramchargers member Dale Reeker designed the hood scoop used exclusively on the T/A. We talked with Reeker when we were driving a T/A at Chelsea. "The 'Scat Scoop' is totally functional. It's located above the slow-moving boundary layer of air, ducting cool air directly to the hood-mated air cleaner. The AAR Cuda has a more traditional hood scoop."

A lot of effort went into the suspension of these E-body twins. Front suspensions had special K-frames with skid plates and thicker-than-stock torsion and sway bars. Much of the suspension tweaking utilized springs and components from more powerful 440 and 426 Street Hemi models. Torque boxes were welded to the unibody, ahead of the rear leaf springs, for platform strengthening. Even with all the suspension and chassis upgrades, wheel hop was still a problem when launching four-speed cars.

I loved the way our T/A tester handled: "We found our test T/A with quick-ratio steering, 11-inch rear drum brakes

at 5,000 rpm and 345 lb-ft of torque at 3,400 rpm. They were conceived in the spring of 1969 and materialized as 1970¹/₂ models. There were no plans for a 1971 model, although dealers did sell new leftovers well into the 1971 model year. Because they were pricey, enthusiasts often opted for more powerful 440 and 426 Street Hemi models for just about the same money. The Challenger T/A we tested for the August 1970 issue of *Hi-Performance CARS* listed for approximately $4,100.

The T/A and AAR existed because Chrysler wanted to race in Trans-Am. Ford had won the series in 1966 and 1967 and Chevrolet dominated in 1968 and 1969. In April 1969, ACCUS/FIA mandated that, for a specific model to be legal for Trans-Am, the carmaker would have to build one for every two dealerships. Since Chrysler projected losing money on every Challenger T/A and AAR 'Cuda, they built just enough to qualify 2,400 T/As and 2,724 AARs. Production started on March 10, 1970, and ended five weeks later.

When new, enthusiasts often thought they were just dressed-up Barracudas and Challengers with tri-power engines. They were extensively modified and fitted with an exclusive powerplant, suspension updates, and styling cues.

TOP: Sam Posey drove the Autodynamics Challenger T/A to third-place finishes at Lime Rock and Elkhart Lake. It was built by Gurney and race-prepped by Autodynamics. This photo was shot at the Trans-Am race at Mount Tremblant. *FCA Archives*

ABOVE: Testing an AAR 'Cuda on the skid pad at Chrysler Proving Ground in 1970. Upgraded suspensions on both Challengers and Barracudas utilized components and tuning from 440 Six-Pack and Street Hemi models.

RIGHT: A rare T/A drag racing car campaigned by McAllister Dodge, photographed with Jim McAllister (right) and driver Nick Haggert. The McAllister family owns McAllister Towing, one of the largest tugboat fleets in the country. I shot this on NYC waterfront with *Grace McAllister* tug in background for the November 3 issue of *Hi-Performance CARS*.

Removing the large air cleaner atop the McAllister T/A's engine reveals three Holley two-barrels with mechanical linkage replacing vacuum setup for end carbs. Response is instant!

One of two AAR race cars, driven by Swede Savage in the 1970 Trans-Am Series. His best finish was a second at Elkhart Lake. Chrysler supplied the acid-dipped body and powertrains. *FCA Archive*

and 11.3-inch front discs with metallic pads to be controllable and boast fantastic directional stability."

In many ways, driving our T/A with close-ratio four-speed and 3.91 Sure-Grip gearing was more fun than driving a heavier 426 Street Hemi Challenger. The T/A offered a much sportier feel, went where you pointed it, and delivered close to big-block performance. My guess was that the 290-horsepower small-block was delivering closer to 335 to 350 horsepower. Our best 0 to 60 time was 6.2 seconds, certainly on a par with many of the hottest pony cars. We never made it to the strip because of inclement weather, but the same car later turned 14.0s at almost 100 miles per hour.

Like all professional race cars built off production models, the Autodynamics Challenger T/A and Dan Gurney AAR 'Cuda race cars had little in common with their donors. Chrysler's Trans-Am Racing Manager Pete Hutchinson shipped three acid-dipped bodies in white and four-speeds and Dana rears to All-American Racers. Engine components were shipped to master race engine builder Keith Black.

Gurney's AAR built three race cars and shipped one, with 475-horsepower, 303.8-inch engine, to Ray Caldwell's Autodynamics for final race prep. The lightened unibody platforms benefitted greatly from roll cages that added much needed structural rigidity. Some cars were fitted with vinyl roof covers for the same reason. Primary drivers for the Chrysler-sponsored teams were Sam Posey at Autodynamics and Swede Savage and Dan Gurney at AAR.

It was a relatively low-budget and not very successful one-year program. The best finish for Swede Savage was a second at Elkhart Lake and, for Sam Posey, thirds at Lime Rock and Elkhart Lake. They didn't win on Sundays and dealers didn't sell T/As and AARs on Monday.

Dodge and Plymouth designed true, head-turning "Day Two" pony cars. T/As and AARs were fast, had great handling, and outperformed more powerful cars. They provided Chrysler the opportunity to showcase its brands in a respected road racing series. Almost half a century later on the historic racing circuit, original Autodynamics T/A and Gurney AAR race cars are still battling Mustangs and Camaros.

1971

The boldest-looking Road Runner was available with Chrysler's boldest engines and drivetrain packages. I drove this 440/385 tri-power coupe at Chelsea, then tested one prepared for us by racer Bill Stiles for the May 1971 issue of *Hi-Performance CARS*. A most impressive ride.

CHAPTER THIRTEEN

THE TURNING POINT

On its path from mean to clean, GM dropped compression ratios and jumped on the politically correct bandwagon. Chrysler and Ford stayed the course. But the handwriting on the wall was loud and clear, "Get 'em while they're hot."

With tightening clean-air standards (which necessitated power-robbing anti-pollution equipment) and the insurance companies gouging under-twenty-five-year-old drivers, the long-term prognosis for performance cars was not encouraging. The muscle car started on the path to becoming an endangered species.

In the August 1970 issue of *Hi-Performance CARS* Editor's Corner, I wrote about carmakers in the 1950s offering Export and/or Marine engine packages that were little more than thinly disguised speed equipment hidden in service parts listings: "Well, it looks like 1971 will be the Year of the Export and Marine options at GM. Ed Cole,

President, GM has pledged that all 1971 production engines will be able to run on non-leaded gas and, of course, will meet Federal emissions standards."

That was the death knell for the 454/450 LS6 Chevy big-block. Other GM small- and big-block performance engines that were retained developed less output, thanks to lower compression ratios and increased smog tuning. If you carefully selected gear ratios, transmissions, and suspension options, you could order a GM car that would deliver very respectable performance.

In road tests conducted for *SUPERCARS '71*, well-tuned GM supercars delivered impressive numbers. A 454/425 LS6 Chevelle SS with cowl induction, automatic, F41 suspension, and 4.10 Posi gears clocked 102 miles per hour in 13.65 seconds.

The big-block with 9.0 compression pumped out 425 horsepower at 5,600 rpm. Unfortunately, LS6 big-blocks appeared only in Chevelles prepared by Chevrolet for early testing during the summer of 1970. The top production option was the LS5 big-block 454/365.

We were pleasantly surprised by a 455/350 W30 Olds 4-4-2 convertible. The 8.5 compression big-block was hooked up to a Hurst-shifted M22 four-speed and 3.91 limited-slip rear. With 350 horsepower at 4,800 rpm, the boldly striped ragtop ran 101 miles per hour in 13.90 seconds and to 60 miles per hour in 7 seconds flat. A Stage I Buick Skylark GS455 with HD suspension, 455/345 engine, beefed automatic, and 3.42 gears was a great road car. It ran 101 miles per hour in 14.50 seconds and sprinted to 60 miles per hour in 7.4 seconds. Not too shabby for smoggers!

LEFT: The March 1971 issue of *Hi-Performance CARS* celebrated the winner of Top Performance Car of the Year: Dodge Charger. For 1971, the Charger got its own 115-inch wheelbase platform and could be ordered with engines up to and including the 426 Street Hemi. It was the last year for a Hemi engine option.

BELOW: The refreshed Barracuda received dual quad headlights and maintained a full array of options on the 426 Street Hemi. Sox & Martin built this Hemi-'Cuda for Brooklyn, New York's Ronnie Lyles. Lyles was one of the country's top Pro Stock competitors. Fred Dellis drove it to win Pro Stock crown at the eighth-annual *CARS* Championship at ATCO Dragway, clocking 141.28 miles per hour in 9.77 seconds.

For 1971, Dodge's Charger—with a full range of high-compression 440 and 426 Street Hemi engine options, bulletproof drivetrains, multiple trim levels, and four distinct striping/paint schemes—was named Top Performance Car of the Year. You could mix and match your Charger options to come up with a truly personalized road and track warrior. Our favorite was the Charger R/T with 440/385 Six-Pack, TorqueFlite, and A34 Super Track Pak 9¾-inch Dana rear with 4.10 Sure-Grip gears. We felt it was *the* supercar for all seasons and reasons!

In the May 1971 issue of *Hi-Performance CARS*, we tested a '71 Road Runner with the exact same powertrain as our favorite Charger R/T. Bill Stiles, a Chrysler factory drag racer best known for his Hemi SS, FX, and Pro Stock Plymouths, professionally prepared the 440/385 RR for us.

We used Englishtown for a day and we probably made a couple of dozen full-throttle passes with the RR. It ran strong and consistent, and it posted a best quarter-mile time of 102 miles per hour in 13.80. Even though gas was cheap and covered by my expense account, its thirst for Sunoco 260 (8 to 9 miles per gallon) warranted a comment in the test article: "You could actually watch the gas gauge go down as the revs went up." To be fair, that was par for the course for big-inch supercars!

Dodge and Plymouth Hemi Pro Stockers continued their winning ways. In stock car racing, Plymouth swept twenty-two NASCAR races and Richard Petty was crowned points champion. It was a great year for Hemi-powered Mopars.

The results of Ford shifting R&D budgets from

TOP: Where there's smoke, there's Oldham. "Mr. Attitude" lights 'em up at E-Town, testing the 429/370 CJ/R Mach I Mustang for *Hi-Performance CARS* in April 1971. Joe ran the best time of 102 miles per hour in 14.15 seconds.

MIDDLE: Courtesy of Ford, Fred Mackerodt, Joe Oldham, Al Root, and myself spent a day driving the hottest 1971 Mustangs and Torino Cobras at E-Town. Oldham got the best time of the day driving the 3,800-pound 429 SCJ Cobra—106 miles per hour in 13.70.

BOTTOM: One of none, the '71 Chevelle is powered by the 454/425 LS6 big-block, at Milford Proving Ground. The engine was an early option but appeared only in a handful of factory test cars. With cowl induction scoop, it ran 102 miles per hour in 13.65 seconds.

racing to safety and emissions, plus Special Vehicles/Kar-Kraft imploding in 1970, hardly affected high-performance offerings. Performance was alive and well in Dearborn thanks to Boss 351 and 429 CJ and SCJ Mustangs and Torino Cobras and Cyclone Spoilers.

The big news was a restyled Mustang. It was longer, wider, lower, and, unfortunately, heavier. Over six model years, the Mustang gained approximately 500 pounds due to restyling and government-mandated safety updates. Even though the new Mustang grew by 22 inches, wheelbase increased by 1 inch, width increased by almost 2$\frac{1}{2}$ inches, and front tread width increased by 3 inches, it retained its pony car appeal. Sexy SportsRoof models had windshields slanted at a 60-degree angle with slope increased by 5$\frac{1}{2}$ degrees. The almost flat backlight diminished driver visibility, but it made the Mustang look even longer and lower.

After spreading the Mustang's front spring towers 3 inches apart, it was able to accommodate 429 CJ and SCJ Drag Pack engines, rated at 370 horsepower at 5,400 rpm and 375 horsepower at 5,600 rpm. The 429, with lightweight thin-wall-cast blocks and round-port heads with canted valves, replaced the 428 Cobra Jet.

The SCJ motor came with four-bolt mains, solid-lifter valvetrain, forged 11.3:1 pistons, beefier rods, and an aluminum manifold with a 780-cfm Holley. Four-speed-only, SCJ Drag Pack Mustangs were available with 3.91 Traction-Lok or 4.11 Detroit Locker gearing. J-Code models came with functional Ram Air.

The Mach 1 and Boss 351 Mustangs were not ready when 1971 models were introduced. The late-release Mach 1 had a flat-black, twin-scoop Ram Air hood, blacked out grille, and color-keyed Urethane front bumper. Ford had a special press preview for the Boss 351 SportsRoof Mustang in November 1970 at Orange County International Raceway.

Fred Freel covered the event, and his story, "The Boss Beat Goes On!" ran in the March 1971 issue of *Hi-Performance CARS*. Available only with four-speed, he track-tested two Boss 351 Mustangs: one with 3.91 Traction-Lok and the other with 4.11 Detroit Locker gears. Of three passes in each car, his best time in the 3.91 car was 103.21 miles per hour in 14.02 seconds, and in the 4.11 car, 102.38 miles per hour in 14.12 seconds. Rev-limiters were factory-set at 6,150 rpm.

The Boss 351/351 high-output engine had a special block and canted-valve Cleveland heads with 429 NASCAR engine Polyangle combustion chambers. It also featured a .467- to .477-inch-lift solid cam, 11.7:1 forged pistons, and an aluminum manifold with a 750-cfm Autolite spread-bore carb. The all-new engine generated 330 horsepower at 5,800 rpm and 380 lb-ft of torque at 3,400 rpm. The Boss 351 was lighter than a 429 CJ model, cheaper to insure—and almost as fast.

Ford had "the right stuff" for the supercar marketplace, but the marketplace was shrinking. The Torino Cobra and Cyclone Spoiler were carried over with new trim and more weight. You could order either with 370-horsepower 429 CJ, four-speed or automatic, and Traction-Lok gearing. We found them to be great road cruisers.

In a 429 CJ Torino Cobra road test, published in *SUPERCARS '71*, I wrote: "It's bigger, heavier and more powerful than many of its competitors. Just how long it's going to be available, however, is anybody's guess." As with the Boss 351 Mustang, the CJ and SCJ 429 Torino Cobra and Cyclone Spoiler would not return in 1972.

It may never win a beauty contest, but the boxy, compact SC/360 Hornet with four-speed could *haul*! We ran 98 miles per hour in 14.22 seconds and sprinted to 60 miles per hour in 7.5 seconds.

A 304-inch destroked 360 AMC engine powered Donohue's '71 Javelin to win the 1971 Trans-Am crown for AMC. It was actually his '70 Penske Javelin rebodied for the new season. *M. M. "Mike" Matune Jr.*

An all-new, longer, wider, and heavier 401/330 Javelin, with unique sculpted lines, did little to enhance AMC's position in the pony car marketplace. Even in AMX trim with engine-turned dash, tasteful rear spoiler, and new 401 engine, it seriously lacked enthusiast appeal, and had quality issues.

The AMC model that pleasantly surprised us was the boxy SC/360 Hornet. It was a true mini-muscle car, powered by a 360/285 four-barrel engine that was available with Hurst-shifted four-speed and 3.91 limited-slip rear. Weighing hundreds of pounds less and cheaper than a Javelin, it delivered solid performance and could easily be insured.

We tested a four-speed SC/360 Hornet with 3.91 gears and an automatic 401 Javelin AMX with 3.54 gears at Michigan International Speedway for *SUPERCARS '71*. The Javelin ran a best quarter-mile time of 96 miles per hour in 14.45 seconds, while the Hornet ran 98 miles per hour in 14.22 seconds. At 7.5 seconds, it was also quicker to 60 miles per hour by a tenth of a second.

In the August 1971 issue of *Hi-Performance CARS*, Joe Oldham tested a similar Javelin and experienced a rear axle failure. He was not happy with the quality and made no bones about it: "If the rattles don't get 'ya, the steering wheel shakes will!"

What cred AMC lacked on the street, it made up for in the high-profile Trans-Am Series. Mark Donahue, driving a Javelin, clinched the 1971 title for AMC. He won seven races and finished in second place twice. With Chevrolet and Ford factory sponsorship bucks drying up, the Javelin team dominated.

Even more restrictive emissions and safety legislation, plus the Department of Transportation investigating speed shops and dealerships modifying new cars, signaled that an era of freewheeling, high-performance days was coming to an end.

1972

Laying down some tracks in a pre-production SS454 LS5 Chevelle in June 1971 at the GM Proving Ground. With automatic and 3.31 Posi gears, the Chevelle was not ideally suited for the quarter-mile. Our loaded production test car with the same powertrain ran 93 miles per hour in 15.10 seconds.

CHAPTER FOURTEEN

Last of the Great Ones

Chrysler and Ford followed GM with a vengeance, not only reducing compression ratios, but killing some great engines and models. This resulted in GM's carryover vehicles, powered by arguably underrated engines, dominating the marketplace. Even though new SAE Net horsepower ratings made almost every new engine look wimpy, performance prevailed.

We presented our Top Performance Car of the Year award to Buick for its GS455 Stage I Skylark. It was the cover story of the April 1972 issue of *Hi-Performance CARS*. In presenting the award, I commented: "Our annual honors go to Buick for its supercar that speaks softly and carries a big stick."

I was interviewed at the presentation by the *The Flint Journal* for its December 10, 1971, edition, and said: "The Stage I GS455 is the year's best overall enthusiast vehicle, offering the best combination of handling, ride, braking, styling, and engine performance. Of all the cars built in this country today, I think GM is building the best cars, and Buick is building the best GM cars."

We tested a GS455 Stage 1 Skylark with automatic and 3.42 gears and recorded a best time of 101 miles per hour in 14.60 seconds and from 0 to 60 in 7.6. That was quick for an air-conditioned car with an 8.5 compression 455-inch engine rated at 270 horsepower at 4,400 rpm and 390 lb-ft torque at 3,000 rpm. It delivered superb ride and handling qualities.

Motor Trend's A. B. Shuman tested a Stage I Skylark for the June 1972 issue and wrote: "Buick has one of the best—if not the best—performance packages now obtainable from Detroit." His Skylark ran 97 miles per hour in 14.10 seconds and from 0 to 60 miles per hour in an incredible 5.8 seconds. He also won his class at the NHRA Winternationals. But it was not production stock. It was a prepared car with open exhausts, larger tires, and 4.30 gears, and it qualified as stock under NHRA rules.

The Bow Tie Brigade's hottest supercar for 1972 was an SS454 Chevelle powered by a hydraulic-lifter LS5 big-block with two-bolt mains rated at 270 horsepower at 4,000 rpm and 390 lb-ft torque at 3,200 rpm.

I ordered a Chevelle SS454 hardtop with LS5, automatic 12-bolt rear with 3.31 Posi gears and AC for a test that ran

in the August issue of *Hi-Performance CARS*. With its F41 suspension and a host of creature comforts, our Midnight Bronze tester was a great road car. The best we were able to do at the track was 93 miles per hour in 15.10 seconds.

We liked everything about the Chevelle except its full-throttle performance, which could have been bolstered with carb-ignition tuning and headers. It ran out of breath over 4,000 rpm. With bold stripes and emblems, plus cowl-induction hood, the SS454 Chevelle still exuded street status.

The GTO came full circle, reverting back to its original option position in Pontiac's midsize lineup. The '71 GTO had been the last exclusive GTO model. By checking off the right LeMans option boxes, you could actually buy a W62 option GTO equipped with supercar powertrain, chassis, and trim. You could opt for the excellent 455 high-output WW5 engine package with Ram Air, a wide- or close-ratio Hurst-shifted four-speed or automatic, Y99 suspension, 15x7-inch Honeycomb mags, and 3.55 Safe-T-Track rear.

I test-drove a "tuned" GTO in 1971 for our annual supercars publication, titled *PERFORMANCE CAR GUIDE '72*. The GTO had the 8.4 compression, 455 high-output engine, rated at 300 horsepower at 4,200 rpm, and 300 lb-ft torque at 3,200 rpm. It had an automatic and 3.55 gears.

Our Stage I GS455 Skylark excelled on the skid pad and slalom course, carving cones like a smaller, well-setup pony car. It was essentially a Sun coupe without production ID. Just 728 Stage I hardtops were built in 1972.

ABOVE: We found the Z/28 Camaro with four-speed, 4.10 Posi gears, F41 suspension, and 9.0 compression 350 with big Holley and solid cam to be one of the best all-around pony cars. With this setup, it was good for 100 miles per hour in 14.50 seconds, plus incredible handling.

LEFT: The top dog LS5 with cowl induction–powered our *Hi-Performance CARS* Chevelle SS454 test car. Over 4,000-rpm performance was disappointing, but it had the right stuff for cruising.

BELOW: Checking out a preproduction GTO with Gen 1–style Firebird rear spoiler that never went into production. The hottest GTO was a Le Mans hardtop/coupe with W62 GTO option, WW5 package with LS5 Ram Air 455 high-output engine, WU3 scooped hood, and Y99 suspension.

Our best quarter-mile time was 100 miles per hour in 14.10 seconds. During 1972, we discovered that similarly equipped GTOs were running mid-high 90s in the 14.50s.

Pontiac Formula and Trans-Am Firebirds were class leaders. With an available 455/300 high-output engine, slick styling, and some of the best suspension tuning in the industry, you would have had difficulty finding a more potent pony car. We drove a unique '72 Trans-Am with prototype louvered hood instead of the Ram Air Shaker hood at Milford that had posted sub-fourteen-second times at 102 miles per hour.

Joe Oldham tested a 455/300 Trans-Am with four-speed and 3.42 gears for the September 1972 issue of *Hi-Performance CARS*. Like the T/A we drove, it too had been tuned. Before tracking it, Oldham brought the T/A to Nunzi's Automotive in Brooklyn, New York, for ignition and carburetor tuning. Oldham registered best times of 103.22 miles per hour in 14.04 seconds.

Like the GTO, Oldsmobile's venerable 4-4-2 was reduced to an option available on a variety of Cutlass models. In order to get maximum 4-4-2 power and image, you had to opt for the W29 Sport/Handling 4-4-2 and the W30 Performance Packages. When you selected the W30, it included the L77 Force-Air 455 rated at 300 horsepower at 4,700 rpm and 410 lb-ft torque at 3,200 rpm. The best part of the W29 option was Oldsmobile's excellent FE2 suspension with heavy-duty *everything*, plus front and rear sway bars. You could order a W25 functionally scooped fiberglass hood, regardless of engine choice.

Oldsmobile engineer Dale Smith supplied the W30 test car with four-speed and 3.91 gears that we featured in *PERFORMANCE CARS '72*. While that car ran 100 miles per hour in 14.30 seconds, production models we drove with similar gearing during the year were off by 2 to 3 miles per hour and a few tenths.

The actual Hurst-Olds that paced the Indy 500 in 1972 was a convertible powered by a blueprinted W30 engine. We tested this loaded, limited-production Cameo White and Hurst Gold hardtop with a stock 455/300 Force-Air W30 engine in the August issue of *Hi-Performance CARS*. It was an automatic with 3.42 gears, and ran 93 miles per hour in 15.30 seconds.

Enthusiasts were left dazed and confused when Ford announced its 1972 lineup. As quickly as Henry Ford II embraced Total Performance and racing a decade earlier, in 1972 he switched gears to safety and fuel economy. Conspicuously missing were Torino Cobra and Cyclone Spoiler Super-cars and Mustangs that had been available with high-compression Boss 351 and 429 CJ and SCJs.

All that remained was a Mustang, powered by an emasculated Boss 351 Cleveland engine dubbed "351 H.O." The solid-cammed, 8.8:1 engine pumped out 275 horsepower at 6,000 rpm. Available in any body style, the 351 high-output Mustang only came with four-speed, 9-inch rear with 3.91 gears and competition suspension with stagger-mount rear shocks. Because of emission and certification problems, a functional Ram Air hood was available only on lower performance Mustangs. At best, it was a sub-100-mile-per-hour, fifteen-second pony car that would have a difficult time fighting off a Z/28 Camaro. Just 398 351 high-output Mustangs were sold compared with 2,575 Z/28 Camaros.

While Chrysler planned on axing the 426 Street Hemi for 1972, it didn't anticipate dropping the excellent 440/385 Six-Pack rated at 330 horsepower. We test drove and reported on a prototype tri-power Road Runner, actually a 1971 model with 1972 sheet metal. With 3.54 gears and four-speed, it ran 102 miles per hour in 14.40 seconds, and was featured in *PERFORMANCE CAR GUIDE '72*.

Unfortunately the tri-power 440 didn't pass EPA testing and was dropped. It is believed that a handful of 1972 440 tri-power Road Runners had been built. We had ordered one for testing, but Chrysler delivered a 440/280 four-barrel RR. Instead of doing a road test, we turned it into a magazine project car. Motion Performance handled the modifications and Alan Root and I reported on progress during the year.

When delivered, our 440 RR with Air Grabber hood, TorqueFlite, and mid-three-series gearing did not impress. We then had Motion modify and dyno-tune it. Joel Rosen

ABOVE: We got overly aggressive testing this 340 'Cuda on the Chelsea Proving Ground skid pad. With a 240-horsepower rating, insurance companies hardly noticed it, but enthusiasts loved its performance.

TOP: Managing Editor Al Root lights up the project Road Runner's G60 Goodyears at ATCO Dragway. With basic intake and exhaust mods, the four-barrel 440 RR ran in the mid-fourteens at 93 to 95 miles per hour. *Bob McClurg*

dialed in 12 degrees initial and 36 degrees total advance at 1,500 rpm. Hooker headers were bolted up to the stock exhaust system and the intake manifold and Carter Thermo-Quad were trashed.

For induction, we chose an Edelbrock manifold with a unique finned aluminum Kendig carb, also used by Don Nicolson on his Ford Pro Stock. While the Kendigerator proved to be less than ideal for daily driving, it excelled at the track. Al Root tested the Road Runner before and after modifications at ATCO Dragway. When delivered, the 440 Road Runner's best time was 14.90 seconds, but most runs were in the 15.20s. Best terminal speed was 88 miles per hour. After basic modifications, Root ran times between 14.30 and 14.55 seconds, with trap speeds of 93 to 95 miles per hour.

I summed the project up in the December issue of *Hi-Performance CARS:* "The most rewarding part of the conversion was that the Road Runner suddenly became fun to drive. It no longer bogged, shuddered and stumbled when called on to perform." Although top performance big-blocks faded away, Chrysler engineers saved the day with a strong-running 340/240. Small-block Barracuda, Challenger, Demon, and Duster models delivered respectable performance and were not on insurance company hit lists. Well-tuned four-speed 340/240 Barracudas or Challengers

with four-speeds and 3.91 gears could run over 90 miles per hour in the 14.30s.

Once again, AMC did not make much headway with its 401-inch Javelin AMX, carried over with few changes. Quality was still an issue and its weak dealer network did little to attract enthusiasts. However, for the second year in a row a Javelin won the Trans-Am Series and gave AMC the championship. Campaigned by Roy Woods Racing and driven by George Follmer, the #1 Javelin ruled. Winning on Sunday did not however translate into selling on Monday.

PONTIAC 455 VENTURA II:
ONE OF NONE

The ultimate 1972 stealth supercar was an unassuming Pontiac Ventura II coupe with a 455 high-output GTO/Firebird engine under its hood. Little more than a grille and badge-engineered Chevy Nova, this screamer, with an EPA-certified engine, would have flown under insurance companies' radar. Pontiac built one and everyone loved it. But it was not to be.

I drove it in June 1971 during Pontiac's 1972 model press preview at GM's Milford Proving Ground. Most writers were much more interested in the new, sexier GTO and Firebird models than a boxy X-platform Nova clone. Once I saw its hood tach, Honeycomb mags with F60 Goodyears, and "455 H.O." fender ID, I couldn't wait to toss it around Black Lake, GM's seemingly endless skid pad.

Unlike most late-model Novas that I had driven, this Pontiac variant cornered extremely flat and was easily controllable through the cones at high speeds. I discovered that this Ventura II had Trans-Am front coil springs and upgraded Sprint power steering and brakes. The engine was

With Firebird Trans-Am front coils, heavy-duty suspension, and Sprint brakes and steering, the M-plated big-block compact excelled on the Black Lake slalom course.

TOP: A one-off Pontiac version of the Chevy Nova with all the good stuff: honeycomb mags with F60 Goodyears, 455/300 high-output GTO Firebird motor with updated Ram Air internals, and a signature hood tach.

RIGHT: The plain Jane engine compartment reveals a basic 1971–1972 high-output 455 with aluminum intake modified Ram Air IV heads and dual snorkel air cleaner. The beefed 400 THM automatic ensured crisp full-throttle upshifts.

a stock 455 high-output engine mated to a beefed THM 400 automatic and 3.42 rear gears.

I wasn't able to run it through the clocks, but the engineer assigned to the car let me know that it had run 14.20s at 101 miles per hour with stock dual exhausts and F60 tires. He was quick to add: "With a little tuning, open exhausts and 3.90 gears, you could expect one-second-quicker elapsed times!"

The 455 Ventura II never went into production. It wouldn't surprise me if Chevrolet had been really concerned after seeing what Pontiac had accomplished with its car and threatened to end X-body platform sharing. Hopefully it survived the crusher.

1973-1974

While not as quick as a Mopar 360/245 Dart or Duster, the '74 Chevy Nova—with L48 small-block 350/185, automatic, 3.42 Posi gears, and F41 suspension—was a great all-around compact. Tested for the July 1974 issue of *Hi-Performance CARS*, an SS350 Nova ran mid-fifteen-second quarters. The billboard side lettering and stripes were a bit much.

CHAPTER FIFTEEN

saven By the super-Duty

At a time when "lean and clean" and downsizing were the mandates in Motown, Pontiac defied all odds and developed the Super-Duty 455, a large-displacement, emissions-legal engine strictly for motorheads.

When we drove 1973 models with ugly, heavy, energy-absorbing front bumpers in June and July 1972, we were aware that 1974 models would only be worse. We also knew that unleaded gas and catalytic converters were on the horizon. What we didn't know was that an Arab oil embargo in 1973 would ignite gas rationing and panic at the pumps, further fueling an industry emphasis on economy.

On Wednesday, June 28, 1972, I attended a press briefing on the Super-Duty 455 engine at GM's Milford Proving Ground. Pontiac Special Projects' Herb Adams, an engineer and racer, and Tom Nell, both key players in the development of the SD-455, revealed details of

All GM midsize coupes came with new Colonnade styling and the GTO featured louvered quarter windows. Even though my GTO arrived with the four-barrel 455, I kept it. It lacked supercar performance, shown here running at Suffolk County Raceway, collecting 15-second time slips.

the engine that would extend GM domination of the performance car marketplace through 1974:

> This morning we can announce a significant step forward in the continuing development of Pontiac's V-8 engines. Two years ago, we set out to develop an engine that would offer excellent performance at a moderate price. The Super-Duty 455 that replaces the 455 H.O. is rated at 310 horsepower and has 6,000-rpm capability. It runs on 91-octane fuel and passes all emissions and noise laws. The engine will be available as optional on the '73 Grand Am, Grand Prix, Trans-Am, Formula and GTO. A 3.42 axle ratio is specified with either Turbo-Hydramatic or M20 four-speed.

Because carmakers had been placing a very low priority on performance cars in view of the latest emission requirements, it was mind-blowing that Pontiac was able to get the SD-455 engine in its 1973 lineup. Even more amazing, it would enjoy an encore performance in 1974.

Magazine road tests confirmed that SD-455 Firebirds were the quickest and fastest 1973 and 1974 cars. The one we tested for *SUPERCARS '73* was fitted with four-speed and

3.42 gears and ran 104 miles per hour in 13.50 seconds. *Hot Rod* tested one and clocked 104.3 miles per hour in 13.54 and *Car and Driver* reported a best time of 103.6 miles per hour in 13.75 in the May 1973 issue. Most magazine test cars had Ram Air IV cams!

When Adams and Nell revealed the SD-455, it was equipped with a Ram Air IV spec .470-inch-lift, 308/320-degree duration camshaft and rated at 310 horsepower. Because they did not pass emissions, only a few engines were built with this cam. Production engines used a milder Ram Air III spec .406-inch-lift, 302/313-duration cam. All 1973 and 1974 SD-455s were hand-assembled, redlined at 5,700 rpm, and rated at 290 horsepower at 4,000 rpm and 395 lb-ft of torque at 3,200 rpm.

The SD-455 utilized a beefed block with reinforced four-bolt main bearing webs, 80-psi oil pump, and provisions for dry sump lube. A nodular iron crank, forged 5140 steel rods with $7/16$-inch bolts, and forged aluminum 8.4:1 TRW pistons ensured durability. Developed at AirFlow Research, the big-valve heads had round exhaust ports matched to high-flow manifolds. A unique 800-cfm Quadrajet was stock.

I rode with Herb Adams in his SD-455 mule and also drove a couple of SD-455 Firebirds. Because of scheduling conflicts, I was not able to drive similarly powered GTO and Grand Am coupes. Joe Oldham filled in for me.

Based on Oldham's SD-455 GTO recommendation for 1973 Top Performance Car of the Year, I made a trip to Pontiac in October and got some seat time in the super-duty GTO that Joe had driven. We were on the same page!

I presented our annual award to Pontiac General Manager Martin J. Casario, who had replaced Jim McDonald. The SD-455 GTO was the April 1973 *Hi-Performance CARS* cover story and I wrote:

> In years of selecting *Top Performance Car of the Year* candidates, flogging them on the open road and under controlled test track conditions and finally selecting the Top Eliminator, never has our job been easier. It is the first time that one car has emerged head and shoulders above every other entry. Pontiac came, saw and conquered. With its all-new SD-455 GTO, Pontiac challenged all of Motown to a Supercar showdown. And, when the tire smoke had cleared, it appeared that once again the GTO was King of the Street.

TOP LEFT: SD-455 Trans Ams offered the best combination of ride, handling, and acceleration in 1973 and 1974. Radial tires were standard on 1974 models, shot here on a GM skid pad.

TOP RIGHT: When Herb Adams introduced the SD-455 in 1972, he had his T/A mule available for rides. It had a modified engine, Radial T/As on trick mags, roll bar, Le Mans fuel filler, and vented trunk. It was track-ready and it wailed.

BELOW: A show-detailed SD-455 with chrome valve covers, in a '74 Formula Firebird. Dyno-testing at Pontiac revealed that this engine could put out a solid 400 gross horsepower. With intake, exhaust, and cam changes, it was possible to coax 600 horsepower from an SD-455.

TOP LEFT: Buick continued to market Stage I GS455 Skylarks that delivered outstanding performance. Cold air induction was no longer available and the coupes got heavier and more luxurious in 1973 and 1974. It didn't take much to light up the tires on this '73 GS455.

TOP RIGHT: Thanks to radial tuned suspension, the one-year-only Ventura GTO was fun to toss around a slalom course. We didn't kill any cones on this pass!

BELOW: Pontiac switched GTO branding from the midsize LeMans to the smaller, lighter Ventura for 1974. Unlike the Firebirds, the shaker hood scoop atop the 350/200 engine was functional.

The SD-455 GTO never went beyond prototype stage, although it was announced for 1973 production. We drove it and loved it enough to award it Top Performance Car of the Year. After I ordered one, the SD-455 option was killed and my GTO came with a 455/250 engine.

After driving the SD-455 GTO, I ordered one! Not waiting for an official order form, I submitted a handwritten order for a loaded GTO with SD-455, automatic, full power, AC, trailer towing, 15-inch G60s, and Y99 suspension. It arrived with everything I ordered except the SD-455 engine. In its place was the dumbed-down 455 rated at 250 horsepower. It didn't perform like a supercar, but it handled better than just about any new midsize coupe. I kept it.

Pontiac engineer and racer Tom Goad explained why the '73 GTO handled so well: "Our philosophy is to maintain standard spring rates and control roll stiffness with front and rear stabilizer bars to maintain a reasonably good ride. That's why we used larger front [1¹⁄₈-inch versus 1-inch] and rear [1-inch versus ⁷⁄₈-inch] stabilizer bars. We think the ride is excellent, considering the '73 GTO's cornering power and

its ability to generate the highest lateral Gs possible in a car of this size and weight."

The SD-455 engine had been released during Jim McDonald's watch, but Martin Casario had no interest in performance cars. The SD-455 GTO was killed before Job One. We had honored a car that didn't exist!

Pontiac's midsize '74 LeMans was much heavier than its predecessor and Pontiac decided to GTO-brand the 111-inch wheelbase X-body Ventura. Since it was already set up for a 350 Pontiac engine, all they did was upgrade L76 power with a four-barrel dual exhaust and a functional Trans-Am Shaker scoop. A 350/200, plus decals, neat wheels, optional hood tach, and new radial tuned suspension, turned a Ventura into a one-year-only GTO. Pontiac sold 7,058 GTO-option Venturas, compared with just 4,806 coupes the year before. Once the X-body GM cars were slated for 350 Buick engines in 1975, Pontiac opted to archive the GTO brand.

There were other bright spots in 1973 and 1974, but nothing to really challenge SD-455 Firebirds. Many performance models were carried over without power upgrades. However, Chevrolet did an excellent job with its Z/28 Camaro.

I left *Hi-Performance CARS* in mid-1973 and my managing editor, Alan Root, took over until being replaced by Fred Mackerodt. Fred evaluated 1974 models for Top Performance Car of the Year and selected the Z/28 Camaro. Joe Oldham tested a four-speed 350/245 Camaro with 3.73 Posi gears, powered by a detuned LT1 small-block and without AC. He clocked 93 miles per hour in 14.82 seconds at Suffolk County Raceway. Any car that ran sub-15-second track times was considered high-performance in 1974.

Carried over with minor cosmetic updates, the Mustang was Ford's only 1973 performance car. Available in Mach I trim with a scooped hood and 351 CJ power, the last full-size Mustang offered decent performance. In early 1973, we drove a prepared 351 CJ Mustang that came directly from the Dearborn Proving Ground. It was a four-speed Mach I with 3.91 gears that ran a best time of 96 miles per hour in 14.80 seconds and was reported on in *SUPERCARS '73*. Most 351 Mustangs tested that year by major magazines couldn't get out of the 16s. A full foot shorter than the '73 Mustang and powered by a four-cylinder engine with a V-6 option, the all-new '74 Mustang II did not appeal to enthusiasts.

Before Motown became mired down in mediocrity, there were some noteworthy cars. Chevrolet built its last Chevelle SS in 1973; it was available with 454/245 LS4 power and Buick showcased its next-to-last Stage I GS455 Skylark. Even

Checking out a '74 Camaro Z/28 at the Milford Proving Ground. Chevrolet managed to save the great LT1 350 engine with four-bolt mains and big-valve heads using a mild hydraulic cam and Q-Jet quad. It was named *Hi-Performance CARS* Top Performance Car of the Year in 1974.

Except for Cibie driving lamps and American mags, my '73 Olds Salon looked stock. Under its hood was a 325-horsepower '72 Olds W30 engine built by Oldsmobile Engineering. Handling and low to midrange acceleration was outstanding. It was a family car for a decade.

without fresh air induction, a Stage I Skylark with automatic and 3.42 gears, tested for *SUPERCARS '73*, ran an impressive 100 miles per hour in 14.60 seconds.

After test-driving a superb-handling '73 Cutlass Salon four-door with 455/250 power on the Milford road course, I suddenly became interested in sedans. An American interpretation of a European touring sedan, Oldsmobile's new 116-inch wheelbase sedan came stock with great multi-adjustable bucket seats, console shifter, radial tires, and a special suspension with fat front and rear stabilizer bars.

After leaving *Hi-Performance CARS*, I purchased a 455 Salon sedan and worked with Oldsmobile engineer Dale Smith on upgrading it. Dale supplied a '72 Olds W30 engine with .474-inch-lift cam, 8.5 pistons, and Marine heads with 69.70cc chambers. He also sent a Hurst Olds automatic and 3.23 Anti-Spin rear. The engine had been built in Lansing and dynoed at 325 horsepower at 4,000 rpm. My Salon was

an incredible road warrior, good for a solid 125 miles per hour with supercar low-end and mid-range acceleration. Coverage of the car and its modifications appeared in a number of publications.

AMC kept the spirit of high-performance alive in 1973 with the 401/255 Matador and Javelin AMX. The Javelin AMX delivered sub-fifteen-second track times, but it was not enough. Javelin production ended after the 1974 model year.

It was the end of an era, but not the end of performance cars. As computer technology advanced, engineers gained the tools needed to develop powerful, clean-burning engines and efficient drivetrains. A decade or so later, Camaros, Firebirds, Mustangs, and the sophisticated turbocharged V-6 Buick Grand National and GNX signaled the return of performance cars. Today we have 500 to 600-plus horsepower production cars and mega-priced 1,000-horsepower exotics. There will always be a need for speed.

INDEX

Abraham, Bill, 39

Adamowicz, Tony, 179

Adams, Herb, 144, 199–201

Alderman, Jerry, 37

Allison, Bobby, 153

AMC, 125–26

  Javelin, 126–27, 171, 189, 196, 205

  Super Javelin, 134–37

Andretti, Mario, 112

Arkus-Duntov, Zora, 57, 109, 143, 146–49, 165

Baker, Buddy, 152–53

Bandrow, Lee, 135, 137

Bauman, John, 131

Bean, Dave, 158

Bell, Jim, 177

Beltz, John, 129, 158, 160

Bimbi, Stefano, 114

Black, Keith, 183

Blanding, Bill, 108

Blocker, Dan, 81

Bonner, Phil, 37

Booth, Wally, 130

Brannan, Dick, 34, 37, 51, 76, 82–83, 96, 133

Brock, Ray, 38, 56

Browne, Fred, 89

Buick, 11, 14

  Bug, 14

  Century, 17, 19–20

  GSX, 150

  Riviera Gran Sport, 78, 80, 112, 174

  Skylark, 80, 106, 111–12, 121–22, 146–47, 174–79, 186, 191–92, 202, 204–5

Bulgari, Nicola, 11

Bullet, 14

Burman, Bob, 14

BVLGARI-Cadillac, 11

Cadillac, 14–15, 38

Caldwell, Ray, 183

Candymatic, 68–70, 75, 87

Casario, Martin J., 200, 203

Castaldo, Charlie, 130–31

Chakmakian, Carl, 134

Chevrolet, 18, 35–36, 41–45, 47

  Bel Air, 34, 43, 113

Biscayne, 29, 34, 48, 70

Camaro, 16, 22, 25–29, 31, 107–9, 113–19, 125–27, 130, 137–39, 142–44, 147–48, 156–58, 164–65, 167, 193, 204

Chevelle, 29–31, 68, 70, 81, 95, 109, 116, 120–22, 143, 165, 169, 175, 186–87, 190, 192–93, 204

Chevy II/Nova, 29–30, 94–96, 143, 198

Corvair Sebring Spyder, 45

Corvette, 16, 29–31, 38, 41, 45, 52, 57–58, 88, 95, 109, 111, 113, 118, 134, 146–49, 156–57, 164–65

El Camino, 43

Impala, 32, 34, 40–43, 53–55, 58, 70

Mark II, 48, 56–58

Monte Carlo, 44–45

RPO Z11, 48, 53–55

SS396, 90

Stinger Corvair, 30

Super Sports, 20

Turbo-Stinger Vega, 30

Z/28, 117–19, 125, 137–39, 142–43, 167, 193, 204

Chevrolet, Arthur, 16

Chevrolet, Louis, 14, 16

Chittenden, Gordon, 80

Chrisman, Jack, 68

Chrysler, 17, 21, 33, 37–38, 47, 62–63, 82, 91, 161, 191, 195

  300F, 20

  300G, 18–19

  426 Hemi, 101

  C-300, 18

  Hemi, 18, 74–76

  Typhoon, 62

Clay, Bill, 53

Cole, Ed, 45, 185–86

Collier, Sam and Miles, 15

Collins, Bill, 66, 144, 146

Color Me Gone, 75–76

Cooper, Gordon, 105

Cunningham, Briggs, 15, 38

Cutler, Fred, 76

Dallafior, John, 85–86

Davies, Scott, 94

DeCou, J. E. "Jack," 178

Dellis, Fred, 186

DeLorean, John, 66, 144, 164–65

Demmer, John, 129

Dixon, "Doc," 31

Dodge, 34, 37–38, 47–49, 51, 64, 68–70, 75–76, 111

  426 Hemi, 84, 92, 130–31, 140

  Challenger, 164, 166–67, 179–83, 196

  Charger, 91–93, 140, 186–87

  Charger Daytona, 144, 150–54, 168–69

  Comet, 105

  Coronet, 9, 82, 87–88, 124, 160, 168–69

  Dart, 36, 82, 130, 179

  Lancer, 89

  Monaco, 130

  Polara, 51

  Super Bee, 124, 144, 160–61, 168

Dodge, Charlie, 88, 98

Donner, Frederick, 48, 56

Donohue, Mark, 118–19, 125, 137–39, 143, 171, 189

Dotterer, Ray, 156, 158

Duesenberg SJ, 12, 16

Durham, Malcolm, 55, 68

Eckstrand, Al, 51

Elliott, John, 112

Engle, Elwood, 62

Estes, Pete, 38, 65–67, 117

Falcon Sprint, 49

Farb, Dilbert Horatio, 10, 24–25

Faubel, Bud, 36

Ferrar, Dennis, 25

Ferrari, GTO, 58, 66

Fisher, Craig, 118

Fisher, Ralph, 41

Follmer, George, 172, 174, 196

Ford, 10, 19–21, 33, 47, 91, 141, 191

  Boss 302, 142, 172–74

  Boss 429, 142–43, 145, 169, 172

  Cobra Jet Mustang, 131–33

  Fairlane, 55, 70, 76, 82, 94, 96, 101, 111–12, 125, 131

  Flathead V-8, 8–10, 14

  Galaxie, 34–35, 37, 40, 49, 51, 53, 70–71, 73–74, 82, 84, 96, 101–5

  GT40, 11

La Galaxie, 62

Model T, 16

Mustang, 71–73, 81–83, 85, 102–3, 108, 111, 117, 125–26, 131, 142, 169, 172, 174, 187–88, 195, 204

Thunderbird, 62

Thunderbolt, 76–77, 96

Torino, 123, 125, 132, 145

Torino Cobra, 142, 166, 172, 174, 187–89, 195

Torino Talladega, 142, 144

Ford, Benson, 71, 73

Ford, Edsel, II, 13–14

Ford, Henry, 13–14, 16, 20

Ford, Henry, II, 33, 48, 105, 195

Foyt, A. J., 58

France, Bill, 58, 75, 82, 87, 92, 101

Freel, Fred, 188

Frey, Donald N., 104

Gardner, Joe "Tex," 39

Garlits, Don "Big Daddy," 75

Gary, Herb, 42, 134

Gee, Russ, 66

General Motors, 21, 33, 38, 47–48, 91, 128, 185–86, 191–92

Genesis, 42, 121, 169

Ghia, 62

Gibb, Fred, 148

Glotzbach, Charlie, 152

Goad, Tom, 203

Golden Commandos, 85–87

Goldenrod, 97

Goldfish, 85–86

Goldsmith, Paul, 58, 74

Gordon, Jack, 48

Gorenstein, Ralph, 17

Gray, Charlie, 76

Grumpy's Toy, 95

Gurney, Dan, 41, 51, 82, 105, 144, 181, 183

Haga, Hank, 164

Hall, Bob, 137

Hall, Jim, 147

Hamilton, Pete, 169

Hanish, Martin, 51

Harrell, Dick, 30–31, 43, 55, 148

Harrison, Ben, 144

Harvey, Jerry, 133

Harvey, Scott, 88–89, 179
Healey, John, 131
Heishman, Hugh, 118
Hernandez, Fran, 50
Hoover, Tom, 37, 130–31
Householder, Ronnie, 82
Howell, Bill, 69, 136
Hudson Hornet, 15, 17, 188
Hulme, Denny, 147
Huntington, Roger, 52, 59, 123
Hurst, George, 128
Hurst-Olds, 128–29, 146, 170, 194
Hutchinson, Pete, 183

Iacocca, Lee, 71
Isaac, Bobby, 150–54, 169
Iskenderian, Ed, 158

Jacolow, Mel, 79
Jarrett, Ned, 51, 82
Jean, Gary, 11
Jeffords, Jim, 30
Jenkins, Ab, 12, 16–17
Jenkins, Bill "Grumpy," 39, 45, 94–96, 127, 169
Jennings, Bruce, 179
Johnson, Junior, 56–58
Jones, Danny, 76
Jones, Parnelli, 172, 174
Joniec, Al, 132–33

Kalitta, Connie, 105
Kaplan, Ronnie, 30
Kayser, Ken, 57, 148
Kehrl, Howard H., 42
Keinath, Richard, 57
Kelley, Lee, 158
Kennedy, Lennie "Pop," 177–78
Kiekhaefer, 18
Kimball, Don, 55
King, Jake, 168
Kirschenbaum, Al, 168
Knapp, Dan, 131
Knowlton, Larry, 131
Knudsen, Semon "Bunkie," 38, 56–58, 61, 81, 124, 139, 142–43
Knudsen, William, 38
Kobe, Ray, 85–86
Kosmala, John, 154, 156
Krause, Bill, 58

Krause, Norman "Mr. Norm," 31
Kroiz, Irwin, 83

LaFon, Pat, 115
Lagana, Bill, 95
Landy, Dick, 75, 130, 169
Lawton, Bill, 37, 55, 76, 131
Le Monstre, 15
Leal, Butch, 43, 55
Leno, Jay, 62
Lindamood, Roger, 74–76
Linstrom, Bruce, 86
Lorenzen, Fred, 51
Lucas, Ted, 129
Lufkin, Jack, 158
Lund, Tiny, 51, 57
Lunn, Roy, 11, 143
Lyles, Ronnie, 186

MacCoon, Grant and Richard, 99–100
Mackerodt, Fred, 24, 79–80, 92, 108, 112, 141, 187, 204
Malco Gasser, 102–3
Manners, Dennis, 146, 178–79
Markowitz, Mack, 30
Marshall, R. E., 144
Martin, Buddy, 169
Martin, Ed, 37, 51
Maselles, Howard, 61
Maserati Ghibli, 164
Mashigan, Charles, 62
Mason, Charlie, 109
Mason, James "Hammer," 76
Maurer, Dave, 158
Maxwell, Dick, 37, 131
McCandless, Dave, 171
McCandless, Herb, 169
McCormack, Al, 95
McDonald, Dave, 41
McDonald, Jim, 200, 203
McIntyre, Tom, 58
McKee, Bob, 160
McKellar, Malcolm "Mac," 61
McLaren, Bruce, 147
McLaren, Stuart, 25
McNulty, Bill, 150
McPherson, Don, 42
Mercedes-Benz, 11
Mercer, Raceabout, 16
Mercury, 9–10

Comet, 70, 83, 95–96, 112
Cougar, 125, 133
Cougar Eliminator, 170, 174
Cyclone, 125, 144
Cyclone Spoiler, 142, 188–89, 195
Marauder, 49–50
Mark II, 70
Meyers, Bruce, 25
MG TC, 8, 10–11
Miller, Ak, 158
Mitchell, Bill, 22, 25, 164
Mitchell, William, 45
Montgomery, "Ohio George," 102–3
Moore, Bud, 96, 105, 174
Morea, Joe, 25
Morgan, Tony, 136
Mormon Meteor, 12, 17
Motion Minicar, 22, 25
Motion Supercar Club, 9
Mueller, Mike, 29
Mullins, Francis "Moon," 67–68, 87, 152
Murray, Phil, 89

Naughton, John, 141
Nell, Tom, 154, 199–200
Nichels, Ray, 38
Nicholson, "Dyno Don," 41, 43, 55, 83, 105, 133, 169, 196

Old Reliable, 41
Old Reliable IV, 55
Oldham, Joe, 24, 26, 112, 143, 146, 167–68, 177, 187, 189, 194, 200, 204
Oldsmobile, 14, 20, 30, 45, 48, 67, 81, 84, 138, 141, 170
    4-4-2, 93, 95, 111–12, 121–23, 146, 172, 175, 186, 194
    Cutlass, 146, 158, 194, 205
    OW-43, 158–60
    Toronado, 99–100
Owens, Cotton, 75, 87–89, 92

Panch, Marvin, 51
Panoz, 11
Pardue, Jimmy, 74
Parks, Wally, 37, 132
Paschal, Jim, 74–75

Passino, Jacque, 76, 105
Pearson, David, 87–89, 92, 143
Penske, Roger, 109, 119, 125, 137–39, 143, 171
Pettitt, Nicholas, 10
Petty, Richard, 74–75, 87–88, 92, 111, 143, 169, 187
Piero Rivolta, 11
Piggins, Vince, 31, 57–58, 96, 109, 117–18, 127, 136, 139, 143–44, 148–49
Pike, Joe, 109
Pitcock, Forrest, 85
Platt, Hubie, 43, 55, 132–33
Plymouth, 20, 34, 36–37, 47–48, 51, 64, 75, 111
    426 Hemi, 96, 98, 130–31
    Barracuda, 85–86, 88–89, 107–9, 130, 164, 167–68, 179–83, 186, 195–96
    Belvedere, 82, 124
    Road Runner, 124, 142, 160–61, 168, 184, 187, 195–96
    Superbird, 168–69, 171
    Valiant, 82
Pontiac, 20, 34–35, 38–40, 42, 47, 51–52, 122, 125
    Bonneville, 9–10, 18, 45, 50
    Catalina, 38, 40, 59
    Firebird, 31, 107–8, 126, 146, 156, 164–65, 167, 194, 196, 200–201, 204
    Grand Prix, 40, 46, 52
    GTO, 14, 16, 21, 23, 31, 39, 61, 65–66, 80–81, 93, 96, 110–11, 115–17, 121, 123–24, 143–44, 150, 154–56, 162, 170, 175, 193–94, 200, 202–4
    Royal Bobcat, 115–16, 123–24
    Super-Duty, 58–61
    Super-Duty 455, 199–201, 203
    Tempest, 16, 31, 45, 58, 61, 65–66, 80
    Trans Am, 164–65, 167
    Ventura, 202–3
    Ventura II, 196–97
Poole, Barrie, 133
Porsche, 22, 25
    917, 147–48
    Carrera Abarth GTL, 58
Porter, Bill, 164
Posey. Sam, 181

Procopio, Al, 146
Proffitt, Hayden, 38, 43, 55, 113, 126

Rausch, John T., 42
Rediker, Frank, 59, 61
Reeker, Dale, 180
Richter, Len, 37, 77
Rickenbacker, Eddie, 16
Ritchey, Les, 37
Roberts, Fireball, 40, 57
Robinson, Pete, 105
Rodger, Bob, 150, 152
Rollert, Edward, 80
Romberg, Gary, 150
Ronda, Gas, 37, 133
Root, Al, 187, 195–96, 204
Rosen, Joel, 8–9, 25, 29, 30, 112, 115–16, 122, 134–35, 137–38, 140, 156–58, 167, 195–96
Rutherford, Johnny, 57–58

Sanders, Frank, 54–55
Satan of Morimar, 15
Satellite, 97
Savage, Swede, 183
Schornack, Milt, 123, 125, 154, 156

Schorr, Marty, 69, 156
Schrewsberry, Bill, 68
Schwartz, Ephraim "Wolf," 146
Shaw, Larry T., 9, 23
Shelby, Carroll, 25, 82, 111, 174
Shettler, John, 165
Shinoda, Larry, 139, 142
Shuman, A. B., 192
Simonin, August, 29
Simonin, Ed, 29
Smith, Ammon, 45
Smith, Dale, 129, 166, 170, 172, 194, 205
Smith, Leroi "Tex," 38
Smith, Nick, 112
Smithson, Bud, 86
Snizek, George, 25, 88, 98
Sox, Ronnie, 55, 68, 130, 169
Stacy, Nelson, 51
Stahl, Jere, 96
Stein, Irwin, 9
Stemple, Bob, 129
Stephani, Edward and Jack, 30
Stiles, Bill, 184, 187
Strickler, Dave, 41, 43, 45, 55, 76, 137–38, 169
Stroppe, Bill, 50, 96, 172–73

Stutz, Bearcat, 16
Summers, Bob, 96–98
Super Snake, 111
Sweepstakes, 14

Tarozzi, Bob, 131
Tasca, Bob, 76, 131, 133
Tasmanian Devil, 25
Teague, Marshall, 15, 17
Thatcher, Norm, 18, 50
Thomas, Bill, 30, 41, 113–15
Thompson, Mickey, 37–38, 44–45, 52, 57–59, 68, 97, 153
Thornton, Jim, 37–38, 68, 70, 74–75, 87
Tinsler, Vern, 76, 96
Titus, Jerry, 82
Tullius, Bob, 179

Unser, Bobby, 145
Usher, Gary, 42, 45

Vanke, Arlen, 31, 39, 130
Vinnie, 25
Volvo, 11
VW, 22, 25

Wallace, George, 150
Walters, Phil, 15
Wangers, Jim, 31, 59, 61, 66–67, 115, 144, 146, 154–55
Warren, Dave, 154
Wasserman, Joel, 9
Watson, Jack "Doc," 128
Weatherly, Joe, 35, 40
Weis, Tony, 153
White, Rex, 35, 58
Williams, Warren, 115
Wilson, Ace, 31, 66
Wilson, Brian, 42, 45
Winton, Alexander, 14
Wren, Dave, 133

Yenko, Don, 30–31, 143–44
Yenko, Frank, 30
Young, Jeff, 144
Yunick, Smokey, 15, 17, 38, 40, 57

Zimmerman, Frank "Zimmy," 53, 76
Zuidema, Gus, 83

Martyn L. Schorr has a history with high-performance cars that dates back to the beginning of Ford's Total Performance era over fifty years ago. He rode with Carroll Shelby and was at the press conference in New York for the debut of the Lola-built Ford GT that became the GT40. Schorr drove the GT40 on streets of New York City and went with Mickey Thompson in 1969 to Bonneville to set a book full of records. He personally knew all the key players from Ford's racing program from his years as a magazine editor. Schorr is the author of *Motion Performance* (Motorbooks, 2009).